PENGUIN BOOKS

BETWEEN PAST AND FUTURE

Hannah Arendt was for many years University Professor of Political Philosophy in the Graduate Faculty of the New School for Social Research and a Visiting Fellow of the Committee on Social Thought at the University of Chicago. She is also the author of *Eichmann in Jerusalem* and *On Revolution* (also published by Penguin Books).

Hannah Arendt

BETWEEN PAST AND FUTURE

Eight Exercises in
Political Thought

PENGUIN BOOKS

PENGUIN BOOKS
Published by the Penguin Group
Viking Penguin Inc., 40 West 23rd Street, New York, New York 10010, U.S.A.
Penguin Books Ltd, 27 Wrights Lane, London W8 5TZ, England
Penguin Books Australia Ltd, Ringwood, Victoria, Australia
Penguin Books Canada Ltd, 2801 John Street,
Markham, Ontario, Canada L3R 1B4
Penguin Books (N.Z.) Ltd, 182–190 Wairau Road,
Auckland 10, New Zealand

Penguin Books Ltd, Registered Offices:
Harmondsworth, Middlesex, England

First published in the United States of America by The Viking Press 1961
First published in Great Britain by Faber and Faber Ltd, 1961
Viking Compass Edition, published with additional text, 1968
Reprinted 1969, 1971, 1973, 1974, 1976
Published in Penguin Books 1977

7   9   11   13   15   14   12   10   8

LIBRARY OF CONGRESS CATALOGING IN PUBLICATION DATA
Arendt, Hannah.
Between past and future.
Reprint of the 1968 ed. published by The Viking Press,
New York.
Includes index.
1. Civilization, Modern—1950—   2. History—
Philosophy. I. Title.
[CB427.A7 1977]   909.82   77-7662
ISBN 0 14 00.4662 3

Printed in the United States of America
Set in Linotype Times Roman

Part of Chapter III was first published in *Nomos I: Authority,* edited by Carl J. Friedrich
for the American Society of Political and Legal Philosophy, copyright © 1958 by the
President and Fellows of Harvard College, published by The Liberal Arts Press, a division
of The Bobbs-Merrill Company, Inc. Part of Chapter VI was first published in *Daedalus,*
copyright © 1960 by the American Academy of Arts and Sciences, and other chapters in
Chicago Review, Partisan Review, and *Review of Politics.*

For Heinrich
after twenty-five years

ACKNOWLEDGMENTS

The essays in this book are revised and enlarged versions of those which appeared in the following magazines: *American Scholar, Chicago Review, Daedalus, Nomos, Partisan Review, The Review of Politics*. "Truth and Politics" originally appeared in *The New Yorker*. "The Crisis in Education" was translated from the German by Denver Lindley.

CONTENTS

BETWEEN PAST AND FUTURE

PREFACE:
THE GAP BETWEEN
PAST AND FUTURE

Notre héritage n'est précédé d'aucun testament—"our inheritance was left to us by no testament"—this is perhaps the strangest of the strangely abrupt aphorisms into which René Char, French poet and writer, compressed the gist of what four years in the *résistance* had come to mean to a whole generation of European writers and men of letters.[1] The collapse of France, to them a totally unexpected event, had emptied, from one day to the next, the political scene of their country, leaving it to the puppet-like antics of knaves or fools, and they who as a matter of course had never participated in the official business of the Third Republic were sucked into politics as though with the force of a vacuum. Thus, without premonition and probably against their conscious inclinations, they had come to constitute willy-nilly a public realm where—without the paraphernalia of officialdom and hidden from the eyes of friend and foe—all relevant business in the affairs of the country was transacted in deed and word.

It did not last long. After a few short years they were liberated from what they originally had thought to be a "burden" and thrown back into what they now knew to be the weightless irrelevance of their personal affairs, once more separated from "the world of reality" by an *épaisseur triste,* the "sad opaqueness" of a private life centered about nothing but itself. And if they refused "to go back to [their] very beginnings, to [their] most indigent behavior," they could only return to the old empty strife of conflicting ideologies which after the defeat of the common enemy once more occupied the political arena to split the former comrades-in-arms into innumerable cliques which were not even factions and to engage them in the endless polemics and intrigues of a paper war. What Char had foreseen, clearly anticipated, while the real fight was still on—"If I survive, I know that I shall have to break with the aroma of these essential years, silently reject (not repress) my treasure" —had happened. They had lost their treasure.

What was this treasure? As they themselves understood it, it seems to have consisted, as it were, of two interconnected parts: they had discovered that he who "joined the Resistance, *found* himself," that he ceased to be "in quest of [himself] without mastery, in naked unsatisfaction," that he no longer suspected himself of "insincerity," of being "a carping, suspicious actor of life," that he could afford "to go naked." In this nakedness, stripped of all masks—of those which society assigns to its members as well as those which the individual fabricates for himself in his psychological reactions against society—they had been visited for the first time in their lives by an apparition of freedom, not, to be sure, because they acted against tyranny and things worse than tyranny —this was true for every soldier in the Allied armies—but because they had become "challengers," had taken the initiative upon themselves and therefore, without knowing or even noticing it, had begun to create that public space between themselves where freedom could appear. "At every meal that we eat together, freedom is invited to sit down. The chair remains vacant, but the place is set."

The men of the European Resistance were neither the first nor the last to lose their treasure. The history of revolutions—from the summer of 1776 in Philadelphia and the summer of 1789 in Paris to the autumn of 1956 in Budapest—which politically spells out the innermost story of the modern age, could be told in parable form as the tale of an age-old treasure which, under the most varied circumstances, appears abruptly, unexpectedly, and disappears again, under different mysterious conditions, as though it were a fata morgana. There exist, indeed, many good reasons to believe that the treasure was never a reality but a mirage, that we deal here not with anything substantial but with an apparition, and the best of these reasons is that the treasure thus far has remained nameless. Does something exist, not in outer space but in the world and the affairs of men on earth, which has not even a name? Unicorns and fairy queens seem to possess more reality than the lost treasure of the revolutions. And yet, if we turn our eyes to the beginnings of this era, and especially to the decades preceding it, we may discover to our surprise that the eighteenth century on both sides of the Atlantic possessed a name for this treasure, a name long since forgotten and lost—one is tempted to say—even before the treasure itself disappeared. The name in America was "public happiness," which, with its overtones of "virtue" and "glory," we understand hardly better than its French counterpart, "public freedom"; the difficulty for us is that in both instances the emphasis was on "public."

However that may be, it is the namelessness of the lost treasure to which the poet alludes when he says that our inheritance was left us by no testament. The testament, telling the heir what will rightfully be his, wills past possessions for a future. Without testament or, to resolve the metaphor, without tradition—which selects and names, which hands down and preserves, which indicates where the treasures are and what their worth is—there seems to be no willed continuity in time and hence, humanly speaking, neither past nor future, only sempiternal change of the world and the biological cycle of living creatures in it. Thus the treasure was lost not because of historical circumstances and the adversity of reality but because no tradition had foreseen its appearance or its reality, because no testament had willed it for the future. The loss, at any rate, perhaps inevitable in terms of political reality, was consummated by oblivion, by a failure of memory, which befell not only the heirs but, as it were, the actors, the witnesses, those who for a fleeting moment had held the treasure in the palms of their hands, in short, the living themselves. For remembrance, which is only one, though one of the most important, modes of thought, is helpless outside a pre-established framework of reference, and the human mind is only on the rarest occasions capable of retaining something which is altogether unconnected. Thus the first who failed to remember what the treasure was like were precisely those who had possessed it and found it so strange that they did not even know how to name it. At the time this did not bother them; if they did not know their treasure, they knew well enough the meaning of what they did and that it was beyond victory and defeat: "Action that has a meaning for the living has value only for the dead, completion only in the minds that inherit and question it." The tragedy began not when the liberation of the country as a whole ruined, almost automatically, the small hidden islands of freedom that were doomed anyhow, but when it turned out that there was no mind to inherit and to question, to think about and to remember. The point of the matter is that the "completion," which indeed every enacted event must have in the minds of those who then are to tell the story and to convey its meaning, eluded them; and without this thinking completion after the act, without the articulation accomplished by remembrance, there simply was no story left that could be told.

There is nothing in this situation that is altogether new. We are only too familiar with the recurring outbursts of passionate exasperation with reason, thought, and rational discourse which are the natural reactions of men who know from their own experiences that thought and reality have parted company, that reality has become opaque for the light of thought and that thought, no longer bound to incident as the circle remains bound to its focus, is liable either to become altogether meaningless or to rehash old verities which have lost all concrete relevance. Even the anticipating recognition of the predicament has by now become familiar. When Tocqueville returned from the New World, which he so superbly knew how to describe and to analyze that his work has remained a classic and survived more than a century of radical change, he was well aware of the fact that what Char called the "completion" of act and event had still eluded him; and Char's "Our inheritance was left to us by no testament" sounds like a variation of Tocqueville's "Since the past has ceased to throw its light upon the future, the mind of man wanders in obscurity." [2] Yet the only exact description of this predicament is to be found, as far as I know, in one of those parables of Franz Kafka which, unique perhaps in this respect in literature, are real παραβολαί, thrown alongside and around the incident like rays of light which, however, do not illuminate its outward appearance but possess the power of X rays to lay bare its inner structure that, in our case, consists of the hidden processes of the mind.

Kafka's parable reads as follows: [3]

He has two antagonists: the first presses him from behind, from the origin. The second blocks the road ahead. He gives battle to both. To be sure, the first supports him in his fight with the second, for he wants to push him forward, and in the same way the second supports him in his fight with the first, since he drives him back. But it is only theoretically so. For it is not only the two antagonists who are there, but he himself as well, and who really knows his intentions? His dream, though, is that some time in an unguarded moment —and this would require a night darker than any night has ever been yet—he will jump out of the fighting line and be promoted, on account of his experience in fighting, to the position of umpire over his antagonists in their fight with each other.

The incident which this parable relates and penetrates follows, in the inner logic of the matter, upon the events whose gist we found contained in René Char's aphorism. It begins, in fact, at precisely the point where our opening aphorism left the sequence of events hanging, as it were, in mid-air. Kafka's fight begins when the course of action has run its course and when the story which was its outcome waits to be completed "in the minds that inherit and question it." The task of the mind is to understand what happened, and this understanding, according to Hegel, is man's way of reconciling himself with reality; its actual end is to be at peace with the world. The trouble is that if the mind is unable to bring peace and to induce reconciliation, it finds itself immediately engaged in its own kind of warfare.

However, historically speaking, this stage in the development of the modern mind was preceded, at least in the twentieth century, by two, rather than one, previous acts. Before the generation of René Char, whom we have chosen here as its representative, found itself thrown out of literary pursuits into the commitments of action, another generation, only slightly older, had turned to politics for the solution of philosophic perplexities and had tried to escape from thought into action. It was this older generation which then became the spokesmen and creators of what they themselves called existentialism; for existentialism, at least in its French version, is primarily an escape from the perplexities of modern philosophy into the unquestioning commitment of action. And since, under the circumstances of the twentieth century, the so-called intellectuals—writers, thinkers, artists, men of letters, and the like—could find access to the public realm only in time of revolution, the revolution came to play, as Malraux once noticed (in *Man's Fate*), "the role which once was played by eternal life": it "saves those that make it." Existentialism, the rebellion of the philosopher against philosophy, did not arise when philosophy turned out to be unable to apply its own rules to the realm of political affairs; this failure of political philosophy as Plato would have understood it is almost as old as the history of Western philosophy and metaphysics; and it did not even arise when it turned out that philosophy was equally unable to perform the task assigned to it by Hegel and the philosophy of history, that is, to understand and grasp conceptually historical reality and the events that made the modern world what it is. The situation, however, became desperate when the old metaphysical questions were shown to be meaningless; that is, when it began to dawn upon modern man that he had come to live in a world in which his mind and his tradition of thought were not even capable of asking adequate, meaningful questions, let alone of giving answers to its own perplexities. In this predicament action, with its involvement and commitment, its being *engagée,* seemed to hold out the hope, not of solving any problems, but of making it possible to live with them without becoming, as Sartre once put it, a *salaud,* a hypocrite.

The discovery that the human mind had ceased, for some mysterious reasons, to function properly forms, so to speak, the first act of the story with which we are concerned here. I mentioned it here, however briefly, because without it the peculiar irony of what was to follow would be lost on us. René Char, writing during the last months of the Resistance, when liberation—which in our context meant liberation from action—loomed large, concluded his reflections with an appeal to thought for the prospective survivors no less urgent and no less passionate than the appeal to action of those who preceded him. If one were to write the intellectual history of our century, not in the form of successive generations, where the historian must be literally true to the sequence of theories and attitudes, but in the form of the biography of a single person, aiming at no more than a metaphorical approximation to what actually happened in the minds of men, this person's mind would stand revealed as having been forced to turn full circle not once but twice, first when he escaped from thought into action, and then again when action, or rather having acted, forced him back into thought. Whereby it would be of some relevance to notice that the appeal to thought arose in the odd in-between period which sometimes inserts itself into historical time when not only the later historians but the actors and witnesses, the living themselves, become aware of an interval in time which is altogether determined by things that are no longer and by things that are not yet. In history, these intervals have shown more than once that they may contain the moment of truth.

We now may return to Kafka, who in the logic of these matters, though not in their chronology, occupies the last and, as it were, the most advanced position. (The riddle of Kafka, who in more than thirty-five years of growing posthumous fame has established himself as one of the foremost writers' writers, is still unsolved; it consists primarily in a kind of breath-taking reversal of the established relationship between experience and thought. While we find it a matter of course to associate richness of concrete detail and dramatic action with the experience of a given reality and to ascribe to mental processes abstract pallor as the price exacted for their order and precision, Kafka, by sheer force of intelligence and spiritual imagination, created out of a bare, "abstract" minimum of experience a kind of thought-landscape which, without losing in precision, harbors all the riches, varieties, and dramatic elements characteristic of "real" life. Because thinking to him was the most vital and the liveliest part of reality, he developed this uncanny gift of anticipation which even today, after almost forty years full of unprecedented and unforeseeable events, does not cease to amaze us.) The story in its utter simplicity and brevity records a mental phenomenon, something which one may call a thought-event. The scene is a battleground on which the forces of the past and the future clash with each other; between them we find the man whom Kafka calls "he," who, if he wants to stand his ground at all, must give battle to both forces. Hence, there are two or even three fights going on simultaneously: the fight between "his" antagonists and the fight of the man in between with each of them. However, the fact that there is a fight at all seems due exclusively to the presence of the man, without whom the forces of the past and of the future, one suspects, would have neutralized or destroyed each other long ago.

The first thing to be noticed is that not only the future—"the wave of the future"—but also the past is seen as a force, and not, as in nearly all our metaphors, as a burden man has to shoulder and of whose dead weight the living can or even must get rid in their march into the future. In the words of Faulkner, "the past is never dead, it is not even past." This past, moreover, reaching all the way back into the origin, does not pull back but presses forward, and it is, contrary to what one would expect, the future which drives us back into the past. Seen from the viewpoint of man, who always lives in the interval between past and future, time is not a continuum, a flow of uninterrupted succession; it is broken in the middle, at the point where "he" stands; and "his" standpoint is not the present as we usually understand it but rather a gap in time which "his" constant fighting, "his" making a stand against past and future, keeps in existence. Only because man is inserted into time and only to the extent that he stands his ground does the flow of indifferent time break up into tenses; it is this insertion—the beginning of a beginning, to put it into Augustinian terms—which splits up the time continuum into forces which then, because they are focused on the particle or body that gives them their direction, begin fighting with each other and acting upon man in the way Kafka describes.

Without distorting Kafka's meaning, I think one may go a step further. Kafka describes how the insertion of man breaks up the unidirectional flow of time but, strangely enough, he does not change the traditional image according to which we think of time as moving in a straight line. Since Kafka retains the traditional metaphor of a rectilinear temporal movement, "he" has barely enough room to stand and whenever "he" thinks of striking out on "his" own "he" falls into the dream of a region over and above the fighting-line—and what else is this dream and this region but the old dream which Western metaphysics has dreamed from Parmenides to Hegel of a timeless, spaceless, suprasensuous realm as the proper region of thought? Obviously what is missing in Kafka's description of a thought-event is a spatial dimension where thinking could exert itself without being forced to jump out of human time altogether. The trouble with Kafka's story in all its magnificence is that it is hardly possible to retain the notion of a rectilinear temporal movement if its unidirectional flow is broken up into antagonistic forces being directed toward and acting upon man. The insertion of man, as he breaks up the continuum, cannot but cause the forces to deflect, however lightly, from their original direction, and if this were the case, they would no longer clash head on but meet at an angle. In other words, the gap where "he" stands is, potentially at least, no simple interval but resembles what the physicists call a parallelogram of forces.

Ideally, the action of the two forces which form the parallelogram of forces where Kafka's "he" has found his battlefield should result in a third force, the resultant diagonal whose origin would be the point at which the forces clash and upon which they act. This diagonal force would in one respect differ from the two forces whose result it is. The two antagonistic forces are both unlimited as to their origins, the one coming from an infinite past and the other from an infinite future; but though they have no known beginning, they have a terminal ending, the point at which they clash. The diagonal force, on the contrary, would be limited as to its origin, its starting-point being the clash of the antagonistic forces, but it would be infinite with respect to its ending by virtue of having resulted from the concerted action of two forces whose origin is infinity. This diagonal force, whose origin is known, whose direction is determined by past and future, but whose eventual end lies in infinity, is the perfect metaphor for the activity of thought. If Kafka's "he" were able to exert his forces along this diagonal, in perfect equidistance from past and future, walking along this diagonal line, as it were, forward and backward, with the slow, ordered movements which are the proper motion for trains of thought, he would not have jumped out of the fighting-line and be above the melee as the parable demands, for this diagonal, though pointing toward the infinite, remains bound to and is rooted in the present; but he would have discovered—pressed as he was by his antagonists into the only direction from which he could properly see and survey what was most his own, what had come into being only with his own, self-inserting appearance—the enormous, ever-changing time-space which is created and limited by the forces of past and future; he would have found the place in time which is sufficiently removed from past and future to offer "the umpire" a position from which to judge the forces fighting with each other with an impartial eye.

But, one is tempted to add, this is "only theoretically so." What is much more likely to happen—and what Kafka in other stories and parables has often described—is that the "he," unable to find the diagonal which would lead him out of the fighting-line and into the space ideally constituted by the parallelogram of forces, will "die of exhaustion," worn out under the pressure of constant fighting, oblivious of his original intentions, and aware only of the existence of this gap in time which, as long as he lives, is the ground on which he must stand, though it seems to be a battle-field and not a home.

To avoid misunderstandings: the imagery I am using here to indicate metaphorically and tentatively the contemporary conditions of thought can be valid only within the realm of mental phenomena. Applied to historical or biographical time, none of these metaphors can possibly make sense because gaps in time do not occur there. Only insofar as he thinks, and that is insofar as he is ageless—a "he" as Kafka so rightly calls him, and not a "somebody"—does man in the full actuality of his concrete being live in this gap of time between past and future. The gap, I suspect, is not a modern phenomenon, it is perhaps not even a historical datum but is coeval with the existence of man on earth. It may well be the region of the spirit or, rather, the path paved by thinking, this small track of non-time which the activity of thought beats within the time-space of mortal men and into which the trains of thought, of remembrance and anticipation, save whatever they touch from the ruin of historical and biographical time. This small non-time-space in the very heart of time, unlike the world and the culture into which we are born, can only be indicated, but cannot be inherited and handed down from the past; each new generation, indeed every new human being as he inserts himself between an infinite past and an infinite future, must discover and ploddingly pave it anew.

The trouble, however, is that we seem to be neither equipped nor prepared for this activity of thinking, of settling down in the gap between past and future. For very long times in our history, actually throughout the thousands of years that followed upon the foundation of Rome and were determined by Roman concepts, this gap was bridged over by what, since the Romans, we have called tradition. That this tradition has worn thinner and thinner as the modern age progressed is a secret to nobody. When the thread of tradition finally broke, the gap between past and future ceased to be a condition peculiar only to the activity of thought and restricted as an experience to those few who made thinking their primary business. It became a tangible reality and perplexity for all; that is, it became a fact of political relevance.

Kafka mentions the experience, the fighting experience gained by "him" who stands his ground between the clashing waves of past and future. This experience is an experience in thinking—since, as we saw, the whole parable concerns a mental phenomenon—and it can be won, like all experience in doing something, only through practice, through exercises. (In this, as in other respects, this kind of thinking is different from such mental processes as deducing, inducing, and drawing conclusions whose logical rules of non-contradiction and inner consistency can be learned once and for all and then need only to be applied.) The following six essays are such exercises, and their only aim is to gain experience in *how* to think; they do not contain prescriptions on what to think or which truths to hold. Least of all do they intend to retie the broken thread of tradition or to invent some newfangled surrogates with which to fill the gap between past and future. Throughout these exercises the problem of truth is kept in abeyance; the concern is solely with how to move in this gap—the only region perhaps where truth eventually will appear.

More specifically, these are exercises in political thought as it arises out of the actuality of political incidents (though such incidents are mentioned only occasionally), and my assumption is that thought itself arises out of incidents of living experience and must remain bound to them as the only guideposts by which to take its bearings. Since these exercises move between past and future, they contain criticism as well as experiment, but the experiments do not attempt to design some sort of utopian future, and the critique of the past, of traditional concepts, does not intend to "debunk." Moreover, the critical and the experimental parts of the following essays are not sharply divided, although, roughly speaking, the first three chapters are more critical than experimental and the last five chapters are more experimental than critical. This gradual shift of emphasis is not arbitrary, because there is an element of experiment in the critical interpretation of the past, an interpretation whose chief aim is to discover the real origins of traditional concepts in order to distill from them anew their original spirit which has so sadly evaporated from the very key words of political language—such as freedom and justice, authority and reason, responsibility and virtue, power and glory—leaving behind empty shells with which to settle almost all accounts, regardless of their underlying phenomenal reality.

It seems to me, and I hope the reader will agree, that the essay as a literary form has a natural affinity to the exercises I have in mind. Like all collections of essays, this book of exercises obviously could contain more or fewer chapters without for that reason changing its character. Their unity—which to me is the justification of publishing them in book form—is not the unity of a whole but of a sequence of movements which, as in a musical suite, are written in the same or related keys. The sequence itself is determined by content. In this respect, the book is divided into three parts. The first part deals with the modern break in tradition and with the concept of history with which the modern age hoped to replace the concepts of traditional metaphysics. The second part discusses two central and interrelated political concepts, authority and freedom; it presupposes the discussion of the first part in the sense that such elementary and direct questions as What is authority? What is freedom? can arise only if no answers, handed down by tradition, are available and valid any longer. The four essays of the last part, finally, are frank attempts at applying the kind of thinking that was tried out in the first two parts of the book to immediate, topical problems with which we are daily confronted, not, to be sure, in order to find definite solutions but in the hope of clarifying the issues and gaining some assurance in confronting specific questions.

I

TRADITION AND
THE MODERN AGE

I

OUR tradition of political thought had its definite beginning in
the teachings of Plato and Aristotle. I believe it came to a
no less definite end in the theories of Karl Marx. The beginning
was made when, in *The Republic*'s allegory of the cave, Plato
described the sphere of human affairs—all that belongs to the
living together of men in a common world—in terms of darkness,
confusion, and deception which those aspiring to true being must
turn away from and abandon if they want to discover the clear
sky of eternal ideas. The end came with Marx's declaration that
philosophy and its truth are located not outside the affairs of men
and their common world but precisely in them, and can be "realized" only in the sphere of living together, which he called "society," through the emergence of "socialized men" (*vergesell-
schaftete Menschen*). Political philosophy necessarily implies the
attitude of the philosopher toward politics; its tradition began with
the philosopher's turning away from politics and then returning

in order to impose his standards on human affairs. The end came
when a philosopher turned away from philosophy so as to "realize"
it in politics. This was Marx's attempt, expressed first in his decision (in itself philosophical) to abjure philosophy, and second
in his intention to "change the world" and thereby the philosophizing minds, the "consciousness" of men.

The beginning and the end of the tradition have this in common: that the elementary problems of politics never come as
clearly to light in their immediate and simple urgency as when
they are first formulated and when they receive their final challenge. The beginning, in Jacob Burckhardt's words, is like a
"fundamental chord" which sounds in its endless modulations
through the whole history of Western thought. Only beginning
and end are, so to speak, pure or unmodulated; and the fundamental chord therefore never strikes its listeners more forcefully
and more beautifully than when it first sends its harmonizing
sound into the world and never more irritatingly and jarringly
than when it still continues to be heard in a world whose sounds—
and thought—it can no longer bring into harmony. A random
remark which Plato made in his last work: "The beginning is like
a god which as long as it dwells among men saves all things"—ἀρχὴ
γὰρ καὶ θεὸς ἐν ἀνθρώποις ἱδρυμένη σώζει πάντα [1] *—is true of our tradition; as long as its beginning was alive, it could save all things
and bring them into harmony. By the same token, it became destructive as it came to its end—to say nothing of the aftermath of
confusion and helplessness which came after the tradition ended
and in which we live today.

In Marx's philosophy, which did not so much turn Hegel upside down as invert the traditional hierarchy of thought and action,
of contemplation and labor, and of philosophy and politics, the
beginning made by Plato and Aristotle proves its vitality by leading Marx into flagrantly contradictory statements, mostly in that
part of his teachings usually called utopian. The most important
are his prediction that under conditions of a "socialized humanity"
the "state will wither away," and that the productivity of labor

---

* Numbered reference notes may be found following the text.

will become so great that labor somehow will abolish itself, thus guaranteeing an almost unlimited amount of leisure time to each member of the society. These statements, in addition to being predictions, contain of course Marx's ideal of the best form of society. As such they are not utopian, but rather reproduce the political and social conditions of the same Athenian city-state which was the model of experience for Plato and Aristotle, and therefore the foundation on which our tradition rests. The Athenian polis functioned without a division between rulers and ruled, and thus was not a state if we use this term, as Marx did, in accordance with the traditional definitions of forms of government, that is, one-man rule or monarchy, rule by the few or oligarchy, and rule by the majority or democracy. Athenian citizens, moreover, were citizens only insofar as they possessed leisure time, had that freedom from labor which Marx predicts for the future. Not only in Athens but throughout antiquity and up to the modern age, those who labored were not citizens and those who were citizens were first of all those who did not labor or who possessed more than their labor power. This similarity becomes even more striking when we look into the actual content of Marx's ideal society. Leisure time is seen to exist under the condition of statelessness, or under conditions where, in Lenin's famous phrase which renders Marx's thought very precisely, the administration of society has become so simplified that every cook is qualified to take over its machinery. Obviously, under such circumstances the whole business of politics, Engels' simplified "administration of things," could be of interest only to a cook, or at best to those "mediocre minds" whom Nietzsche thought best qualified for taking care of public affairs.[2] This, to be sure, is very different from actual conditions in antiquity, where, on the contrary, political duties were considered so difficult and time-consuming that those engaged in them could not be permitted to undertake any tiring activity. (Thus, for instance, the shepherd could qualify for citizenship but the peasant could not; the painter, but not the sculptor, was still recognized as something more than a βάναυσος, the distinction being drawn in either case simply by applying the criterion of effort and fatigue.) It is against the time-consuming political life of an average full-fledged citizen of the Greek polis that the philosophers, especially Aristotle, established their ideal of σχολή, of leisure time, which in antiquity never meant freedom from ordinary labor, a matter of course anyhow, but time free from political activity and the business of the state.

In Marx's ideal society these two different concepts are inextricably combined: the classless and stateless society somehow realizes the general ancient conditions of leisure from labor and, at the same time, leisure from politics. This is supposed to come about when the "administration of things" has taken the place of government and political action. This twofold leisure from labor as well as politics had been for the philosophers the condition of a βίος θεωρητικός, a life devoted to philosophy and knowledge in the widest sense of the word. Lenin's cook, in other words, lives in a society providing her with as much leisure from labor as the free ancient citizens enjoyed in order to devote their time to πολιτεύεσθαι, as well as as much leisure from politics as the Greek philosophers had demanded for the few who wanted to devote all their time to philosophizing. The combination of a stateless (apolitical) and almost laborless society loomed so large in Marx's imagination as the very expression of an ideal humanity because of the traditional connotation of leisure as σχολή and *otium,* that is, a life devoted to aims higher than work or politics.

Marx himself regarded his so-called utopia as simple prediction, and it is true that this part of his theories corresponds to certain developments which have come fully to light only in our time. Government in the old sense has given way in many respects to administration, and the constant increase in leisure for the masses is a fact in all industrialized countries. Marx clearly perceived certain trends inherent in the era ushered in by the Industrial Revolution, although he was wrong in assuming that these trends would assert themselves only under conditions of socialization of the means of production. The hold which the tradition had over him lies in his viewing this development in an idealized light, and in understanding it in terms and concepts having their origin in an altogether different historical period. This blinded him to the authentic and very perplexing problems inherent in the modern world and gave his accurate predictions their utopian quality. But the utopian ideal of a classless, stateless, and laborless society was born out of the marriage of two altogether non-utopian elements: the perception of certain trends in the present which could no longer be understood in the framework of the tradition, and the traditional concepts and ideals by which Marx himself understood and integrated them.

Marx's own attitude to the tradition of political thought was one of conscious rebellion. In a challenging and paradoxical mood he therefore framed certain key statements which, containing his political philosophy, underlie and transcend the strictly scientific part of his work (and as such curiously remained the same throughout his life, from the early writings to the last volume of *Das Kapital*). Crucial among them are the following: "Labor created man" (in a formulation by Engels, who, contrary to an opinion current among some Marx scholars, usually rendered Marx's thought adequately and succinctly).[3] "Violence is the midwife of every old society pregnant with a new one," hence: violence is the midwife of history (which occurs in both the writings of Marx and of Engels in many variations).[4] Finally, there is the famous last thesis on Feuerbach: "The philosophers have only interpreted the world differently; the point is, however, to change it," which, in the light of Marx's thought, one could render more adequately as: The philosophers have interpreted the world long enough; the time has come to change it. For this last statement is in fact only a variation of another, occurring in an early manuscript: "You cannot *aufheben* [i.e., elevate, conserve, and abolish in the Hegelian sense] philosophy without realizing it." In the later work the same attitude to philosophy appears in the prediction that the working class will be the only legitimate heir of classical philosophy.

None of these statements can be understood in and by itself. Each acquires its meaning by contradicting some traditionally accepted truth whose plausibility up to the beginning of the modern age had been beyond doubt. "Labor created man" means first that labor and not God created man; second, it means that man, insofar as he is human, creates himself, that his humanity is the result of his own activity; it means, third, that what distinguishes man from animal, his *differentia specifica,* is not reason, but labor, that he is not an *animal rationale,* but an *animal laborans;* it means, fourth, that it is not reason, until then the highest attribute of man, but labor, the traditionally most despised human activity, which contains the humanity of man. Thus Marx challenges the traditional God, the traditional estimate of labor, and the traditional glorification of reason.

That violence is the midwife of history means that the hidden forces of development of human productivity, insofar as they depend upon free and conscious human action, come to light only through the violence of wars and revolutions. Only in those violent periods does history show its true face and dispel the fog of mere ideological, hypocritical talk. Again the challenge to tradition is clear. Violence is traditionally the *ultima ratio* in relationships between nations and the most disgraceful of domestic actions, being always considered the outstanding characteristic of tyranny. (The few attempts to save violence from disgrace, chiefly by Machiavelli and Hobbes, are of great relevance for the problem of power and quite illuminative of the early confusion of power with violence, but they exerted remarkably little influence on the tradition of political thought prior to our own time.) To Marx, on the contrary, violence or rather the possession of the means of violence is the constituent element of all forms of government; the state is the instrument of the ruling class by means of which it oppresses and exploits, and the whole sphere of political action is characterized by the use of violence.

The Marxian identification of action with violence implies another fundamental challenge to tradition which may be more difficult to perceive, but of which Marx, who knew Aristotle very well, must have been aware. The twofold Aristotelian definition of man as a ζῷον πολιτικόν and a ζῷον λόγον ἔχον, a being attaining his highest possibility in the faculty of speech and the life in a polis.

was designed to distinguish the Greek from the barbarian and the free man from the slave. The distinction was that Greeks, living together in a polis, conducted their affairs by means of speech, through persuasion (πείθειν), and not by means of violence, through mute coercion. Hence, when free men obeyed their government, or the laws of the polis, their obedience was called πειθαρχία, a word which indicates clearly that obedience was obtained by persuasion and not by force. Barbarians were ruled by violence and slaves forced to labor, and since violent action and toil are alike in that they do not need speech to be effective, barbarians and slaves were ἄνευ λόγου, that is, they did not live with each other primarily by means of speech. Labor was to the Greeks essentially a nonpolitical, private affair, but violence was related to and established a contact, albeit negative, with other men. Marx's glorification of violence therefore contains the more specific denial of λόγος, of speech, the diametrically opposite and traditionally most human form of intercourse. Marx's theory of ideological superstructures ultimately rests on this anti-traditional hostility to speech and the concomitant glorification of violence.

For traditional philosophy it would have been a contradiction in terms to "realize philosophy" or to change the world in accordance with philosophy—and Marx's statement implies that change is preceded by interpretation, so that the philosophers' interpretation of the world has indicated how it should be changed. Philosophy might have prescribed certain rules of action, though no great philosopher ever took this to be his most important concern. Essentially, philosophy from Plato to Hegel was "not of this world," whether it was Plato describing the philosopher as the man whose body only inhabits the city of his fellow men, or Hegel admitting that, from the point of view of common sense, philosophy is a world stood on its head, a *verkehrte Welt*. The challenge to tradition, this time not merely implied but directly expressed in Marx's statement, lies in the prediction that the world of common human affairs, where we orient ourselves and think in common-sense terms, will one day become identical with the realm of ideas where the philosopher moves, or that philosophy, which has always been only "for the few," will one day be the common-sense reality for everybody.

These three statements are framed in traditional terms which they, however, explode; they are formulated as paradoxes and meant to shock us. They are in fact even more paradoxical and led Marx into greater perplexities than he himself had anticipated. Each contains one fundamental contradiction which remained insoluble in his own terms. If labor is the most human and most productive of man's activities, what will happen when, after the revolution, "labor is abolished" in "the realm of freedom," when man has succeeded in emancipating himself from it? What productive and what essentially human activity will be left? If violence is the midwife of history and violent action therefore the most dignified of all forms of human action, what will happen when, after the conclusion of class struggle and the disappearance of the state, no violence will even be possible? How will men be able to act at all in a meaningful, authentic way? Finally, when philosophy has been both realized and abolished in the future society, what kind of thought will be left?

Marx's inconsistencies are well known and noted by almost all Marx scholars. They usually are summarized as discrepancies "between the scientific point of view of the historian and the moral point of view of the prophet" (Edmund Wilson), between the historian seeing in the accumulation of capital "a material means for the increase of productive forces" (Marx) and the moralist who denounced those who performed "the historical task" (Marx) as exploiters and dehumanizers of man. This and similar inconsistencies are minor when compared with the fundamental contradiction between the glorification of labor and action (as against contemplation and thought) and of a stateless, that is, actionless and (almost) laborless society. For this can be neither blamed on the natural difference between a revolutionary young Marx and the more scientific insights of the older historian and economist, nor resolved through the assumption of a dialectical movement which needs the negative or evil to produce the positive or the good.

Such fundamental and flagrant contradictions rarely occur in second-rate writers, in whom they can be discounted. In the work of great authors they lead into the very center of their work and are the most important clue to a true understanding of their problems and new insights. In Marx, as in the case of other great authors of the last century, a seemingly playful, challenging, and paradoxical mood conceals the perplexity of having to deal with new phenomena in terms of an old tradition of thought outside of whose conceptual framework no thinking seemed possible at all. It is as though Marx, not unlike Kierkegaard and Nietzsche, tried desperately to think against the tradition while using its own conceptual tools. Our tradition of political thought began when Plato discovered that it is somehow inherent in the philosophical experience to turn away from the common world of human affairs; it ended when nothing was left of this experience but the opposition of thinking and acting, which, depriving thought of reality and action of sense, makes both meaningless.

II

The strength of this tradition, its hold on Western man's thought, has never depended on his consciousness of it. Indeed, only twice in our history do we encounter periods in which men are conscious and over-conscious of the fact of tradition, identifying age as such with authority. This happened, first, when the Romans adopted classical Greek thought and culture as their own spiritual tradition and thereby decided historically that tradition was to have a permanent formative influence on European civilization. Before the Romans such a thing as tradition was unknown; with them it became and after them it remained the guiding thread through the past and the chain to which each new generation knowingly or unknowingly was bound in its understanding of the world and its own experience. Not until the Romantic period do we again encounter an exalted consciousness and glorification of tradition. (The discovery of antiquity in the Renaissance was a first attempt to break the fetters of tradition, and by going to the sources themselves to establish a past over which tradition would have no hold.) Today tradition is sometimes considered an essentially romantic concept, but Romanticism did no more than place the discussion of tradition on the agenda of the nineteenth century; its glorification of the past only served to mark the moment when the modern age was about to change our world and general circumstances to such an extent that a matter-of-course reliance on tradition was no longer possible.

The end of a tradition does not necessarily mean that traditional concepts have lost their power over the minds of men. On the contrary, it sometimes seems that this power of well-worn notions and categories becomes more tyrannical as the tradition loses its living force and as the memory of its beginning recedes; it may even reveal its full coercive force only after its end has come and men no longer even rebel against it. This at least seems to be the lesson of the twentieth-century aftermath of formalistic and compulsory thinking, which came after Kierkegaard, Marx, and Nietzsche had challenged the basic assumptions of traditional religion, traditional political thought, and traditional metaphysics by consciously inverting the traditional hierarchy of concepts. However, neither the twentieth-century aftermath nor the nineteenth-century rebellion against tradition actually caused the break in our history. This sprang from a chaos of mass-perplexities on the political scene and of mass-opinions in the spiritual sphere which the totalitarian movements, through terror and ideology, crystallized into a new form of government and domination. Totalitarian domination as an established fact, which in its unprecedentedness cannot be comprehended through the usual categories of political thought, and whose "crimes" cannot be judged by traditional moral standards or punished within the legal framework of our civilization, has broken the continuity of Occidental history. The break in our tradition is now an accomplished fact. It is neither the result of anyone's deliberate choice nor subject to further decision.

The attempts of great thinkers after Hegel to break away from patterns of thought which had ruled the West for more than two thousand years may have foreshadowed this event and certainly can help to illuminate it, but they did not cause it. The event itself marks the division between the modern age—rising with the natural sciences in the seventeenth century, reaching its political climax in the revolutions of the eighteenth, and unfolding its general implications after the Industrial Revolution of the nineteenth—and the world of the twentieth century, which came into existence through the chain of catastrophes touched off by the First World War. 'To hold the thinkers of the modern age, especially the nineteenth-century rebels against tradition, responsible for the structure and conditions of the twentieth century is even more dangerous than it is unjust. The implications apparent in the actual event of totalitarian domination go far beyond the most radical or most adventurous ideas of any of these thinkers. Their greatness lay in the fact that they perceived their world as one invaded by new problems and perplexities which our tradition of thought was unable to cope with. In this sense their own departure from tradition, no matter how emphatically they proclaimed it (like children whistling louder and louder because they are lost in the dark), was no deliberate act of their own choosing either. What frightened them about the dark was its silence, not the break in tradition. This break, when it actually occurred, dispelled the darkness, so that we can hardly listen any longer to the overloud, "pathetic" style of their writing. But the thunder of the eventual explosion has also drowned the preceding ominous silence that still answers us whenever we dare to ask, not "What are we fighting *against*" but "What are we fighting *for?*"

Neither the silence of the tradition nor the reaction of thinkers against it in the nineteenth century can ever explain what actually happened. The non-deliberate character of the break gives it an irrevocability which only events, never thoughts, can have. The rebellion against tradition in the nineteenth century remained strictly within a traditional framework; and on the level of mere thought, which could hardly be concerned then with more than the essentially negative experiences of foreboding, apprehension, and ominous silence, only radicalization, not a new beginning and reconsideration of the past, was possible.

Kierkegaard, Marx, and Nietzsche stand at the end of the tradition, just before the break came. Their immediate predecessor was Hegel. He it was who for the first time saw the whole of world history as one continuous development, and this tremendous achievement implied that he himself stood outside all authority-claiming systems and beliefs of the past, that he was held only by the thread of continuity in history itself. The thread of historical continuity was the first substitute for tradition; by means of it, the overwhelming mass of the most divergent values, the most contradictory thoughts and conflicting authorities, all of which had somehow been able to function together, were reduced to a unilinear, dialectically consistent development actually designed to repudiate not tradition as such, but the authority of all traditions. Kierkegaard, Marx, and Nietzsche remained Hegelians insofar as they saw the history of past philosophy as one dialectically developed whole; their great merit was that they radicalized this new approach toward the past in the only way it could still be further developed, namely, in questioning the conceptual hierarchy which had ruled Western philosophy since Plato and which Hegel had still taken for granted.

Kierkegaard, Marx, and Nietzsche are for us like guideposts to a past which has lost its authority. They were the first who dared to think without the guidance of any authority whatsoever; yet, for better and worse, they were still held by the categorical framework of the great tradition. In some respects we are better off. We need no longer be concerned with their scorn for the "educated philistines," who all through the nineteenth century tried to make up for the loss of authentic authority with a spurious glorification of culture. To most people today this culture looks like a field of ruins which, far from being able to claim any authority, can hardly command their interest. This fact may be deplorable, but implicit in it is the great chance to look upon the past with eyes undistracted by any tradition, with a directness which has disappeared from Occidental reading and hearing ever since Roman civilization submitted to the authority of Greek thought.

III

The destructive distortions of the tradition were all caused by men who had experienced something new which they tried almost instantaneously to overcome and resolve into something old. Kierkegaard's leap from doubt into belief was a reversal and a distortion of the traditional relationship between reason and faith. It was the answer to the modern loss of faith, not only in God but in reason as well, which was inherent in Descartes' *de omnibus dubitandum est,* with its underlying suspicion that things may not be as they appear and that an evil spirit may willfully and forever hide truth from the minds of man. Marx's leap from theory into action, and from contemplation into labor, came after Hegel had transformed metaphysics into a philosophy of history and changed the philosopher into the historian to whose backward glance eventually, at the end of time, the meaning of becoming and motion, not of being and truth, would reveal itself. Nietzsche's leap from the nonsensuous transcendent realm of ideas and measurements into the sensuousness of life, his "inverted Platonism" or "trans-valuation of values," as he himself would call it, was the last attempt to turn away from the tradition, and it succeeded only in turning tradition upside down.

Different as these rebellions against tradition are in content and intention, their results have an ominous similarity: Kierkegaard, jumping from doubt into belief, carried doubt into religion, transformed the attack of modern science on religion into an inner religious struggle, so that since then sincere religious experience has seemed possible only in the tension between doubt and belief, in torturing one's beliefs with one's doubts and relaxing from this torment in the violent affirmation of the absurdity of both the human condition and man's belief. No clearer symptom of this modern religious situation can be found than the fact that Dostoevski, perhaps the most experienced psychologist of modern religious beliefs, portrayed pure faith in the character of Myshkin "the idiot," or of Alyosha Karamazov, who is pure in heart because he is simple-minded.

Marx, when he leaped from philosophy into politics, carried the theories of dialectics into action, making political action more theoretical, more dependent upon what we today would call an ideology, than it ever had been before. Since, moreover, his springboard was not philosophy in the old metaphysical sense, but as specifically Hegel's philosophy of history as Kierkegaard's springboard had been Descartes' philosophy of doubt, he superimposed the "law of history" upon politics and ended by losing the significance of both, of action no less than of thought, of politics no less than of philosophy, when he insisted that both were mere functions of society and history.

Nietzsche's inverted Platonism, his insistence on life and the sensuously and materially given as against the suprasensuous and transcendent ideas which, since Plato, had been supposed to measure, judge, and give meaning to the given, ended in what is commonly called nihilism. Yet Nietzsche was no nihilist but, on the contrary, was the first to try to overcome the nihilism inherent not in the notions of the thinkers but in the reality of modern life. What he discovered in his attempt at "trans-valuation" was that within this categorical framework the sensuous loses its very *raison d'être* when it is deprived of its background of the suprasensuous and transcendent. "We abolished the true world: which world has remained? perhaps the world of appearances? . . . But no! together with the true world we abolished the world of appearances." [5] This insight in its elementary simplicity is relevant for all the turning-about operations in which the tradition found its end.

What Kierkegaard wanted was to assert the dignity of faith against modern reason and reasoning, as Marx desired to assert again the dignity of human action against modern historical contemplation and relativization, and as Nietzsche wanted to assert the dignity of human life against the impotence of modern man. The traditional oppositions of *fides* and *intellectus,* and of theory and practice, took their respective revenges upon Kierkegaard and Marx, just as the opposition between the transcendent and the sensuously given took its revenge upon Nietzsche, not because these oppositions still had roots in valid human experience, but, on the contrary, because they had become mere concepts, outside of which, however, no comprehensive thought seemed possible at all.

That these three outstanding and conscious rebellions against a tradition which had lost its ἀρχή, its beginning and principle, should have ended in self-defeat is no reason to question the greatness of the enterprises nor their relevance to the understanding of the modern world. Each attempt, in its particular way, took account of those traits of modernity which were incompatible with our tradition, and this even before modernity in all its aspects had fully revealed itself. Kierkegaard knew that the incompatibility of modern science with traditional beliefs does not lie in any specific scientific findings, all of which can be integrated into religious systems and absorbed by religious beliefs for the reason that they will never be able to answer the questions which religion raises. He knew that this incompatibility lay, rather, in the conflict between a spirit of doubt and distrust which ultimately can trust only what it has made itself, and the traditional unquestioning confidence in what has been given and appears in its true being to man's reason and senses. Modern science, in Marx's words, would "be superfluous if the appearance and the essence of things coincided." [6] Because our traditional religion is essentially a revealed religion and holds, in harmony with ancient philosophy, that truth is what reveals itself, that truth *is* revelation (even though the meanings of this revelation may be as different as the philosophers' ἀλήθεια and δήλωσις are from the early Christians' eschatological expectations for an ἀποκάλυψις in the Second Coming),[7] modern science has become a much more formidable enemy of religion than traditional philosophy, even in its most rationalistic versions, ever could be. Yet Kierkegaard's attempt to save faith from the onslaught of modernity made even religion modern, that is, subject to doubt and distrust. Traditional beliefs disintegrated into absurdity when Kierkegaard tried to reassert them on the assumption that man cannot trust the truth-receiving capacity of his reason or of his senses.

Marx knew that the incompatibility between classical political thought and modern political conditions lay in the accomplished fact of the French and Industrial Revolutions, which together had raised labor, traditionally the most despised of all human activities, to the highest rank of productivity and pretended to be able to assert the time-honored ideal of freedom under unheard-of conditions of universal equality. He knew that the question was only superficially posed in the idealistic assertions of the equality of man, the inborn dignity of every human being, and only superficially answered by giving laborers the right to vote. This was not a problem of justice that could be solved by giving the new class of workers its due, after which the old order of *suum cuique* would be restored and function as in the past. There is the fact of the basic incompatibility between the traditional concepts making labor itself the very symbol of man's subjection to necessity, and the modern age which saw labor elevated to express man's positive freedom, the freedom of productivity. It is from the impact of labor, that is to say, of necessity in the traditional sense, that Marx endeavored to save philosophical thought, deemed by the tradition to be the freest of all human activities. Yet when he proclaimed that "you cannot abolish philosophy without realizing it," he began subjecting thought also to the inexorable despotism of necessity, to the "iron law" of productive forces in society.

Nietzsche's devaluation of values, like Marx's labor theory of value, arises from the incompatibility between the traditional "ideas," which, as transcendent units, had been used to recognize and measure human thoughts and actions, and modern society, which had dissolved all such standards into relationships between its members, establishing them as functional "values." Values are social commodities that have no significance of their own but, like other commodities, exist only in the ever-changing relativity of social linkages and commerce. Through this relativization both the things which man produces for his use and the standards according to which he lives undergo a decisive change: they become entities of exchange, and the bearer of their "value" is society and not man, who produces and uses and judges. The "good" loses its character as an idea, the standard by which the good and the bad can be measured and recognized; it has become a value which can be exchanged with other values, such as those of expediency or of power. The holder of values can refuse this exchange and become an "idealist," who prices the value of "good" higher than the value of expediency; but this does not make the "value" of good any less relative.

The term "value" owes its origin to the sociological trend which even before Marx was quite manifest in the relatively new science of classical economy. Marx was still aware of the fact, which the social sciences have since forgotten, that nobody "seen in his isolation produces values," but that products "become values only in their social relationship." [8] His distinction between "use value" and "exchange value" reflects the distinction between things as men use and produce them and their value in society, and his insistence on the greater authenticity of use values, his frequent description of the rise of exchange value as a kind of original sin at the beginning of market production reflect his own helpless and, as it were, blind recognition of the inevitability of an impending "devaluation of all values." The birth of the social sciences can be located at the moment when all things, "ideas" as well as material objects, were equated with values, so that everything derived its existence from and was related to society, the *bonum* and *malum* no less than tangible objects. In the dispute as to whether capital or labor is the source of values, it is generally overlooked that at no time prior to the incipient Industrial Revolution was it held that values, and not things, are the result of man's productive capacity, or was everything that exists related to society and not to man "seen in his isolation." The notion of "socialized men," whose emergence Marx projected into the future classless society, is in fact the underlying assumption of classical as well as Marxian economy.

It is therefore only natural that the perplexing question which has plagued all later "value-philosophies," where to find the one supreme value by which to measure all others, should first appear in the economic sciences which, in Marx's words, try to "square the circle—to find a commodity of unchanging value which would serve as a constant standard for others." Marx believed he had found this standard in labor-time, and insisted that use values "which can be acquired without labor have no exchange value" (though they retain their "natural usefulness"), so that the earth itself is of "no value"; it does not represent "objectified labor." [9] With this conclusion we come to the threshold of a radical nihilism, to that denial of everything given of which the nineteenth-century rebellions against tradition as yet knew little and which arises only in twentieth-century society.

Nietzsche seems to have been unaware of the origin as well as of the modernity of the term "value" when he accepted it as a key notion in his assault on tradition. But when he began to devaluate the current values of society, the implications of the whole enterprise quickly became manifest. Ideas in the sense of absolute units had become identified with social values to such an extent that they simply ceased to exist once their value-character, their social status, was challenged. Nobody knew his way better than Nietzsche through the meandering paths of the modern spiritual labyrinth, where recollections and ideas of the past are hoarded up as though they had always been values which society depreciated whenever it needed better and newer commodities. Also, he was well aware of the profound nonsense of the new "value-free" science which was soon to degenerate into scientism and general scientific superstition and which never, despite all protests to the contrary, had anything in common with the Roman historians' attitude of *sine ira et studio*. For while the latter demanded judgment without scorn and truthfinding without zeal, the *wertfreie Wissenschaft,* which could no longer judge because it had lost its standards of judgment and could no longer find truth because it doubted the existence of truth, imagined that it could produce meaningful results if only it abandoned the last remnants of those absolute standards. And when Nietzsche proclaimed that he had discovered "new and higher values," he was the first to fall prey to delusions which he himself had helped to destroy, accepting the old traditional notion of measuring with transcendent units in its newest and most hideous form, thereby again carrying the relativity and exchangeability of values into the very matters whose absolute dignity he had wanted to assert—power and life and man's love of his earthly existence.

IV

Self-defeat, the result of all three challenges to tradition in the nineteenth century, is only one and perhaps the most superficial thing Kierkegaard, Marx, and Nietzsche have in common. More important is the fact that each of their rebellions seems to be concentrated on the same ever-repeated subject: Against the alleged abstractions of philosophy and its concept of man as an *animal rationale,* Kierkegaard wants to assert concrete and suffering men; Marx confirms that man's humanity consists of his productive and active force, which in its most elementary aspect he calls labor-power; and Nietzsche insists on life's productivity, on man's will and will-to-power. In complete independence of one another—none of them ever knew of the others' existence—they arrive at the conclusion that this enterprise in terms of the tradition can be achieved only through a mental operation best described in the images and similes of leaps, inversions, and turning concepts upside down: Kierkegaard speaks of his leap from doubt into belief; Marx turns Hegel, or rather "Plato and the whole Platonic tradition" (Sidney Hook), "right side up again," leaping "from the realm of necessity into the realm of freedom"; and Nietzsche understands his philosophy as "inverted Platonism" and "transformation of all values."

The turning operations with which the tradition ends bring the beginning to light in a twofold sense. The very assertion of one side of the opposites—*fides* against *intellectus,* practice against theory, sensuous, perishable life against permanent, unchanging, suprasensuous truth—necessarily brings to light the repudiated opposite and

shows that both have meaning and significance only in this opposition. Furthermore, to think in terms of such opposites is not a matter
of course, but is grounded in a first great turning operation on
which all others ultimately are based because it established the opposites in whose tension the tradition moves. This first turning-about
is Plato's περιαγωγὴ τῆς ψυχῆς, the turning-about of the whole human
being, which he tells—as though it were a story with beginning and
end and not merely a mental operation—in the parable of the cave
in *The Republic*.

The story of the cave unfolds in three stages: the first turning-
about takes place in the cave itself when one of the inhabitants frees
himself from the fetters which chain the cave dwellers' "legs and
necks" so that "they can only see before them," their eyes glued to
the screen on which shadows and images of things appear; he now
turns around to the rear of the cave, where an artificial fire illuminates the things in the cave as they really are. There is, second, the
turning from the cave to the clear sky, where the ideas appear as
the true and eternal essences of the things in the cave, illuminated
by the sun, the idea of ideas, enabling man to see and the ideas to
shine forth. Finally, there is the necessity of returning to the cave, of
leaving the realm of eternal essences and moving again in the realm
of perishable things and mortal men. Each of these turnings is accomplished by a loss of sense and orientation: the eyes accustomed
to the shadowy appearances on the screen are blinded by the fire
in the cave; the eyes then adjusted to the dim light of the artificial
fire are blinded by the light that illuminates the ideas; finally, the
eyes adjusted to the light of the sun must readjust to the dimness of
the cave.

Behind these turnings-about, which Plato demands only of the
philosopher, the lover of truth and light, lies another inversion indicated generally in Plato's violent polemics against Homer and the
Homeric religion, and in particular in the construction of his story
as a kind of reply to and reversal of Homer's description of Hades
in the eleventh book of the *Odyssey*. The parallel between the images
of the cave and Hades (the shadowy, unsubstantial, senseless movements of the soul in Homer's Hades correspond to the ignorance and

senselessness of the bodies in the cave) is unmistakable because it is stressed by Plato's use of the words εἴδωλον, image, and σκία, shadow, which are Homer's own key words for the description of life after death in the underworld. The reversal of the Homeric "position" is obvious; it is as though Plato were saying to him: Not the life of bodyless souls, but the life of the bodies takes place in an underworld; compared to the sky and the sun, the earth is like Hades; images and shadows are the objects of bodily senses, not the surroundings of bodyless souls; the true and real is not the world in which we move and live and which we have to part from in death, but the ideas seen and grasped by the eyes of the mind. In a sense, Plato's περιαγωγή was a turning-about by which everything that was commonly believed in Greece in accordance with the Homeric religion came to stand on its head. It is as though the underworld of Hades had risen to the surface of the earth.[10] But this reversal of Homer did not actually turn Homer upside down or downside up, since the dichotomy within which such an operation alone can take place is almost as alien to Plato's thought, which did not yet operate with predetermined opposites, as it is alien to the Homeric world. (No turning about of the tradition can therefore ever land us in the original Homeric "position," which seems to have been Nietzsche's error; he probably thought that his inverted Platonism could lead him back into pre-Platonic modes of thought.) It was solely for political purposes that Plato set forth his doctrine of ideas in the form of a reversal of Homer; but thereby he established the framework within which such turning operations are not far-fetched possibilities but predetermined by the conceptual structure itself. The development of philosophy in late antiquity in the various schools, which fought one another with a fanaticism unequaled in the pre-Christian world, consists of turnings-about and shifting emphases on one of two opposite terms, made possible by Plato's separation of a world of mere shadowy appearance and the world of eternally true ideas. He himself had given the first example in the turning from the cave to the sky. When Hegel finally, in a last gigantic effort, had gathered together into one consistent self-developing whole the various strands of traditional philosophy as they had developed from

Plato's original concept, the same splitting up into two conflicting schools of thought, though on a much lower level, took place, and right-wing and left-wing, idealistic and materialistic Hegelians could for a short while dominate philosophical thought.

The significance of Kierkegaard's, Marx's, and Nietzsche's challenges to the tradition—though none of them would have been possible without the synthesizing achievement of Hegel and his concept of history—is that they constitute a much more radical turning-about than the mere upside-down operations with their weird oppositions between sensualism and idealism, materialism and spiritualism, and even immanentism and transcendentalism imply. If Marx had been merely a "materialist" who brought Hegel's "idealism" down to earth, his influence would have been as short-lived and limited to scholarly quarrels as that of his contemporaries. Hegel's basic assumption was that the dialectical movement of thought is identical with the dialectical movement of matter itself. Thus he hoped to bridge the abyss which Descartes had opened between man, defined as *res cogitans,* and the world, defined as *res extensa,* between cognition and reality, thinking and being. The spiritual homelessness of modern man finds its first expressions in this Cartesian perplexity and the Pascalian answer. Hegel claimed that the discovery of the dialectical movement as a universal law, ruling both man's reason and human affairs *and* the inner "reason" of natural events, accomplished even more than a mere correspondence between *intellectus* and *res,* whose coincidence pre-Cartesian philosophy had defined as truth. By introducing the spirit and its self-realization in movement, Hegel believed he had demonstrated an ontological identity of matter and idea. To Hegel, therefore, it would have been of no great importance whether one started this movement from the viewpoint of consciousness, which at one moment begins to "materialize," or whether one chose as starting point matter, which, moving in the direction of "spiritualization," becomes conscious of itself. (How little Marx doubted these fundamentals of his teacher appears from the role he ascribed to self-consciousness in the form of class-consciousness in history.) In other words, Marx was no more a "dialectical materialist" than Hegel was a "dialectical idealist"; the very concept of dialectical *movement,* as Hegel conceived it as a universal law, and as Marx accepted it, makes the terms "idealism" and "materialism" as philosophical systems meaningless. Marx, especially in his earlier writings, is quite conscious of this and knows that his repudiation of the tradition and of Hegel does not lie in his "materialism," but in his refusal to assume that the difference between man and animal life is *ratio,* or thought, that, in Hegel's words, "man is essentially spirit"; for the young Marx man is essentially a natural being endowed with the faculty of action (*ein tätiges Naturwesen*), and his action remains "natural" because it consists of laboring—the metabolism between man and nature.[11] His turning-about, like Kierkegaard's and Nietzsche's, goes to the core of the matter; they all question the traditional hierarchy of human capabilities, or, to put it another way, they ask again what the specifically human quality of man is; they do not intend to build systems or *Weltanschauungen* on this or that premise.

Since the rise of modern science, whose spirit is expressed in the Cartesian philosophy of doubt and mistrust, the conceptual framework of the tradition has not been secure. The dichotomy between contemplation and action, the traditional hierarchy which ruled that truth is ultimately perceived only in speechless and actionless seeing, could not be upheld under conditions in which science became active and *did* in order to know. When the trust that things appear as they really are was gone, the concept of truth as revelation had become doubtful, and with it the unquestioning faith in a revealed God. The notion of "theory" changed its meaning. It no longer meant a system of reasonably connected truths which as such had been not made but given to reason and the senses. Rather it became the modern scientific theory, which is a working hypothesis, changing in accordance with the results it produces and depending for its validity not on what it "reveals" but on whether it "works." By the same process, Plato's ideas lost their autonomous power to illuminate the world and the universe. First they became what they had been for Plato only in their relationship to the political realm, standards and measurements, or the regulating, limiting forces of man's own reasoning mind, as they appear in Kant. Then, after the priority of reason over doing, of the mind's prescribing its rules to the actions of men, had been lost in the transformation of the whole world by the Industrial Revolution—a transformation the success of which seemed to prove that man's doings and fabrications prescribe their rules to reason—these ideas finally became mere values whose validity is determined not by one or many men but by society as a whole in its ever-changing functional needs.

These values in their ex- and inter-changeability are the only "ideas" left to (and understood by) "socialized men." These are men who have decided never to leave what to Plato was "the cave" of everyday human affairs, and never to venture on their own into a world and a life which, perhaps, the ubiquitous functionalization of modern society has deprived of one of its most elementary characteristics—the instilling of wonder at that which is as it is. This very real development is reflected and foreshadowed in Marx's political thought. Turning the tradition upside down within its own framework, he did not actually get rid of Plato's ideas, though he did record the darkening of the clear sky where those ideas, as well as many other presences, had once become visible to the eyes of men.

2

THE CONCEPT
OF HISTORY

Ancient and Modern

I: History and Nature

LET us begin with Herodotus, whom Cicero called *pater historiae* and who has remained father of Western history.[1] He tells us in the first sentence of the Persian Wars that the purpose of his enterprise is to preserve that which owes its existence to men, τὰ γενόμενα ἐξ ἀνθρώπων, lest it be obliterated by time, and to bestow upon the glorious, wondrous deeds of Greeks and barbarians sufficient praise to assure their remembrance by posterity and thus make their glory shine through the centuries.

This tells us a great deal and yet does not tell us enough. For us, concern with immortality is not a matter of course, and Herodotus, since this was a matter of course to him, does not tell us much about it. His understanding of the task of history—to save human deeds from the futility that comes from oblivion—was rooted in the Greek concept and experience of nature, which comprehended all things

41

that come into being by themselves without assistance from men or gods—the Olympian gods did not claim to have created the world [2] —and therefore are immortal. Since the things of nature are ever-present, they are not likely to be overlooked or forgotten; and since they are forever, they do not need human remembrance for their further existence. All living creatures, man not excepted, are contained in this realm of being-forever, and Aristotle explicitly assures us that man, insofar as he is a natural being and belongs to the species of mankind, possesses immortality; through the recurrent cycle of life, nature assures the same kind of being-forever to things that are born and die as to things that are and do not change. "Being for living creatures is Life," and being-forever ($\grave{\alpha}\epsilon\grave{\iota}$ $\epsilon\hat{\iota}\nu\alpha\iota$) corresponds to $\grave{\alpha}\epsilon\iota\gamma\epsilon\nu\acute{\epsilon}s$, procreation.[3]

No doubt this eternal recurrence "is the closest possible approximation of a world of becoming to that of being," [4] but it does not, of course, make individual men immortal; on the contrary, embedded in a cosmos in which everything was immortal, it was mortality which became the hallmark of human existence. Men are "the mortals," the only mortal things there are, for animals exist only as members of their species and not as individuals. The mortality of man lies in the fact that individual life, a $\beta\acute{\iota}os$ with a recognizable life-story from birth to death, rises out of biological life, $\zeta\omega\acute{\eta}$. This individual life is distinguished from all other things by the rectilinear course of its movement, which, so to speak, cuts through the circular movements of biological life. This is mortality: to move along a rectilinear line in a universe where everything, if it moves at all, moves in a cyclical order. Whenever men pursue their purposes, tilling the effortless earth, forcing the free-flowing wind into their sails, crossing the ever-rolling waves, they cut across a movement which is purposeless and turning within itself. When Sophocles (in the famous chorus of *Antigone*) says that there is nothing more awe-inspiring than man, he goes on to exemplify this by evoking purposeful human activities which do violence to nature because they disturb what, in the absence of mortals, would be the eternal quiet of being-forever that rests or swings within itself.

What is difficult for us to realize is that the great deeds and works of which mortals are capable, and which become the topic of historical narrative, are not seen as parts of either an encompassing whole or a process; on the contrary, the stress is always on single instances and single gestures. These single instances, deeds or events, interrupt the circular movement of daily life in the same sense that the rectilinear βίος of the mortals interrupts the circular movement of biological life. The subject matter of history is these interruptions—the extraordinary, in other words.

When in late antiquity speculations began about the nature of history in the sense of a historical process and about the historical fate of nations, their rise and fall, where the particular actions and events were engulfed in a whole, it was at once assumed that these processes must be circular. The historical movement began to be construed in the image of biological life. In terms of ancient philosophy, this could mean that the world of history had been reintegrated into the world of nature, the world of the mortals into the universe that is forever. But in terms of ancient poetry and historiography it meant that the earlier sense of the greatness of mortals, as distinguished from the undoubtedly higher greatness of the gods and nature, had been lost.

In the beginning of Western history the distinction between the mortality of men and the immortality of nature, between man-made things and things which come into being by themselves, was the tacit assumption of historiography. All things that owe their existence to men, such as works, deeds, and words, are perishable, infected, as it were, by the mortality of their authors. However, if mortals succeeded in endowing their works, deeds, and words with some permanence and in arresting their perishability, then these things would, to a degree at least, enter and be at home in the world of everlastingness, and the mortals themselves would find their place in the cosmos, where everything is immortal except men. The human capacity to achieve this was remembrance, Mnemosyne, who therefore was regarded as the mother of all the other muses.

In order to understand quickly and with some measure of clarity how far we today are removed from this Greek understanding of the relationship between nature and history, between the cosmos and men, we may be permitted to quote four lines from Rilke and leave them in their original language; their perfection seems to defy translation.

> Berge ruhn, von Sternen überprächtigt;
> aber auch in ihnen flimmert Zeit.
> Ach, in meinem wilden Herzen nächtigt
> obdachlos die Unvergänglichkeit.[5]

Here even the mountains only seem to rest under the light of the stars; they are slowly, secretly devoured by time; nothing is forever, immortality has fled the world to find an uncertain abode in the darkness of the human heart that still has the capacity to remember and to say: forever. Immortality or imperishability, if and when it occurs at all, is homeless. If one looks upon these lines through Greek eyes it is almost as though the poet had tried consciously to reverse the Greek relationships: everything has become perishable, except perhaps the human heart; immortality is no longer the medium in which mortals move, but has taken its homeless refuge in the very heart of mortality; immortal things, works and deeds, events and even words, though men might still be able to externalize, reify as it were, the remembrance of their hearts, have lost their home in the world; since the world, since nature is perishable and since man-made things, once they have come into being, share the fate of all being—they begin to perish the moment they have come into existence.

With Herodotus words and deeds and events—that is, those things that owe their existence exclusively to men—became the subject matter of history. Of all man-made things, these are the most futile. The works of human hands owe part of their existence to the material nature provides and therefore carry within themselves some measure of permanence, borrowed, as it were, from the being-forever of nature. But what goes on between mortals directly, the spoken word and all the actions and deeds which the Greeks called πράξεις or πράγματα, as distinguished from ποίησις, fabrication, can never outlast the moment of their realization, would never leave any trace without the help of remembrance. The task of the poet and

historiographer (both of whom Aristotle still puts in the same category because their subject is πρᾶξις) [6] consists in making something
lasting out of remembrance. They do this by translating πρᾶξις and
λέξις, action and speech, into that kind of ποίησις or fabrication
which eventually becomes the written word.

History as a category of human existence is of course older than
the written word, older than Herodotus, older even than Homer.
Not historically but poetically speaking, its beginning lies rather in
the moment when Ulysses, at the court of the king of the Phaeacians,
listened to the story of his own deeds and sufferings, to the story
of his life, now a thing outside himself, an "object" for all to see
and to hear. What had been sheer occurrence now became "history."
But the transformation of single events and occurrences into history
was essentially the same "imitation of action" in words which was
later employed in Greek tragedy,[7] where, as Burckhardt once remarked, "external action is hidden from the eye" through the re-
ports of messengers, even though there was no objection at all to
showing the horrible.[8] The scene where Ulysses listens to the story
of his own life is paradigmatic for both history and poetry; the
"reconciliation with reality," the catharsis, which, according to Aristotle, was the essence of tragedy, and, according to Hegel, was the
ultimate purpose of history, came about through the tears of remembrance. The deepest human motive for history and poetry appears here in unparalleled purity: since listener, actor, and sufferer
are the same person, all motives of sheer curiosity and lust for new
information, which, of course, have always played a large role in
both historical inquiry and aesthetic pleasure, are naturally absent
in Ulysses himself, who would have been bored rather than moved
if history were only news and poetry only entertainment.

Such distinctions and reflections may seem commonplace to modern ears. Implied in them, however, is one great and painful paradox
which contributed (perhaps more than any other single factor) to
the tragic aspect of Greek culture in its greatest manifestations. The
paradox is that, on the one hand, everything was seen and measured
against the background of the things that are forever, while, on the
other, true human greatness was understood, at least by the pre-

Platonic Greeks, to reside in deeds and words, and was rather represented by Achilles, "the doer of great deeds and the speaker of great words," than by the maker and fabricator, even the poet and writer. This paradox, that greatness was understood in terms of permanence while human greatness was seen in precisely the most futile and least lasting activities of men, has haunted Greek poetry and historiography as it has perturbed the quiet of the philosophers.

The early Greek solution of the paradox was poetic and non-philosophical. It consisted in the immortal fame which the poets could bestow upon word and deed to make them outlast not only the futile moment of speech and action but even the mortal life of their agent. Prior to the Socratic school—with the possible exception of Hesiod—we encounter no real criticism of immortal fame; even Heraclitus thought that it was the greatest of all human aspirations, and while he denounced with violent bitterness the political conditions in his native Ephesus, it never would have occurred to him to condemn the realm of human affairs as such or doubt its potential greatness.

The change, prepared by Parmenides, came about with Socrates and reached its culmination in Plato's philosophy, whose teaching regarding a potential immortality of mortal men become authoritative for all philosophy schools in antiquity. To be sure, Plato was still confronted with the same paradox and he seems to have been the first who considered "the desire to become famous and not to lie in the end without a name" on the same level as the natural desire for children through which nature secures the immortality of the species, though not the ἀθανασία of the individual person. In his political philosophy, therefore, he proposed to substitute the latter for the former, as though the desire for immortality through fame could as well be fulfilled when men "are immortal because they leave children's children behind them, and partake of immortality through the unity of a sempiternal becoming"; when he declared the begetting of children to be a law he obviously hoped this would be sufficient for the "common man's" natural yearning for death-lessness. For neither Plato nor Aristotle any longer believed that mortal men could "immortalize" (ἀθανατίζειν, in the Aristotelian terminology, an activity whose object is by no means necessarily one's own self, the immortal fame of the name, but includes a variety of occupations with immortal things in general) through great deeds and words.[9] They had discovered, in the activity of thought itself, a hidden human capacity for turning away from the whole realm of human affairs which should not be taken too seriously by men (Plato) because it was patently absurd to think that man is the highest being there is (Aristotle). While begetting might be enough for the many, to "immortalize" meant for the philosopher to dwell in the neighborhood of those things which are forever, to be there and present in a state of active attention, but without doing anything, without performance of deeds or achievement of works. Thus the proper attitude of mortals, once they had reached the neighborhood of the immortal, was actionless and even speechless contemplation: the Aristotelian νοῦς, the highest and most human capacity of pure vision, cannot translate into words what it beholds,[10] and the ultimate truth which the vision of ideas disclosed to Plato is likewise an ἄρρητον, something which cannot be caught in words.[11] Hence the old paradox was resolved by the philosophers by denying to man not the capacity to "immortalize," but the capability of measuring himself and his own deeds against the everlasting greatness of the cosmos, of matching, as it were, the immortality of nature and the gods with an immortal greatness of his own. The solution clearly comes about at the expense of "the doer of great deeds and the speaker of great words."

The distinction between the poets and historians on one side and the philosophers on the other was that the former simply accepted the common Greek concept of greatness. Praise, from which came glory and eventually everlasting fame, could be bestowed only upon things already "great," that is, things that possessed an emerging, shining quality which distinguished them from all others and made glory possible. The great was that which deserved immortality, that which should be admitted to the company of things that lasted forever, surrounding the futility of mortals with their unsurpassable majesty. Through history men almost became the equals of nature, and only those events, deeds, or words that rose by themselves to the ever-present challenge of the natural universe were what we would call historical. Not only the poet Homer and not only the storyteller Herodotus, but even Thucydides, who in a much more sober mood was the first to set standards for historiography, tells us explicitly in the beginning of the *Peloponnesian War* that he wrote his work because of the war's "greatness," because "this was the greatest movement yet known in history, not only of the Hellenes, but of a large part of the barbarian world . . . almost mankind."

The concern with greatness, so prominent in Greek poetry and historiography, is based on the most intimate connection between the concepts of nature and history. Their common denominator is immortality. Immortality is what nature possesses without effort and without anybody's assistance, and immortality is what the mortals therefore must try to achieve if they want to live up to the world into which they were born, to live up to the things which surround them and to whose company they are admitted for a short while. The connection between history and nature is therefore by no means an opposition. History receives into its remembrance those mortals who through deed and word have proved themselves worthy of nature, and their everlasting fame means that they, despite their mortality, may remain in the company of the things that last forever.

Our modern concept of history is no less intimately connected with our modern concept of nature than the corresponding and very different concepts which stand at the beginning of our history. They too can be seen in their full significance only if their common root is discovered. The nineteenth-century opposition of the natural and historical sciences, together with the allegedly absolute objectivity and precision of the natural scientists, is today a thing of the past. The natural sciences now admit that with the experiment, testing natural processes under prescribed conditions, and with the observer, who in watching the experiment becomes one of its conditions, a "subjective" factor is introduced into the "objective" processes of nature.

The most important new result of nuclear physics was the recognition of the possibility of applying quite different types of natural laws, without contradiction, to one and the same physical event. This is due to the fact that within a system of laws which are based on certain fundamental ideas only certain quite definite ways of asking questions make sense, and thus, that such a system is separated from others which allow different questions to be put.[12]

In other words, the experiment "being a question put before nature" (Galileo),[13] the answers of science will always remain replies to questions asked by men; the confusion in the issue of "objectivity" was to assume that there could be answers without questions and results independent of a question-asking being. Physics, we know today, is no less a man-centered inquiry into what is than historical research. The old quarrel, therefore, between the "subjectivity" of historiography and the "objectivity" of physics has lost much of its relevance.[14]

The modern historian as a rule is not yet aware of the fact that the natural scientist, against whom he had to defend his own "scientific standards" for so many decades, finds himself in the same position, and he is quite likely to state and restate in new, seemingly more scientific terms the old distinction between a science of nature and a science of history. The reason is that the problem of objectivity in the historical sciences is more than a mere technical, scientific perplexity. Objectivity, the "extinction of the self" as the condition of "pure vision" (*das reine Sehen der Dinge*—Ranke) meant the historian's abstention from bestowing either praise or blame, together with an attitude of perfect distance with which he would follow the course of events as they were revealed in his documentary sources. To him the only limitation of this attitude, which Droysen once denounced as "eunuchic objectivity," [15] lay in the necessity of selecting material from a mass of facts which, compared with the limited capacity of the human mind and the limited time of human life, appeared infinite. Objectivity, in other words, meant noninterference as well as nondiscrimination. Of these two, nondiscrimination, abstention from praise and blame, was obviously much easier to achieve than noninterference; every selection of material in a sense interferes with history, and all criteria for selection put the historical course of events under certain man-made conditions, which are quite similar to the conditions the natural scientist prescribes to natural processes in the experiment.

We have stated here the problem of objectivity in modern terms, as it arose during the modern age, which believed it had discovered in history a "new science" which then would have to comply to the standards of the "older" science of nature. This, however, was a self-misunderstanding. Modern natural science developed quickly into an even "newer" science than history, and both sprang, as we shall see, from exactly the same set of "new" experiences with the exploration of the universe, made at the beginning of the modern age. The curious and still confusing point about the historical sciences was that they did not take their standards from the natural sciences of their own age, but harked back to the scientific and, in the last analysis, philosophical attitude which the modern age had just begun to liquidate. Their scientific standards, culminating in the "extinction of the self," had their roots in Aristotelian and medieval natural science, which consisted mainly in observing and cataloguing observed facts. Before the rise of the modern age it was a matter of course that quiet, actionless, and selfless contemplation of the miracle of being, or of the wonder of God's creation, should also be the proper attitude for the scientist, whose curiosity about the particular had not yet parted company with the wonder before the general from which, according to the ancients, sprang philosophy.

With the modern age this objectivity lost its fundament and therefore was constantly on the lookout for new justifications. For the historical sciences the old standard of objectivity could make sense only if the historian believed that history in its entirety was either a cyclical phenomenon which could be grasped as a whole through contemplation (and Vico, following the theories of late antiquity, was still of this opinion) or that it was guided by some divine providence for the salvation of mankind, whose plan was revealed, whose beginnings and ends were known, and therefore could be again contemplated as a whole. Both these concepts, however, were actually quite alien to the new consciousness of history in the modern age; they were only the old traditional framework into which the new experiences were pressed and from which the new science had risen. The problem of scientific objectivity, as the nineteenth century posed it, owed so much to historical self-misunderstanding and philosophical confusion that the real issue at stake, the issue of impartiality, which is indeed decisive not only for the "science" of history but for all historiography from poetry and storytelling onward, has become difficult to recognize.

Impartiality, and with it all true historiography, came into the world when Homer decided to sing the deeds of the Trojans no less than those of the Achaeans, and to praise the glory of Hector no less than the greatness of Achilles. This Homeric impartiality, as it is echoed by Herodotus, who set out to prevent "the great and wonderful actions of the Greeks *and* the barbarians from losing their due meed of glory," is still the highest type of objectivity we know. Not only does it leave behind the common interest in one's own side and one's own people which, up to our own days, characterizes almost all national historiography, but it also discards the alternative of victory or defeat, which moderns have felt expresses the "objective" judgment of history itself, and does not permit it to interfere with what is judged to be worthy of immortalizing praise. Somewhat later, and most magnificently expressed in Thucydides, there appears in Greek historiography still another powerful element that contributes to historical objectivity. It could come to the foreground only after long experience in polis-life, which to an incredibly large extent consisted of citizens talking with one another. In this incessant talk the Greeks discovered that the world we have in common is usually regarded from an infinite number of different standpoints, to which correspond the most diverse points of view. In a sheer inexhaustible flow of arguments, as the Sophists presented them to the citizenry of Athens, the Greek learned to exchange his own viewpoint, his own "opinion"—the way the world appeared and opened up to him (δοκεῖ μοι, "it appears to me," from which comes δόξα, or "opinion")—with those of his fellow citizens. Greeks learned to *understand*—not to understand one another as individual persons, but to look upon the same world from one another's standpoint, to see the same in very different and frequently opposing aspects. The speeches in which Thucydides makes articulate the standpoints and interests of the warring parties are still a living testimony to the extraordinary degree of this objectivity.

What has obscured the modern discussion of objectivity in the historical sciences and prevented its ever touching the fundamental issues involved seems to be the fact that none of the conditions of either Homeric impartiality or Thucydidean objectivity are present in the modern age. Homeric impartiality rested upon the assumption that great things are self-evident, shine by themselves; that the poet (or later the historiographer) has only to preserve their glory, which is essentially futile, and that he would destroy, instead of preserving, if he were to forget the glory that was Hector's. For the short duration of their existence great deeds and great words were, in their greatness, as real as a stone or a house, there to be seen and heard by everybody present. Greatness was easily recognizable as that which by itself aspired to immortality—that is, negatively speaking, as a heroic contempt for all that merely comes and passes away, for all individual life, one's own included. This sense of greatness could not possibly survive intact into the Christian era for the very simple reason that, according to Christian teachings, the relationship between life and world is the exact opposite to that in Greek and Latin antiquity: in Christianity neither the world nor the ever-recurring cycle of life is immortal, only the single living individual. It is the world that will pass away; men will live forever. The Christian reversal is based, in its turn, upon the altogether different teachings of the Hebrews, who always held that life itself is sacred, more sacred than anything else in the world, and that man is the supreme being on earth.

Connected with this inner conviction of the sacredness of life as such, which has remained with us even after security of the Christian faith in life after death has passed away, is the stress on the all-importance of self-interest, still so prominent in all modern political philosophy. In our context this means that the Thucydidean type of objectivity, no matter how much it may be admired, no longer has any basis in real political life. Since we have made life our supreme and foremost concern, we have no room left for an activity based on contempt for one's own life-interest. Selflessness may still be a religious or a moral virtue; it can hardly be a political one. Under these conditions objectivity lost its validity in experience, was divorced from real life, and became that "lifeless" academic affair which Droysen rightly denounced as being eunuchic.

Moreover, the birth of the modern idea of history not only coincided with but was powerfully stimulated by the modern age's doubt of the reality of an outer world "objectively" given to human perception as an unchanged and unchangeable object. In our context the most important consequence of this doubt was the emphasis on sensation *qua* sensation as more "real" than the "sensed" object and, at any rate, the only safe ground of experience. Against this subjectivization, which is but one aspect of the still growing world-alienation of man in the modern age, no judgments could hold out: they were all reduced to the level of sensations and ended on the level of the lowest of all sensations, the sensation of taste. Our vocabulary is a telling testimony to this degradation. All judgments not inspired by moral principle (which is felt to be old-fashioned) or not dictated by some self-interest are considered matters of "taste," and this in hardly a different sense from what we mean by saying that the preference for clam chowder over pea soup is a matter of taste. This conviction, the vulgarity of its defenders on the theoretical level notwithstanding, has disturbed the conscience of the historian much more deeply because it has much deeper roots in the general spirit of the modern age than the allegedly superior scientific standards of his colleagues in the natural sciences.

Unfortunately it is in the nature of academic quarrels that methodological problems are likely to overshadow more fundamental issues. The fundamental fact about the modern concept of history is that it arose in the same sixteenth and seventeenth centuries which ushered in the gigantic development of the natural sciences. Foremost among the characteristics of that age, which are still alive and present in our own world, is the world-alienation of man, which I mentioned before and which is so difficult to perceive as a basic condition of our whole life because out of it, and partly at least out of its despair, did arise the tremendous structure of the human artifice we inhabit today, in whose framework we have even discovered the means of destroying it together with all non-man-made things on earth.

The shortest and most fundamental expression this world-alienation ever found is contained in Descartes' famous *de omnibus dubitandum est,* for this rule signifies something altogether different from the skepticism inherent in the self-doubt of all true thought. Descartes came to his rule because the then recent discoveries in the natural sciences had convinced him that man in his search for truth and knowledge can trust neither the given evidence of the senses, nor the "innate truth" of the mind, nor the "inner light of reason." This mistrust of the human capacities has been ever since one of the most elementary conditions of the modern age and the modern world; but it did not spring, as is usually assumed, from a sudden mysterious dwindling of faith in God, and its cause was originally not even a suspicion of reason as such. Its origin was simply the highly justified loss of confidence in the truth-revealing capacity of the senses. Reality no longer was disclosed as an outer phenomenon to human sensation, but had withdrawn, so to speak, into the sensing of the sensation itself. It now turned out that without confidence in the senses neither faith in God nor trust in reason could any longer be secure, because the revelation of both divine and rational truth had always been implicitly understood to follow the awe-inspiring simplicity of man's relationship with the world: I open my eyes and behold the vision, I listen and hear the sound, I move my body and touch the tangibility of the world. If we begin to doubt the fundamental truthfulness and reliability of this relationship, which of course does not exclude errors and illusions but, on the contrary, is the condition of their eventual correction, none of the traditional metaphors for suprasensual truth—be it the eyes of the mind which can see the sky of ideas or the voice of conscience listened to by the human heart—can any longer carry its meaning.

The fundamental experience underlying Cartesian doubt was the discovery that the earth, contrary to all direct sense experience, revolves around the sun. The modern age began when man, with the help of the telescope, turned his bodily eyes toward the universe, about which he had speculated for a long time—seeing with the eyes of the mind, listening with the ears of the heart, and guided by the inner light of reason—and learned that his senses were not fitted for the universe, that his everyday experience, far from being able to constitute the model for the reception of truth and the acquisition of knowledge, was a constant source of error and delusion. After this deception—whose enormity we find difficult to realize because it was centuries before its full impact was felt everywhere and not only in the rather restricted milieu of scholars and philosophers—suspicions began to haunt modern man from all sides. But its most immediate consequence was the spectacular rise of natural science, which for a long time seemed to be liberated by the discovery that our senses by themselves do not tell the truth. Henceforth, sure of the unreliability of sensation and the resulting insufficiency of mere observation, the natural sciences turned toward the experiment, which, by directly interfering with nature, assured the development whose progress has ever since appeared to be limitless.

Descartes became the father of modern philosophy because he generalized the experience of the preceding as well as his own generation, developed it into a new method of thinking, and thus became the first thinker thoroughly trained in that "school of suspicion" which, according to Nietzsche, constitutes modern philosophy. Suspicion of the senses remained the core of scientific pride until in our time it has turned into a source of uneasiness. The trouble is that "we find nature behaving so differently from what we observe in the visible and palpable bodies of our surroundings that *no* model shaped after our large-scale experiences can ever be 'true' "; at this point the indissoluble connection between our thinking and our sense perception takes its revenge, for a model that would leave sense experience altogether out of account and, therefore, be completely adequate to nature in the experiment is not only "practically inaccessible but not even thinkable." [16] The trouble, in other words, is not that the modern physical universe cannot be visualized, for this is a matter of course under the assumption that nature does not reveal itself to the human senses; the uneasiness begins when nature turns out to be inconceivable, that is, unthinkable in terms of pure reasoning as well.

The dependence of modern thought upon factual discoveries of the natural sciences shows itself most clearly in the seventeenth century. It is not always admitted as readily as by Hobbes, who attributed his philosophy exclusively to the results of the work of Copernicus and Galileo, Kepler, Gassendi, and Mersenne, and who denounced all past philosophy as nonsense with a violence matched perhaps only by Luther's contempt for the *"stulti philosophi."* One does not need the radical extremism of Hobbes's conclusion, not that man may be evil by nature, but that a distinction between good and evil makes no sense, and that reason, far from being an inner light disclosing truth, is a mere "faculty of reckoning with consequences"; for the basic suspicion that man's earthbound experience presents a caricature of truth is no less present in Descartes' fear that an evil spirit may rule the world and withhold truth forever from the mind of a being so manifestly subject to error. In its most harmless form, it permeates English empiricism, where the meaningfulness of the sensibly given is dissolved into data of sense perception, disclosing their meaning only through habit and repeated experiences, so that in an extreme subjectivism man is ultimately imprisoned in a non-world of meaningless sensations that no reality and no truth can penetrate. Empiricism is only seemingly a vindication of the senses; actually it rests on the assumption that only common-sense arguing can give them meaning, and it always starts with a declaration of non-confidence in the truth- or reality-revealing capacity of the senses. Puritanism and empiricism, in fact, are only two sides of the same coin. The same fundamental suspicion finally inspired Kant's gigantic effort to re-examine the human faculties in such a way that the question of a *Ding an sich,* that is the truth-revealing faculty of experience in an absolute sense, could be left in abeyance.

Of much more immediate consequence for our concept of history was the positive version of subjectivism which arose from the same predicament: Although it seems that man is unable to recognize the given world which he has not made himself, he nevertheless must be capable of knowing at least what he made himself. This pragmatic attitude is already the fully articulated reason why Vico turned his attention to history and thus became one of the fathers of modern historical consciousness. He said: *Geometrica demonstramus quia facimus; si physica demonstrare possemus, faceremus.*[17] ("Mathematical matters we can prove because we ourselves make them; to prove the physical, we would have to make it.") Vico turned to the sphere of history only because he still believed it impossible "to make nature." No so-called humanist considerations inspired his turning away from nature, but solely the belief that history is "made" by men just as nature is "made" by God; hence historical truth can be known by men, the makers of history, but physical truth is reserved for the Maker of the universe.

It has frequently been asserted that modern science was born when attention shifted from the search after the "what" to the investigation of "how." This shift of emphasis is almost a matter of course if one assumes that man can know only what he has made himself, insofar as this assumption in turn implies that I "know" a thing whenever I understand how it has come into being. By the same token, and for the same reasons, the emphasis shifted from interest in things to interest in processes, of which things were soon to become almost accidental by-products. Vico lost interest in nature because he assumed that to penetrate the mystery of Creation it would be necessary to understand the creative process, whereas all previous ages had taken it for granted that one can very well understand the universe without ever knowing how God created it, or, in the Greek version, how the things that are by themselves came into being. Since the seventeenth century the chief preoccupation of all scientific inquiry, natural as well as historical, has been with processes; but only modern technology (and no mere science, no matter how highly developed), which began with substituting mechanical processes for human activities—laboring and working—and ended with starting new natural processes, would have been wholly adequate to Vico's ideal of knowledge. Vico, who is regarded by many as the father of modern history, would hardly have turned to history under modern conditions. He would have turned to technology; for our technology does indeed what Vico thought divine action did in the realm of nature and human action in the realm of history.

In the modern age history emerged as something it never had been before. It was no longer composed of the deeds and sufferings of men, and it no longer told the story of events affecting the lives of men; it became a man-made process, the only all-comprehending process which owed its existence exclusively to the human race. Today this quality which distinguished history from nature is also a thing of the past. We know today that though we cannot "make" nature in the sense of creation, we are quite capable of starting new natural processes, and that in a sense therefore we "make nature," to the extent, that is, that we "make history." It is true we have reached this stage only with the nuclear discoveries, where natural forces are let loose, unchained, so to speak, and where the natural processes which take place would never have existed without direct interference of human action. This stage goes far beyond not only the pre-modern age, when wind and water were used to substitute for and multiply human forces, but also the industrial age, with its steam engine and internal-combustion motor, where natural forces were imitated and utilized as man-made means of production.

The contemporary decline of interest in the humanities, and especially in the study of history, which seems inevitable in all completely modernized countries, is quite in accord with the first impulses that led to modern historical science. What is definitely out of place today is the resignation which led Vico into the study of history. We can do in the natural-physical realm what he thought we could do only in the realm of history. We have begun to act into nature as we used to act into history. If it is merely a question of processes, it has turned out that man is as capable of starting natural processes which would not have come about without human interference as he is of starting something new in the field of human affairs.

Since the beginning of the twentieth century, technology has emerged as the meeting ground of the natural and historical sciences, and although hardly a single great scientific discovery has ever been made for pragmatic, technical, or practical purposes (pragmatism in the vulgar sense of the word stands refuted by the factual record of scientific development), this final outcome is in perfect accord with the innermost intentions of modern science. The comparatively new social sciences, which so quickly became to history what technology had been to physics, may use the experiment in a much cruder and less reliable way than do the natural sciences, but the method is the same: they too prescribe conditions, conditions to human behavior, as modern physics prescribes conditions to natural processes. If their vocabulary is repulsive and their hope to close the alleged gap between our scientific mastery of nature and our deplored impotence to "manage" human affairs through an engineering science of human relations sounds frightening, it is only because they have decided to treat man as an entirely natural being whose life process can be handled the same way as all other processes.

In this context, however, it is important to be aware how decisively the technological world we live in, or perhaps begin to live in, differs from the mechanized world as it arose with the Industrial Revolution. This difference corresponds essentially to the difference between action and fabrication. Industrialization still consisted primarily of the mechanization of work processes, the improvement in the making of objects, and man's attitude to nature still remained that of *homo faber,* to whom nature gives the material out of which the human artifice is erected. The world we have now come to live in, however, is much more determined by man acting into nature, creating natural processes and directing them into the human artifice and the realm of human affairs, than by building and preserving the human artifice as a relatively permanent entity.

Fabrication is distinguished from action in that it has a definite beginning and a predictable end: it comes to an end with its end product, which not only outlasts the activity of fabrication but from then on has a kind of "life" of its own. Action, on the contrary, as the Greeks were the first to discover, is in and by itself utterly futile; it never leaves an end product behind itself. If it has any consequences at all, they consist in principle in an endless new chain of happenings whose eventual outcome the actor is utterly incapable of knowing or controlling beforehand. The most he may be able to do is to force things into a certain direction, and even of this he can never be sure. None of these characteristics is present in fabrication. Compared with the futility and fragility of human action, the world fabrication erects is of lasting permanence and tremendous solidity. Only insofar as the end product of fabrication is incorporated into the human world, where its use and eventual "history" can never be entirely predicted, does even fabrication start a process whose outcome cannot be entirely foreseen and is therefore beyond the control of its author. This means only that man is never exclusively *homo faber,* that even the fabricator remains at the same time an acting being, who starts processes wherever he goes and with whatever he does.

Up to our own age human action with its man-made processes was confined to the human world, whereas man's chief preoccupation with regard to nature was to use its material in fabrication, to build with it the human artifice and defend it against the overwhelming force of the elements. The moment we started natural processes of our own—and splitting the atom is precisely such a man-made natural process—we not only increased our power over nature, or became more aggressive in our dealings with the given forces of the earth, but for the first time have taken nature into the human world as such and obliterated the defensive boundaries between natural elements and the human artifice by which all previous civilizations were hedged in.[18]

The dangers of this acting into nature are obvious if we assume that the aforementioned characteristics of human action are part and parcel of the human condition. Unpredictability is not lack of foresight, and no engineering management of human affairs will ever be able to eliminate it, just as no training in prudence can ever lead to the wisdom of knowing what one does. Only total conditioning, that is, the total abolition of action, can ever hope to cope with unpredictability. And even the predictability of human behavior which political terror can enforce for relatively long periods of time is hardly able to change the very essence of human affairs once and for all; it can never be sure of its own future. Human action, like all strictly political phenomena, is bound up with human plurality, which is one of the fundamental conditions of human life insofar as it rests on the fact of natality, through which the human world is constantly invaded by strangers, newcomers whose actions and reactions cannot be foreseen by those who are already there and are going to leave in a short while. If, therefore, by starting natural processes, we have begun to act *into* nature, we have manifestly begun to carry our own unpredictability into that realm which we used to think of as ruled by inexorable laws. The "iron law" of history was always only a metaphor borrowed from nature; and the fact is that this metaphor no longer convinces us because it has turned out that natural science can by no means be sure of an unchallengeable rule of law in nature as soon as men, scientists and technicians, or simply builders of the human artifice, decide to interfere and no longer leave nature to herself.

Technology, the ground on which the two realms of history and nature have met and interpenetrated each other in our time, points back to the connection between the concepts of nature and history as they appeared with the rise of the modern age in the sixteenth and seventeenth centuries. The connection lies in the concept of process: both imply that we think and consider everything in terms of processes and are not concerned with single entities or individual occurrences and their special separate causes. The key words of modern historiography—"development" and "progress"—were, in the nineteenth century, also the key words of the then new branches of natural science, particularly biology and geology, one dealing with animal life and the other even with non-organic matter in terms of historical processes. Technology, in the modern sense, was preceded by the various sciences of natural history, the history of biological life, of the earth, of the universe. A mutual adjustment of terminology of the two branches of scientific inquiry had taken place before the quarrel between the natural and historical sciences preoccupied the scholarly world to such an extent that it confused the fundamental issues.

Nothing seems more likely to dispel this confusion than the latest developments in the natural sciences. They have brought us back to the common origin of both nature and history in the modern age and demonstrate that their common denominator lies indeed in the concept of process—no less than the common denominator of nature and history in antiquity lay in the concept of immortality. But the experience which underlies the modern age's notion of process, unlike the experience underlying the ancient notion of immortality, is by no means primarily an experience which man made in the world surrounding him; on the contrary, it sprang from the despair of ever experiencing and knowing adequately all that is given to man and not made by him. Against this despair modern man summoned up the full measure of his own capacities; despairing of ever finding truth through mere contemplation, he began to try out his capacities for action, and by doing so he could not help becoming aware that wherever man acts he starts processes. The notion of process does not denote an objective quality of either history or nature; it is the inevitable result of human action. The first result of men's acting into history is that history becomes a process, and the most cogent argument for men's acting into nature in the guise of scientific inquiry is that today, in Whitehead's formulation, "nature is a process."

To act into nature, to carry human unpredictability into a realm where we are confronted with elemental forces which we shall perhaps never be able to control reliably, is dangerous enough. Even more dangerous would it be to ignore that for the first time in our history the human capacity for action has begun to dominate all others—the capacity for wonder and thought in contemplation no less than the capacities of *homo faber* and the human *animal laborans*. This, of course, does not mean that men from now on will no longer be able to fabricate things or to think or to labor. Not the capabilities of man, but the constellation which orders their mutual relationships can and does change historically. Such changes can best be observed in the changing self-interpretations of man throughout history, which, though they may be quite irrelevant for the ultimate "what" of human nature, are still the briefest and most succinct witnesses to the spirit of whole epochs. Thus, schematically speaking, Greek classic antiquity agreed that the highest form of human life was spent in a polis and that the supreme human capacity was speech—ζῷον πολιτικόν and ζῷον λόγον ἔχον, in Aristotle's famous twofold definition; Rome and medieval philosophy defined man as the *animal rationale;* in the initial stages of the modern age, man was thought of primarily as *homo faber,* until, in the nineteenth century, man was interpreted as an *animal laborans* whose metabolism with nature would yield the highest productivity of which human life is capable. Against the background of these schematic definitions, it would be adequate for the world we have come to live in to define man as a being capable of action; for this capacity seems to have become the center of all other human capabilities.

It is beyond doubt that the capacity to act is the most dangerous of all human abilities and possibilities, and it is also beyond doubt that the self-created risks mankind faces today have never been faced before. Considerations like these are not at all meant to offer solutions or to give advice. At best, they might encourage sustained and closer reflection on the nature and the intrinsic potentialities of action, which never before has revealed its greatness and its dangers so openly.

II: History and Earthly Immortality

The modern concept of process pervading history and nature alike separates the modern age from the past more profoundly than any other single idea. To our modern way of thinking nothing is meaningful in and by itself, not even history or nature taken each as a whole, and certainly not particular occurrences in the physical order or specific historical events. There is a fateful enormity in this state of affairs. Invisible processes have engulfed every tangible thing, every individual entity that is visible to us, degrading them into functions of an over-all process. The enormity of this change is likely to escape us if we allow ourselves to be misled by such generalities as the disenchantment of the world or the alienation of man, generalities that often involve a romanticized notion of the

past. What the concept of process implies is that the concrete and
the general, the single thing or event and the universal meaning,
have parted company. The process, which alone makes meaningful whatever it happens to carry along, has thus acquired a monopoly
of universality and significance.

Certainly nothing more sharply distinguishes the modern concept
of history from that of antiquity. For this distinction does not hinge
on whether or not antiquity had a concept of world history or an
idea of mankind as a whole. What is much more relevant is that
Greek and Roman historiography, much as they differ from each
other, both take it for granted that the meaning or, as the Romans
would say, the lesson of each event, deed, or occurrence is revealed
in and by itself. This, to be sure, does not exclude either causality
or the context in which something occurs; antiquity was as aware
of these as we are. But causality and context were seen in a light
provided by the event itself, illuminating a specific segment of human
affairs; they were not envisaged as having an independent existence
of which the event would be only the more or less accidental though
adequate expression. Everything that was done or happened contained and disclosed its share of "general" meaning within the
confines of its individual shape and did not need a developing and
engulfing process to become significant. Herodotus wanted "to say
what is" (λέγειν τὰ ἐόντα) because saying and writing stabilize the
futile and perishable, "fabricate a memory" for it, in the Greek
idiom: μνήμην ποιεῖσθαι; yet he never would have doubted that each
thing that is or was carries its meaning within itself and needs only
the word to make it manifest (λόγοις δηλοῦν, "to disclose through
words"), to "display the great deeds in public," ἀπόδειξις ἔργων
μεγάλων. The flux of his narrative is sufficiently loose to leave room
for many stories, but there is nothing in this flux indicative that the
general bestows meaning and significance on the particular.

For this shift of emphasis it is immaterial whether Greek poetry
and historiography saw the meaning of the event in some surpassing
greatness justifying its remembrance by posterity, or whether the
Romans conceived of history as a storehouse of examples taken
from actual political behavior, demonstrating what tradition, the

authority of ancestors, demanded from each generation and what the past had accumulated for the benefit of the present. Our notion of historical process overrules both concepts, bestowing upon mere time-sequence an importance and dignity it never had before.

Because of this modern emphasis upon time and time-sequence, it has often been maintained that the origin of our historical consciousness lies in the Hebrew-Christian tradition, with its rectilinear time-concept and its idea of a divine providence giving to the whole of man's historical time the unity of a plan of salvation—an idea which indeed stands as much in contrast to the insistence on individual events and occurrences of classical antiquity as to the cyclical time-speculations of late antiquity. A great deal of evidence has been cited in support of the thesis that the modern historical consciousness has a Christian religious origin and came into being through a secularization of originally theological categories. Only our religious tradition, it is said, knows of a beginning and, in the Christian version, an end of the world; if human life on earth follows a divine plan of salvation, then its mere sequence must harbor a significance independent of and transcending all single occurrences. Therefore, the argument runs, a "well-defined outline of world history" did not appear prior to Christianity, and the first philosophy of history is presented in Augustine's *De Civitate Dei*. And it is true that in Augustine we find the notion that history itself, namely that which has meaning and makes sense, can be separated from the single historical events related in chronological narrative. He states explicitly that "although the past institutions of men are related in historical narrative, history itself is not to be counted among human institutions." [19]

This similarity between the Christian and the modern concept of history is deceptive, however. It rests on a comparison with the cyclical history-speculations of late antiquity and overlooks the classical history-concepts of Greece and Rome. The comparison is supported by the fact that Augustine himself, when he refuted pagan time-speculations, was primarily concerned with the cyclical time-theories of his own era, which indeed no Christian could accept because of the absolute uniqueness of Christ's life and death on earth: "Once Christ died for our sins; and rising from the dead, he dieth no more." [20] What modern interpreters are liable to forget is that Augustine claimed this uniqueness of event, which sounds so familiar to our ears, for this one event only—the supreme event in human history, when eternity, as it were, broke into the course of earthly mortality; he never claimed such uniqueness, as we do, for ordinary secular events. The simple fact that the problem of history arose in Christian thought only with Augustine should make us doubt its Christian origin, and this all the more as it arose, in terms of Augustine's own philosophy and theology, because of an accident. The fall of Rome, occurring in his lifetime, was interpreted by Christians and pagans alike as a decisive event, and it was to the refutation of this belief that Augustine devoted thirteen years of his life. The point, as he saw it, was that no purely secular event could or should ever be of central import to man. His lack of interest in what we call history was so great that he devoted only one book of the *Civitas Dei* to secular events; and in commissioning his friend and pupil Orosius to write a "world history" he had no more in mind than a "true compilation of the evils of the world." [21]

Augustine's attitude toward secular history is essentially no different from that of the Romans, albeit the emphasis is inverted: history remains a storehouse of examples, and the location of events in time within the secular course of history remains without importance. Secular history repeats itself, and the only story in which unique and unrepeatable events take place begins with Adam and ends with the birth and death of Christ. Thereafter secular powers rise and fall as in the past and will rise and fall until the world's end, but no fundamentally new truth will ever again be revealed by such mundane events, and Christians are not supposed to attach particular significance to them. In all truly Christian philosophy man is a "pilgrim on earth," and this fact alone separates it from our own historical consciousness. To the Christian, as to the Roman, the significance of secular events lay in their having the character of examples likely to repeat themselves, so that action could follow certain standardized patterns. (This, incidentally, is also very far removed from the Greek notion of the heroic deed, related by poets and historians, which serves as a kind of yardstick with which to measure one's own capacities for greatness. The difference between the faithful following of a recognized example and the attempt to measure oneself against it is the difference between Roman-Christian morality and what has been called the Greek agonal spirit, which did not know any "moral" considerations but only an ἀεὶ ἀριστεύειν, an unceasing effort always to be the best of all.) For us, on the other hand, history stands and falls on the assumption that the process in its very secularity tells a story of its own and that, strictly speaking, repetitions cannot occur.

Even more alien to the modern concept of history is the Christian notion that mankind has a beginning and an end, that the world was created in time and will ultimately perish, like all things temporal. Historical consciousness did not arise when the creation of the world was taken as the starting point for chronological enumeration, by the Jews in the Middle Ages; nor did it arise in the sixth century when Dionysus Exiguus began counting time from the birth of Christ. We know of similar schemes of chronology in Oriental civilization, and the Christian calendar imitated the Roman practice of counting time from the year of the foundation of Rome. In stark contrast stands the modern computation of historical dates, introduced only at the end of the eighteenth century, that takes the birth of Christ as a turning point from which to count time both backward and forward. This chronological reform is presented in the textbooks as a mere technical improvement, needed for scholarly purposes to facilitate the exact fixing of dates in ancient history without referring to a maze of different time-reckonings. In more recent times, Hegel inspired an interpretation which sees in the modern time system a truly Christian chronology because the birth of Christ now seems to have become the turning point of world history.[22]

Neither of these explanations is satisfactory. Chronological reforms for scholarly purposes have occurred many times in the past without being accepted in everyday life, precisely because they were invented for scholarly convenience only and did not correspond to any changed time-concept in society at large. The decisive thing in our system is not that the birth of Christ now appears as the turning point of world history, for it had been recognized as such and with greater force many centuries before without any similar effect upon our chronology, but rather that now, for the first time, the history of mankind reaches back into an infinite past to which we can add at will and into which we can inquire further as it stretches ahead into an infinite future. This twofold infinity of past and future eliminates all notions of beginning and end, establishing mankind in a potential earthly immortality. What at first glance looks like a Christianization of world history in fact eliminates all religious time-speculations from secular history. So far as secular history is concerned we live in a process which knows no beginning and no end and which thus does not permit us to entertain eschatological expectations. Nothing could be more alien to Christian thought than this concept of an earthly immortality of mankind.

The great impact of the notion of history upon the consciousness of the modern age came relatively late, not before the last third of the eighteenth century, finding with relative quickness its climactic consummation in Hegel's philosophy. The central concept of Hegelian metaphysics is history. This alone places it in the sharpest possible opposition to all previous metaphysics, which, since Plato, had looked for truth and the revelation of eternal Being everywhere except in the realm of human affairs—τὰ τῶν ἀνθρώπων πράγματα— of which Plato speaks with such contempt precisely because no permanence could be found in it and therefore it could not be expected to disclose truth. To think, with Hegel, that truth resides and reveals itself in the time-process itself is characteristic of all modern historical consciousness, however it expresses itself, in specifically Hegelian terms or not. The rise of the humanities in the nineteenth century was inspired by the same feeling for history and is hence clearly distinguished from the recurrent revivals of antiquity that took place in previous periods. Men now began to read, as Meinecke pointed out, as nobody had ever read before. They "read in order to force from history the ultimate truth it could offer to God-seeking people"; but this ultimate truth was no longer supposed to reside in a single book, whether the Bible or some substitute for it. History itself was considered such a book, the book "of the human soul in times and nations," as Herder defined it.[23]

Recent historical research has shed much new light on the transitional period between the Middle Ages and modern times, with the result that the modern age, previously assumed to have begun with the Renaissance, has been traced back into the very heart of the Middle Ages. This greater insistence on an unbroken continuity, valuable though it is, has one drawback, that by trying to bridge the gulf separating a religious culture from the secular world we live in, it bypasses, rather than solves, the great riddle of the sudden undeniable rise of the secular. If by "secularization" one means no more than the rise of the secular and the concomitant eclipse of a transcendent world, then it is undeniable that modern historical consciousness is very intimately connected with it. This, however, in no way implies the doubtful transformation of religious and transcendent categories into immanent earthly aims and standards on which the historians of ideas have recently insisted. Secularization means first of all simply the separation of religion and politics, and this affected both sides so fundamentally that nothing is less likely to have taken place than the gradual transformation of religious categories into secular concepts which the defenders of unbroken continuity try to establish. The reason they can succeed to some extent in convincing us lies in the nature of ideas in general rather than in the period with which they deal; the moment one separates an idea entirely from its basis in real experience, it is not difficult to establish a connection between it and almost any other idea. In other words, if we assume that something like an independent realm of pure ideas exists, all notions and concepts cannot but be interrelated, because then they all owe their origin to the same source: a human mind seen in its extreme subjectivity, forever playing with its own images, unaffected by experience and with no relationship to the world, whether the world is conceived as nature or as history.

However, if we understand by secularization an event that can be dated in historical time rather than a change of ideas, then the question is not whether Hegel's "cunning of reason" was a secularization of divine providence or whether Marx's classless society represents a secularization of the Messianic Age. The fact is that the separation of church and state occurred, eliminating religion from public life, removing all religious sanctions from politics, and causing religion to lose that political element it had acquired in the centuries when the Roman Catholic Church acted as the heir of the Roman Empire. (It does not follow that this separation converted religion into an entirely "private affair." This type of privacy in religion comes about when a tyrannical regime prohibits the public functioning of churches, denying the believer the public space in which he can appear with others and be seen by them. The public-secular domain, or the political sphere, properly speaking, comprehends and has room for the public-religious sphere. A believer can be a member of a church and at the same time act as a citizen in the larger unit constituted by all belonging to the City.) This secularization was frequently brought about by men who did not doubt in the least the truth of traditional religious teaching (even Hobbes died in mortal fear of "hell-fire," and Descartes prayed to the Holy Virgin) and nothing in the sources justifies us in considering all those who prepared or helped to establish a new independent secular sphere as secret or unconscious atheists. All that we can say is that, whatever their faith or lack of it, it was without influence on the secular. Thus the political theorists of the seventeenth century accomplished secularization by separating political thinking from theology, and by insisting that the rules of natural law provided a basis for the body politic even if God did not exist. It was the same thought which made Grotius say that "even God cannot cause two times two not to make four." The point was not to deny the existence of God but to discover in the secular realm an independent, immanent meaning which even God could not alter.

It has been pointed out before that the most important consequence of the rise of the secular realm in the modern age was that belief in individual immortality—whether it be the immortality of the soul or, more importantly, the resurrection of the body—lost its politically binding force. Now indeed "it was inevitable that earthly posterity should once again become the principal substance of hope," but it does not follow from this that a secularization of the belief in a hereafter occurred or that the new attitude was essentially nothing but "a redisposition of the Christian ideas which it seeks to displace." [24] What actually happened was that the problem of politics regained that grave and decisive relevance for the existence of men which it had been lacking since antiquity because it was irreconcilable with a strictly Christian understanding of the secular. For Greeks and Romans alike, all differences notwithstanding, the foundation of a body politic was brought about by man's need to overcome the mortality of human life and the futility of human deeds. Outside the body politic, man's life was not only and not even primarily insecure, i.e., exposed to the violence of others; it was without meaning and dignity because under no circumstances could it leave any traces behind it. That was the reason for the curse laid by Greek thinking on the whole sphere of private life, the "idiocy" of which consisted in its being concerned solely with survival, just as it was the reason for Cicero's contention that only through building and preserving political communities could human virtue attain to the ways of the gods.[25] In other words, the secularization of the modern age once more brought to the fore that activity which Aristotle had called ἀθανατίζειν, a term for which we have no ready equivalent in our living languages. The reason I mention this word again is that it points to an activity of "immortalizing" rather than to the object which is to become immortal. To strive for immortality can mean, as it certainly did in early Greece, the immortalization of oneself through famous deeds and the acquisition of immortal fame; it can also mean the addition to the human artifice of something more permanent than we are ourselves; and it can mean, as it did with the philosophers, the spending of one's life with things immortal. In any event, the word designated an activity and not a belief, and what the activity required was an imperishable space guaranteeing that "immortalizing" would not be in vain.[26]

To us, who have been accustomed to the idea of immortality only through the lasting appeal of works of art and perhaps through the relative permanence we ascribe to all great civilizations, it may appear implausible that the drive toward immortality should lie at the foundation of political communities.[27] To the Greeks, however, the latter might very well have been much more taken for granted than the former. Did not Pericles think that the highest praise he could bestow upon Athens was to claim that it no longer needed "a Homer or others of his craft," but that, thanks to the polis, Athenians everywhere would leave "imperishable monuments" behind them? [28] What Homer had done was to immortalize human deeds,[29] and the polis could dispense with the service of "others of his craft" because it offered each of its citizens that public-political space that it assumed would confer immortality upon his acts. The growing apolitism of the philosophers after Socrates' death, their demand to be freed from political activities and their insistence on performing a nonpractical, purely theoretical ἀθανατίζειν outside the sphere of political life had philosophical as well as political causes, but among the political ones was certainly the increasing decay of polis life, making even the permanence, let alone immortality, of this particular body politic more and more doubtful.

The apolitism of ancient philosophy foreshadowed the much more radical anti-political attitude of early Christianity, which, however, in its very extremism survived only so long as the Roman Empire provided a stable body politic for all nations and all religions. During these early centuries of our era the conviction that things earthly are perishable remained a religious matter and was the belief of those who wanted to have nothing to do with political affairs. This changed decisively with the crucial experience of the fall of Rome, the sacking of the Eternal City, after which no age ever again believed that any human product, least of all a political structure, could endure forever. As far as Christian thought was concerned, this was a mere reaffirmation of its beliefs. It was of no great relevance, as Augustine pointed out. To Christians only individual men were immortal, but nothing else of this world, neither mankind as a whole nor the earth itself, least of all the human artifice. Only by transcending this world could immortalizing activities be performed, and the only institution that could be justified within the secular realm was the Church, the *Civitas Dei* on earth, to which had fallen the burden of political responsibility and into which all genuinely political impulses could be drawn. That this transformation of Christianity and its earlier anti-political impulses into a great and stable political institution was possible at all without complete perversion of the Gospel is almost wholly due to Augustine, who, though hardly the father of our concept of history, is probably the spiritual author and certainly the greatest theorist of Christian politics. What was decisive in this respect was that he, still firmly rooted in the Roman tradition, could add to the Christian notion of an everlasting life the idea of a future *civitas*, a *Civitas Dei*, where men even in the hereafter would continue to live in a community. Without this reformulation of Christian thoughts through Augustine, Christian politics might have remained what they had been in the early centuries, a contradiction in terms. Augustine could solve the dilemma because the language itself came to his help: in Latin the word "to live" had always coincided with *inter homines esse*, "to be in the company of men," so that an everlasting life in Roman interpretation was bound to mean that no man would ever have to part from human company even though in death he had to leave the earth. Thus the fact of the plurality of men, one of the fundamental prerequisites of political life, bound human "nature" even under the conditions of individual immortality, and was not among the characteristics which this "nature" had acquired after Adam's fall and which made politics in the mere secular sense a necessity for the sinful life on earth. Augustine's conviction that some kind of political life must exist even under conditions of sinlessness, and indeed sanctity, he summed up in one sentence: *Socialis est vita sanctorum*, even the life of the saints is a life together with other men.[30]

If the insight into the perishability of all human creations had no great relevance for Christian thought and could even in its greatest thinker be in accord with a conception of politics beyond the secular realm, it became very troublesome in the modern age when the secular sphere of human life had emancipated itself from religion. The separation of religion and politics meant that no matter what an individual might believe as a member of a church, as a citizen he acted and behaved on the assumption of human mortality. Hobbes's fear of hell-fire did not influence in the least his construction of government as the Leviathan, a mortal god to overawe all men. Politically speaking, within the secular realm itself secularization meant nothing more or less than that men once more had become mortals. If this led them to a rediscovery of antiquity, which we call humanism, and in which Greek and Roman sources spoke again a much more familiar language corresponding to experiences much more similar to their own, it certainly did not allow them in practice to mold their behavior in accordance with either the Greek or the Roman example. The ancient trust in the world's being more permanent than individual men and in political structures as a guarantee of earthly survival after death did not return, so that the ancient opposition of a mortal life to a more or less immortal world failed them. Now both life and world had become perishable, mortal, and futile.

Today we find it difficult to grasp that this situation of absolute mortality could be unbearable to men. However, looking back upon the development of the modern age up to the beginning of our own, the modern world, we see that centuries passed before we became accustomed to the notion of absolute mortality, so that the thought of it no longer bothers us and the old alternative between an individual immortal life in a mortal world and a mortal life in an immortal world has ceased to be meaningful. In this respect, however, as in many others, we differ from all previous ages. Our concept of history, though essentially a concept of the modern age, owes its existence to the transition period when religious confidence in immortal life had lost its influence upon the secular and the new indifference toward the question of immortality had not yet been born.

If we leave aside the new indifference and stay within the limits of the traditional alternative, bestowing immortality either upon life or upon the world, then it is obvious that ἀθανατίζειν, immortalizing, as an activity of mortal men, can be meaningful only if there is no guarantee of life in the hereafter. At that moment, however, it becomes almost a necessity as long as there is any concern with immortality whatsoever. It was therefore in the course of its search for a strictly secular realm of enduring permanence that the modern age discovered the potential immortality of mankind. This is what is manifestly expressed in our calendar; it is the actual content of our concept of history. History, stretching into the twofold infinity of past and future, can guarantee immortality on earth in much the same way as the Greek polis or the Roman republic had guaranteed that human life and human deeds, insofar as they disclosed something essential and something great, would receive a strictly human and earthly permanence in this world. The great advantage of this concept has been that the twofold infinity of the historical process establishes a time-space in which the very notion of an end is virtually inconceivable, whereas its great disadvantage, compared with ancient political theory, seems to be that permanence is entrusted to a flowing process, as distinguished from a stable structure. At the same time the immortalizing process has become independent of cities, states, and nations; it encompasses the whole of mankind, whose history Hegel was consequently able to see as one uninterrupted development of the Spirit. Therewith mankind ceases to be only a species of nature, and what distinguishes man from the animals is no longer merely that he has speech ($\lambda\acute{o}\gamma o\nu$ $\acute{\epsilon}\chi\omega\nu$), as in the Aristotelian definition, or that he has reason, as in the medieval definition (*animal rationale*): his very life now distinguishes him, the one thing that in the traditional definition he was supposed to share with the animals. In the words of Droysen, who was perhaps the most thoughtful of the nineteenth-century historians: "What their species is for animals and plants . . . that is history for human beings." [31]

III: History and Politics

While it is obvious that our historical consciousness would never have been possible without the rise of the secular realm to a new dignity, it was not so obvious that the historical process would eventually be called upon to bestow the necessary new meaning and significance upon men's deeds and sufferings on earth. And indeed,

at the beginning of the modern age everything pointed to an eleva-
tion of political action and political life, and the sixteenth and seventeenth centuries, so rich in new political philosophies, were still quite
unaware of any special emphasis on history as such. Their concern,
on the contrary, was to get rid of the past rather than to rehabilitate
the historical process. The distinguishing trait of Hobbes's philosophy is his single-minded insistence on the future and the resulting
teleological interpretation of thought as well as of action. The conviction of the modern age that man can know only that which he
himself has made seems to be in accordance with a glorification of
action rather than with the basically contemplative attitude of the
historian and of historical consciousness in general.

Thus one of the reasons for Hobbes's break with traditional philosophy was that while all previous metaphysics had followed Aristotle in holding that the inquiry into the first causes of everything
that is comprises the chief task of philosophy, it was Hobbes's contention that, on the contrary, the task of philosophy was to guide
purposes and aims and to establish a reasonable teleology of action.
So important was this point to Hobbes that he insisted that animals
too are capable of discovering causes and that therefore this cannot
be the true distinction between human and animal life; he found
the distinction instead in the ability to reckon with "the effects of
some present or past cause . . . of which I have not at any time
seen any sign but in man only." [32] The modern age not only produced
at its very start a new and radical political philosophy—Hobbes is
only one example, though perhaps the most interesting—it also produced for the first time philosophers willing to orient themselves
according to the requirements of the political realm; and this new
political orientation is present not only in Hobbes but, *mutatis mutandis,* in Locke and Hume as well. It can be said that Hegel's
transformation of metaphysics into a philosophy of history was preceded by an attempt to get rid of metaphysics for the sake of a philosophy of politics.

In any consideration of the modern concept of history one of the
crucial problems is to explain its sudden rise during the last third

of the eighteenth century and the concomitant decrease of interest in purely political thinking. (Vico must be said to be a forerunner whose influence was not felt until more than two generations after his death.) Where a genuine interest in political theory still survived it ended in despair, as in Tocqueville, or in the confusion of politics with history, as in Marx. For what else but despair could have inspired Tocqueville's assertion that "since the past has ceased to throw its light upon the future the mind of man wanders in obscurity"? This is actually the conclusion of the great work in which he had "delineated the society of the modern world" and in the introduction to which he had proclaimed that "a new science of politics is needed for a new world." [33] And what else but confusion —a merciful confusion for Marx himself and a fatal one for his followers—could have led to Marx's identification of action with "the making of history"?

Marx's notion of "making history" had an influence far beyond the circle of convinced Marxists or determined revolutionaries. Although it is closely connected with Vico's idea that history was made by man, as distinguished from "nature," which was made by God, the difference between them is still decisive. For Vico, as later for Hegel, the importance of the concept of history was primarily theoretical. It never occurred to either of them to apply this concept directly by using it as a principle of action. Truth they conceived of as being revealed to the contemplative, backward-directed glance of the historian, who, by being able to see the process as a whole, is in a position to overlook the "narrow aims" of acting men, concentrating instead on the "higher aims" that realize themselves behind their backs (Vico). Marx, on the other hand, combined this notion of history with the teleological political philosophies of the earlier stages of the modern age, so that in his thought the "higher aims"—which according to the philosophers of history revealed themselves only to the backward glance of the historian and philosopher—could become intended aims of political action. The point is that Marx's political philosophy was based not upon an analysis of action and acting men but, on the contrary, on the Hegelian con-

cern with history. It was the historian and the philosopher of history
who were politicized. By the same token, the age-old identification of action with making and fabricating was supplemented and
perfected, as it were, through identifying the contemplative gaze of
the historian with the contemplation of the model (the εἶδος or
"shape" from which Plato had derived his "ideas") that guides the
craftsmen and precedes all making. And the danger of these combi-
nations did not lie in making immanent what was formerly transcendent, as is often alleged, as though Marx attempted to establish on
earth a paradise formerly located in the hereafter. The danger of
transforming the unknown and unknowable "higher aims" into
planned and willed intentions was that meaning and meaningfulness
were transformed into ends—which is what happened when Marx
took the Hegelian meaning of all history—the progressive unfolding
and actualization of the idea of Freedom—to be an end of human
action, and when he furthermore, in accordance with tradition,
viewed this ultimate "end" as the end-product of a manufacturing
process. But neither freedom nor any other meaning can ever be the
product of a human activity in the sense in which the table is clearly
the end-product of the carpenter's activity.

The growing meaninglessness of the modern world is perhaps
nowhere more clearly foreshadowed than in this identification of
meaning and end. Meaning, which can never be the aim of action
and yet, inevitably, will rise out of human deeds after the action itself
has come to an end, was now pursued with the same machinery of
intentions and of organized means as were the particular direct aims
of concrete action—with the result that it was as though meaning
itself had departed from the world of men and men were left with
nothing but an unending chain of purposes in whose progress the
meaningfulness of all past achievements was constantly canceled out
by future goals and intentions. It is as though men were stricken
suddenly blind to fundamental distinctions such as the distinction
between meaning and end, between the general and the particular,
or, grammatically speaking, the distinction between "for the sake
of . . ." and "in order to . . ." (as though the carpenter, for in-

stance, forgot that only his particular acts in making a table are performed in the mode of "in order to," but that his whole life as a carpenter is ruled by something quite different, namely an encompassing notion "for the sake of" which he became a carpenter in the first place). And the moment such distinctions are forgotten and meanings are degraded into ends, it follows that ends themselves are no longer safe because the distinction between means and ends is no longer understood, so that finally all ends turn and are degraded into means.

In this version of deriving politics from history, or rather, political conscience from historical consciousness—by no means restricted to Marx in particular, or even to pragmatism in general—we can easily detect the age-old attempt to escape from the frustrations and fragility of human action by construing it in the image of making. What distinguishes Marx's own theory from all others in which the notion of "making history" has found a place is only that he alone realized that if one takes history to be the object of a process of fabrication or making, there must come a moment when this "object" is completed, and that if one imagines that one can "make history," one cannot escape the consequence that there will be an end to history. Whenever we hear of grandiose aims in politics, such as establishing a new society in which justice will be guaranteed forever, or fighting a war to end all wars or to make the whole world safe for democracy, we are moving in the realm of this kind of thinking.

In this context, it is important to see that here the process of history, as it shows itself in our calendar's stretching into the infinity of the past and the future, has been abandoned for the sake of an altogether different kind of process, that of making something which has a beginning as well as an end, whose laws of motion, therefore, can be determined (for instance as dialectical movement) and whose innermost content can be discovered (for instance as class struggle). This process, however, is incapable of guaranteeing men any kind of immortality because its end cancels out and makes unimportant whatever went before: in the classless society the best mankind can do with history is to forget the whole unhappy affair, whose only purpose was to abolish itself. It cannot bestow meaning on particular occurrences either, because it has dissolved all of the particular into means whose meaningfulness ends the moment the end-product is finished: single events and deeds and sufferings have no more meaning here than hammer and nails have with respect to the finished table.

We know the curious ultimate meaninglessness arising from all the strictly utilitarian philosophies that were so common and so characteristic of the earlier industrial phase of the modern age, when men, fascinated by the new possibilities of manufacturing, thought of everything in terms of means and ends, i.e., categories whose validity had its source and justification in the experience of producing use-objects. The trouble lies in the nature of the categorical framework of ends and means, which changes every attained end immediately into the means to a new end, thereby, as it were, destroying meaning wherever it is applied, until in the midst of the seemingly unending utilitarian questioning, What is the use of . . . ? in the midst of the seemingly unending progress where the aim of today becomes the means of a better tomorrow, the one question arises which no utilitarian thinking can ever answer: "And what is the use of use?" as Lessing once succinctly put it.

This meaninglessness of all truly utilitarian philosophies could escape Marx's awareness because he thought that after Hegel in his dialectics had discovered the law of all movements, natural and historical, he himself had found the spring and content of this law in the historical realm and thereby the concrete meaning of the story history has to tell. Class struggle—to Marx this formula seemed to unlock all the secrets of history, just as the law of gravity had appeared to unlock all the secrets of nature. Today, after we have been treated to one such history-construction after another, to one such formula after another, the question for us is no longer whether this or that particular formula is correct. In all such attempts what is considered to be a meaning is in fact no more than a pattern, and within the limitations of utilitarian thought nothing but patterns can make sense, because only patterns can be "made," whereas meanings cannot be, but, like truth, will only disclose or reveal themselves. Marx was only the first—and still the greatest, among historians—to mistake a pattern for a meaning, and he certainly could hardly have been expected to realize that there was almost no pattern into which the events of the past would not have fitted as neatly and consistently as they did into his own. Marx's pattern at least was based on one important historical insight; since then we have seen historians freely imposing upon the maze of past facts almost any pattern they wish, with the result that the ruin of the factual and particular through the seemingly higher validity of general "meanings" has even undermined the basic factual structure of all historical process, that is, chronology.

Moreover, Marx construed his pattern as he did because of his concern with action and impatience with history. He is the last of those thinkers who stand at the borderline between the modern age's earlier interest in politics and its later preoccupation with history. One might mark the point where the modern age abandoned its earlier attempts to establish a new political philosophy for its rediscovery of the secular by recalling the moment at which the French Revolutionary calendar was given up, after one decade, and the Revolution was reintegrated, as it were, into the historical process with its twofold extension toward infinity. It was as though it was conceded that not even the Revolution, which, along with the promulgation of the American Constitution, is still the greatest event in modern political history, contained sufficient independent meaning in itself to begin a new historical process. For the Republican calendar was abandoned not merely because of Napoleon's wish to rule an empire and to be considered the equal of the crowned heads of Europe. The abandonment also implied the refusal, despite the re-establishment of the secular, to accept the conviction of the ancients that political actions are meaningful regardless of their historical location, and especially a repudiation of the Roman faith in the sacredness of foundations with the accompanying custom of numbering time from the foundation date. Indeed, the French Revolution, which was inspired by the Roman spirit and appeared to the world, as Marx liked to say, in Roman dress, reversed itself in more than one sense.

An equally important landmark in the shift from the earlier concern with politics to the later concern with history is encountered in Kant's political philosophy. Kant, who had greeted in Rousseau "the Newton of the moral world," and had been greeted by his contemporaries as the theorist of the Rights of Man,[34] still had great difficulty in coping with the new idea of history, which had probably come to his attention in the writings of Herder. He is one of the last philosophers to complain in earnest about the "meaningless course of human affairs," the "melancholy haphazardness" of historical events and developments, this hopeless, senseless "mixture of error and violence," as Goethe once defined history. Yet Kant also saw what others had seen before him, that once you look at history in its entirety (*im Grossen*), rather than at single events and the ever-frustrated intentions of human agents, everything suddenly makes sense, because there is always at least a story to tell. The process as a whole appears to be guided by an "intention of nature" unknown to acting men but comprehensible to those who come after them. By pursuing their own aims without rhyme or reason men seem to be led by "the guiding thread of reason." [35]

It is of some importance to notice that Kant, like Vico before him, was already aware of what Hegel later called "the cunning of reason" (Kant occasionally called it "the ruse of nature"). He even had some rudimentary insight into historical dialectics, as when he pointed out that nature pursues its over-all aims through "the antagonism of men in society . . . without which men, good-natured like the sheep they tend, would hardly know how to give a higher value to their own existence than is possessed by their cattle." This shows to what extent the very idea of history as a process suggests that in their actions men are led by something of which they are not necessarily conscious and which finds no direct expression in the action itself. Or, to put it another way, it shows how extremely useful the modern concept of history proved to be in giving the secular political realm a meaning which it otherwise seemed to be devoid of. In

Kant, in contrast to Hegel, the motive for the modern escape from politics into history is still quite clear. It is the escape into the "whole," and the escape is prompted by the meaninglessness of the particular. And since Kant's primary interest was still in the nature and principles of political (or, as he would say, moral) action, he was able to perceive the crucial drawback of the new approach, the one great stumbling block which no philosophy of history and no concept of progress can ever remove. In Kant's own words: "It will always remain bewildering . . . that the earlier generations seem to carry on their burdensome business only for the sake of the later . . . and that only the last should have the good fortune to dwell in the [completed] building." [36]

The bewildered regret and great diffidence with which Kant resigned himself to introducing a concept of history into his political philosophy indicates with rare precision the nature of the perplexities which caused the modern age to shift its emphasis from a theory of politics—apparently so much more appropriate to its belief in the superiority of action to contemplation—to an essentially contemplative philosophy of history. For Kant was perhaps the only great thinker to whom the question "What shall I do?" was not only as relevant as the two other questions of metaphysics, "What can I know?" and "What may I hope?" but formed the very center of his philosophy. Therefore he was not troubled, as even Marx and Nietzsche were still troubled, by the traditional hierarchy of contemplation over action, the *vita contemplativa* over the *vita activa;* his problem was rather another traditional hierarchy which, because it is hidden and rarely articulate, has proved much more difficult to overcome, the hierarchy within the *vita activa* itself, where the acting of the statesman occupies the highest position, the making of the craftsman and artist an intermediary, and the laboring which provides the necessities for the functioning of the human organism the lowest. (Marx was later to reverse this hierarchy too, although he wrote explicitly only about elevating action over contemplation and changing the world as against interpreting it. In the course of this reversal he had to upset the traditional hierarchy within the *vita activa* as well, by putting the lowest of human activities, the activity of labor, into the highest place. Action now appeared to be no more than a function of "the productive relationships" of mankind brought about by labor.) It is true that traditional philosophy often pays only lip service to the estimate of action as the highest activity of man, preferring the so much more reliable activity of making, so that the hierarchy within the *vita activa* has hardly ever been fully articulated. It is a sign of the political rank of Kant's philosophy that the old perplexities inherent in action were brought to the fore again.

However that may be, Kant could not but become aware of the fact that action fulfilled neither of the two hopes the modern age was bound to expect from it. If the secularization of our world implies the revival of the old desire for some kind of earthly immortality, then human action, especially in its political aspect, must appear singularly inadequate to meet the demands of the new age. From the point of view of motivation, action appears to be the least interesting and most futile of all human pursuits: "Passions, private aims, and the satisfaction of selfish desires, are . . . the most effective springs of action," [37] and "the facts of known history," taken by themselves, "possess neither a common basis nor continuity nor coherence" (Vico). From the viewpoint of achievement, on the other hand, action appears at once to be more futile and more frustrating than the activities of laboring and of producing objects. Human deeds, unless they are remembered, are the most futile and perishable things on earth; they hardly outlast the activity itself and certainly by themselves can never aspire to that permanence which even ordinary use-objects possess when they outlast their maker's life, not to mention works of art, which speak to us over the centuries. Human action, projected into a web of relationships where many and opposing ends are pursued, almost never fulfills its original intention; no act can ever be recognized by its author as his own with the same happy certainty with which a piece of work of any kind can be recognized by its maker. Whoever begins to act must know that he has started something whose end he can never foretell, if only because his own deed has already changed everything and made it even more unpredictable. That is what Kant had in mind when he spoke of the "melancholy haphazardness" (*trostlose Ungefähr*) which is so striking in the record of political history. "Action: one does not know its origin, one does not know its consequences:—therefore, does action possess any value at all?" [38] Were not the old philosophers right, and was it not madness to expect any meaning to arise out of the realm of human affairs?

For a long time it seemed that these inadequacies and perplexities within the *vita activa* could be solved by ignoring the peculiarities of action and by insisting upon the "meaningfulness" of the process of history in its entirety, which seemed to give to the political sphere that dignity and final redemption from "melancholy haphazardness" so obviously required. History—based on the manifest assumption that no matter how haphazard single actions may appear in the present and in their singularity, they inevitably lead to a sequence of events forming a story that can be rendered through intelligible narrative the moment the events are removed into the past—became the great dimension in which men could become "reconciled" with reality (Hegel), the reality of human affairs, i.e., of things which owe their existence exclusively to men. Moreover, since history in its modern version was conceived primarily as a process, it showed a peculiar and inspiring affinity to action, which, indeed, in contrast to all other human activities, consists first of all of starting processes —a fact of which human experience has of course always been aware, even though the preoccupation of philosophy with making as the model of human activity has prevented the elaboration of an articulate terminology and precise description. The very notion of process, which is so highly characteristic of modern science, both natural and historical, probably had its origin in this fundamental experience of action, to which secularization lent an emphasis such as it had not known since the very early centuries of Greek culture, even before the rise of the polis and certainly before the victory of the Socratic school. History in its modern version could come to terms with this experience; and though it failed to save politics itself from the old disgrace, though the single deeds and acts constituting the realm of politics, properly speaking, were left in limbo, it has at least bestowed upon the record of past events that share of earthly immortality to which the modern age necessarily aspired, but which its acting men no longer dared to claim from posterity.

Epilogue

Today the Kantian and Hegelian way of becoming reconciled to reality through understanding the innermost meaning of the entire historical process seems to be quite as much refuted by our experience as the simultaneous attempt of pragmatism and utilitarianism to "make history" and impose upon reality the preconceived meaning and law of man. While trouble throughout the modern age has as a rule started with the natural sciences and has been the consequence of experience gained in the attempt to know the universe, this time the refutation rises simultaneously out of the physical and political fields. The trouble is that almost every axiom seems to lend itself to consistent deductions and this to such an extent that it is as though men were in a position to prove almost any hypothesis they might choose to adopt, not only in the field of purely mental constructions like the various over-all interpretations of history which are all equally well supported by facts, but in the natural sciences as well.[39]

As far as natural science is concerned, this brings us back to the previously quoted statement by Heisenberg (pp. 48–49), whose consequence he once formulated in a different context as the paradox that man, whenever he tries to learn about things which neither are himself nor owe their existence to him, will ultimately encounter nothing but himself, his own constructions, and the patterns of his own actions.[40] This is no longer a question of academic objectivity. It cannot be solved by the reflection that man as a question-asking being naturally can receive only answers to match his own questions. If nothing more was involved, then we would be satisfied that different questions put "to one and the same physical event" reveal different but objectively equally "true" aspects of the same phenomenon, just as the table around which a number of people have taken their places is seen by each of them in a different aspect, without thereby ceasing to be the object common to all of them. One could even imagine that a theory of theories, like the old *mathesis universalis,* might eventually be able to determine how many such questions are possible or how many "different types of natural law" can be applied to the same natural universe without contradiction.

The matter would become somewhat more serious if it turned out that no question exists at all which does not lead to a consistent set of answers—a perplexity we mentioned earlier when we discussed the distinction between pattern and meaning. In this instance the very distinction between meaningful and meaningless questions would disappear together with absolute truth, and the consistency we would be left with could just as well be the consistency of an asylum for paranoiacs or the consistency of the current demonstrations of the existence of God. However, what is really undermining the whole modern notion that meaning is contained in the process as a whole, from which the particular occurrence derives its intelligibility, is that not only can we prove this, in the sense of consistent deduction, but we can take almost any hypothesis and *act* upon it, with a sequence of results in reality which not only make sense but *work*. This means quite literally that everything is possible not only in the realm of ideas but in the field of reality itself.

In my studies of totalitarianism I tried to show that the totalitarian phenomenon, with its striking anti-utilitarian traits and its strange disregard for factuality, is based in the last analysis on the conviction that everything is possible—and not just permitted, morally or otherwise, as was the case with early nihilism. The totalitarian systems tend to demonstrate that action can be based on any hypothesis and that, in the course of consistently guided action, the particular hypothesis will become true, will become actual, factual reality. The assumption which underlies consistent action can be as mad as it pleases; it will always end in producing facts which are then "objectively" true. What was originally nothing but a hypothesis, to be proved or disproved by actual facts, will in the course of consistent action always turn into a fact, never to be disproved. In other words, the axiom from which the deduction is started does not need to be, as traditional metaphysics and logic supposed, a self-evident truth; it does not have to tally at all with the facts as given in the objective world at the moment the action starts; the process of action, if it is consistent, will proceed to create a world in which the assumption becomes axiomatic and self-evident.

The frightening arbitrariness with which we are confronted whenever we decide to embark upon this type of action, which is the exact counterpart of consistent logical processes, is even more obvious in the political than in the natural realm. But it is more difficult to convince people that this holds true for past history. The historian, by gazing backward into the historical process, has been so accustomed to discovering an "objective" meaning, independent of the aims and awareness of the actors, that he is liable to overlook what actually happened in his attempt to discern some objective trend. He will, for example, overlook the particular characteristics of Stalin's totalitarian dictatorship in favor of the industrialization of the Soviet empire or of the nationalistic aims of traditional Russian foreign policy.

Within the natural sciences things are not essentially different, but they appear more convincing because they are so far removed from the competence of the layman and his healthy, stubborn common sense, which refuses to see what it cannot understand. Here too, thinking in terms of processes, on the one hand, and the conviction, on the other, that I know only what I have myself made, has led to the complete meaninglessness inevitably resulting from the insight that I can choose to do whatever I want and some kind of "meaning" will always be the consequence. In both instances the perplexity is that the particular incident, the observable fact or single occurrence of nature, or the reported deed and event of history, have ceased to make sense without a universal process in which they are supposedly embedded; yet the moment man approaches this process in order to escape the haphazard character of the particular, in order to find meaning—order and necessity—his effort is rebutted by the answer from all sides: Any order, any necessity, any meaning you wish to impose will do. This is the clearest possible demonstration that under these conditions there is neither necessity nor meaning. It is as though the "melancholy haphazardness" of the particular had now caught up with us and were pursuing us into the very region where the generations before us had fled in order to escape it. The decisive factor in this experience, both in nature and in history, is not the patterns with which we tried to "explain," and which in the social and historical sciences cancel each other out more quickly, because they can all be consistently proved, than they do in the natural sciences, where matters are more complex and for this technical reason less open to the irrelevant arbitrariness of irresponsible opinions. These opinions, to be sure, have an altogether different source, but are liable to becloud the very relevant issue of contingency, with which we are everywhere confronted today. What is decisive is that our technology, which nobody can accuse of not functioning, is based on these principles, and that our social techniques, whose real field of experimentation lies in the totalitarian countries, have only to overcome a certain time-lag to be able to do for the world of human relations and human affairs as much as has already been done for the world of human artifacts.

The modern age, with its growing world-alienation, has led to a situation where man, wherever he goes, encounters only himself. All the processes of the earth and the universe have revealed themselves either as man-made or as potentially man-made. These processes, after having devoured, as it were, the solid objectivity of the given, ended by rendering meaningless the one over-all process which originally was conceived in order to give meaning to them, and to act, so to speak, as the eternal time-space into which they could all flow and thus be rid of their mutual conflicts and exclusiveness. This is what happened to our concept of history, as it happened to our concept of nature. In the situation of radical world-alienation, neither history nor nature is at all conceivable. This twofold loss of the world—the loss of nature and the loss of human artifice in the widest sense, which would include all history—has left behind it a society of men who, without a common world which would at once relate and separate them, either live in desperate lonely separation or are pressed together into a mass. For a mass-society is nothing more than that kind of organized living which automatically establishes itself among human beings who are still related to one another but have lost the world once common to all of them.

3

WHAT IS AUTHORITY?

I

IN order to avoid misunderstanding, it might have been wiser to
ask in the title: What was—and not what is—authority? For it
is my contention that we are tempted and entitled to raise this question because authority has vanished from the modern world. Since
we can no longer fall back upon authentic and undisputable experiences common to all, the very term has become clouded by controversy and confusion. Little about its nature appears self-evident or
even comprehensible to everybody, except that the political scientist
may still remember that this concept was once fundamental to political theory, or that most will agree that a constant, ever-widening
and deepening crisis of authority has accompanied the development
of the modern world in our century.

This crisis, apparent since the inception of the century, is political in origin and nature. The rise of political movements intent
upon replacing the party system, and the development of a new
totalitarian form of government, took place against a background
of a more or less general, more or less dramatic breakdown of all
traditional authorities. Nowhere was this breakdown the direct result

of the regimes or movements themselves; it rather seemed as though totalitarianism, in the form of movements as well as of regimes, was best fitted to take advantage of a general political and social atmosphere in which the party system had lost its prestige and the government's authority was no longer recognized.

The most significant symptom of the crisis, indicating its depth and seriousness, is that it has spread to such prepolitical areas as child-rearing and education, where authority in the widest sense has always been accepted as a natural necessity, obviously required as much by natural needs, the helplessness of the child, as by political necessity, the continuity of an established civilization which can be assured only if those who are newcomers by birth are guided through a pre-established world into which they are born as strangers. Because of its simple and elementary character, this form of authority has, throughout the history of political thought, served as a model for a great variety of authoritarian forms of government, so that the fact that even this prepolitical authority which ruled the relations between adults and children, teachers and pupils, is no longer secure signifies that all the old time-honored metaphors and models for authoritarian relations have lost their plausibility. Practically as well as theoretically, we are no longer in a position to know what authority really *is*.

In the following reflections I assume that the answer to this question cannot possibly lie in a definition of the nature or essence of "authority in general." The authority we have lost in the modern world is no such "authority in general," but rather a very specific form which had been valid throughout the Western World over a long period of time. I therefore propose to reconsider what authority was historically and the sources of its strength and meaning. Yet, in view of the present confusion, it seems that even this limited and tentative approach must be preceded by a few remarks on what authority never was, in order to avoid the more common misunderstandings and make sure that we visualize and consider the same phenomenon and not any number of connected or unconnected issues.

Since authority always demands obedience, it is commonly mistaken for some form of power or violence. Yet authority precludes the use of external means of coercion; where force is used, authority itself has failed. Authority, on the other hand, is incompatible with persuasion, which presupposes equality and works through a process of argumentation. Where arguments are used, authority is left in abeyance. Against the egalitarian order of persuasion stands the authoritarian order, which is always hierarchical. If authority is to be defined at all, then, it must be in contradistinction to both coercion by force and persuasion through arguments. (The authoritarian relation between the one who commands and the one who obeys rests neither on common reason nor on the power of the one who commands; what they have in common is the hierarchy itself, whose rightness and legitimacy both recognize and where both have their predetermined stable place.) This point is of historical importance; one aspect of our concept of authority is Platonic in origin, and when Plato began to consider the introduction of authority into the handling of public affairs in the polis, he knew he was seeking an alternative to the common Greek way of handling domestic affairs, which was persuasion (πείθειν) as well as to the common way of handling foreign affairs, which was force and violence (βία).

Historically, we may say that the loss of authority is merely the final, though decisive, phase of a development which for centuries undermined primarily religion and tradition. Of tradition, religion, and authority—whose interconnectedness we shall discuss later—authority has proved to be the most stable element. With the loss of authority, however, the general doubt of the modern age also invaded the political realm, where things not only assume a more radical expression but become endowed with a reality peculiar to the political realm alone. What perhaps hitherto had been of spiritual significance only for the few now has become a concern of one and all. Only now, as it were after the fact, the loss of tradition and of religion have become political events of the first order.

When I said that I did not wish to discuss "authority in general," but only the very specific concept of authority which has been dominant in our history, I wished to hint at some distinctions which we are liable to neglect when we speak too sweepingly of the crisis of our time, and which I may perhaps more easily explain in terms of the related concepts of tradition and religion. Thus the undeniable loss of tradition in the modern world does not at all entail a loss of the past, for tradition and past are not the same, as the believers in tradition on one side and the believers in progress on the other would have us believe—whereby it makes little difference that the former deplore this state of affairs while the latter extend their congratulations. With the loss of tradition we have lost the thread which safely guided us through the vast realms of the past, but this thread was also the chain fettering each successive generation to a predetermined aspect of the past. It could be that only now will the past open up to us with unexpected freshness and tell us things no one has yet had ears to hear. But it cannot be denied that without a securely anchored tradition—and the loss of this security occurred several hundred years ago—the whole dimension of the past has also been endangered. We are in danger of forgetting, and such an oblivion— quite apart from the contents themselves that could be lost—would mean that, humanly speaking, we would deprive ourselves of one dimension, the dimension of depth in human existence. For memory and depth are the same, or rather, depth cannot be reached by man except through remembrance.

It is similar with the loss of religion. Ever since the radical criticism of religious beliefs in the seventeenth and eighteenth centuries, it has remained characteristic of the modern age to doubt religious truth, and this is true for believers and nonbelievers alike. Since Pascal and, even more pointedly, since Kierkegaard, doubt has been carried into belief, and the modern believer must constantly guard his beliefs against doubts; not the Christian faith as such, but Christianity (and Judaism, of course) in the modern age is ridden by paradoxes and absurdity. And whatever else may be able to survive absurdity—philosophy perhaps can—religion certainly cannot. Yet this loss of belief in the dogmas of institutional religion need not necessarily imply a loss or even a crisis of faith, for religion and faith, or belief and faith, are by no means the same. Only belief, but not faith, has an inherent affinity with and is constantly exposed to doubt. But who can deny that faith too, for so many centuries securely protected by religion, its beliefs and its dogmas, has been gravely endangered through what is actually only a crisis of institutional religion?

Some similar qualifications seem to me to be necessary regarding the modern loss of authority. Authority, resting on a foundation in the past as its unshaken cornerstone, gave the world the permanence and durability which human beings need precisely because they are mortals—the most unstable and futile beings we know of. Its loss is tantamount to the loss of the groundwork of the world, which indeed since then has begun to shift, to change and transform itself with ever-increasing rapidity from one shape into another, as though we were living and struggling with a Protean universe where everything at any moment can become almost anything else. But the loss of worldly permanence and reliability—which politically is identical with the loss of authority—does not entail, at least not necessarily, the loss of the human capacity for building, preserving, and caring for a world that can survive us and remain a place fit to live in for those who come after us.

It is obvious that these reflections and descriptions are based on the conviction of the importance of making distinctions. To stress such a conviction seems to be a gratuitous truism in view of the fact that, at least as far as I know, nobody has yet openly stated that distinctions are nonsense. There exists, however, a silent agreement in most discussions among political and social scientists that we can ignore distinctions and proceed on the assumption that everything can eventually be called anything else, and that distinctions are meaningful only to the extent that each of us has the right "to define his terms." Yet does not this curious right, which we have come to grant as soon as we deal with matters of importance—as though it were actually the same as the right to one's own opinion—already indicate that such terms as "tyranny," "authority," "totalitarianism" have simply lost their common meaning, or that we have ceased to live in a common world where the words we have in common possess an unquestionable meaningfulness, so that, short of being condemned to live verbally in an altogether meaningless world, we grant each other the right to retreat into our own worlds of meaning, and demand only that each of us remain consistent within his own private terminology? If, in these circumstances, we assure ourselves that we still understand each other, we do not mean that together we understand a world common to us all, but that we understand the consistency of arguing and reasoning, of the process of argumentation in its sheer formality.

However that may be, to proceed under the implicit assumption that distinctions are not important or, better, that in the social-political-historical realm, that is, in the sphere of human affairs, things do not possess that distinctness which traditional metaphysics used to call their "otherness" (their *alteritas*), has become the hallmark of a great many theories in the social, political, and historical sciences. Among these, two seem to me to deserve special mention because they touch the subject under discussion in an especially significant manner.

The first concerns the ways in which, since the nineteenth century, liberal and conservative writers have dealt with the problem of authority and, by implication, with the related problem of freedom in the realm of politics. Generally speaking, it has been quite typical of liberal theories to start from the assumption that "the constancy of progress . . . in the direction of organized and assured freedom is the characteristic fact of modern history" [1] and to look upon each deviation from this course as a reactionary process leading in the opposite direction. This makes them overlook the differences in principle between the restriction of freedom in authoritarian regimes, the abolition of political freedom in tyrannies and dictatorships, and the total elimination of spontaneity itself, that is, of the most general and most elementary manifestation of human freedom, at which only totalitarian regimes aim by means of their various methods of conditioning. The liberal writer, concerned with history and the progress of freedom rather than with forms of government, sees only differences in degree here, and ignores that authoritarian government committed to the restriction of liberty remains tied to the freedom it limits to the extent that it would lose its very substance if it abolished it altogether, that is, would change into tyranny. The same is true for the distinction between legitimate and illegitimate power on which all authoritarian government hinges. The liberal writer is apt to pay little attention to it because of his conviction that all power corrupts and that the constancy of progress requires constant loss of power, no matter what its origin may be.

Behind the liberal identification of totalitarianism with authoritarianism, and the concomitant inclination to see "totalitarian" trends in every authoritarian limitation of freedom, lies an older confusion of authority with tyranny, and of legitimate power with violence. The difference between tyranny and authoritarian government has always been that the tyrant rules in accordance with his own will and interest, whereas even the most draconic authoritarian government is bound by laws. Its acts are tested by a code which was made either not by man at all, as in the case of the law of nature or God's Commandments or the Platonic ideas, or at least not by those actually in power. The source of authority in authoritarian government is always a force external and superior to its own power; it is always this source, this external force which transcends the political realm, from which the authorities derive their "authority," that is, their legitimacy, and against which their power can be checked.

Modern spokesmen of authority, who, even in the short intervals when public opinion provides a favorable climate for neo-conservatism, remain well aware that theirs is an almost lost cause, are of course eager to point to this distinction between tyranny and authority. Where the liberal writer sees an essentially assured progress in the direction of freedom, which is only temporarily interrupted by some dark forces of the past, the conservative sees a process of doom which started with the dwindling of authority, so that freedom, after it lost the restricting limitations which protected its boundaries, became helpless, defenseless, and bound to be destroyed. (It is hardly fair to say that only liberal political thought is primarily interested in freedom; there is hardly a school of political thought in our history which is not centered around the idea of freedom, much as the concept of liberty may vary with different writers and in different political circumstances. The only exception of any consequence to this statement seems to me to be the political philosophy of Thomas Hobbes, who, of course, was anything but a conservative.) Tyranny and totalitarianism are again identified, except that now totalitarian government, if it is not directly identified with democracy, is seen as its almost inevitable result, that is, the result of the disappearance of all traditionally recognized authorities. Yet the differences between tyranny and dictatorship on one side, and totalitarian domination on the other, are no less distinct than those between authoritarianism and totalitarianism.

These structural differences become apparent the moment we leave the over-all theories behind and concentrate our attention on the apparatus of rule, the technical forms of administration, and the organization of the body politic. For brevity's sake, it may be permitted to sum up the technical-structural differences between authoritarian, tyrannical, and totalitarian government in the image of three different representative models. As an image for authoritarian government, I propose the shape of the pyramid, which is well known in traditional political thought. The pyramid is indeed a particularly fitting image for a governmental structure whose source of authority lies outside itself, but whose seat of power is located at the top, from which authority and power is filtered down to the base in such a way that each successive layer possesses some authority, but less than the one above it, and where, precisely because of this careful filtering process, all layers from top to bottom are not only firmly integrated into the whole but are interrelated like converging rays whose common focal point is the top of the pyramid as well as the transcending source of authority above it. This image, it is true, can be used only for the Christian type of authoritarian rule as it developed through and under the constant influence of the Church during the Middle Ages, when the focal point above and beyond the earthly pyramid provided the necessary point of reference for the Christian type of equality, the strictly hierarchical structure of life on earth notwithstanding. The Roman understanding of political authority, where the source of authority lay exclusively in the past, in the foundation of Rome and the greatness of ancestors, leads into institutional structures whose shape requires a different kind of image—about which more later (p. 124). In any event, an authoritarian form of government with its hierarchical structure is the least egalitarian of all forms; it incorporates inequality and distinction as its all-permeating principles.

All political theories concerning tyranny agree that it belongs strictly among the egalitarian forms of government; the tyrant is the ruler who rules as one against all, and the "all" he oppresses are all equal, namely equally powerless. If we stick to the image of the pyramid, it is as though all intervening layers between top and bottom were destroyed, so that the top remains suspended, supported only by the proverbial bayonets, over a mass of carefully isolated, disintegrated, and completely equal individuals. Classical political theory used to rule the tyrant out of mankind altogether, to call him a "wolf in human shape" (Plato), because of this position of one against all, in which he had put himself and which sharply distinguished his rule, the rule of one, which Plato still calls indiscriminately μον-αρχία or tyranny, from various forms of kingship or βασιλεία.

In contradistinction to both tyrannical and authoritarian regimes, the proper image of totalitarian rule and organization seems to me to be the structure of the onion, in whose center, in a kind of empty space, the leader is located; whatever he does—whether he integrates the body politic as in an authoritarian hierarchy, or oppresses his subjects like a tyrant—he does it from within, and not from without or above. All the extraordinarily manifold parts of the movement: the front organizations, the various professional societies, the party membership, the party bureaucracy, the elite formations and police groups, are related in such a way that each forms the façade in one direction and the center in the other, that is, plays the role of normal outside world for one layer and the role of radical extremism for another. The great advantage of this system is that the movement provides for each of its layers, even under conditions of totalitarian rule, the fiction of a normal world along with a consciousness of being different from and more radical than it. Thus, the sympathizers in the front organizations, whose convictions differ only in intensity from those of the party membership, sur-

round the whole movement and provide a deceptive façade of nor-
mality to the outside world because of their lack of fanaticism and
extremism, while, at the same time, they represent the normal world
to the totalitarian movement, whose members come to believe that
their convictions differ only in degree from those of other people,
so that they need never be aware of the abyss which separates their
own world from that which actually surrounds it. The onion structure makes the system organizationally shock-proof against the
factuality of the real world.[2]

However, while both liberalism and conservatism fail us the
moment we try to apply their theories to factually existing political
forms and institutions, it can hardly be doubted that their over-all
assertions carry a high amount of plausibility. Liberalism, we saw,
measures a process of receding freedom, and conservatism measures
a process of receding authority; both call the expected end-result
totalitarianism and see totalitarian trends wherever either one or the
other is present. No doubt, both can produce excellent documenta-
tion for their findings. Who would deny the serious threats to freedom from all sides since the beginning of the century, and the rise
of all kinds of tyranny, at least since the end of the First World War?
Who can deny, on the other hand, that disappearance of practically
all traditionally established authorities has been one of the most
spectacular characteristics of the modern world? It seems as though
one has only to fix his glance on either of these two phenomena to
justify a theory of progress or a theory of doom according to his
own taste or, as the phrase goes, according to his own "scale of
values." If we look upon the conflicting statements of conservatives
and liberals with impartial eyes, we can easily see that the truth is
equally distributed between them and that we are in fact confronted
with a simultaneous recession of both freedom and authority in the
modern world. As far as these processes are concerned, one can even
say that the numerous oscillations in public opinion, which for more
than a hundred and fifty years has swung at regular intervals from
one extreme to the other, from a liberal mood to a conservative one
and back to a more liberal again, at times attempting to reassert
authority and at others to reassert freedom, have resulted only in

further undermining both, confusing the issues, blurring the distinctive lines between authority and freedom, and eventually destroying the political meaning of both.

Both liberalism and conservatism were born in this climate of violently oscillating public opinion, and they are tied together, not only because each would lose its very substance without the presence of its opponent in the field of theory and ideology, but because both are primarily concerned with restoration, with restoring either freedom or authority, or the relationship between both, to its traditional position. It is in this sense that they form the two sides of the same coin, just as their progress-or-doom ideologies correspond to the two possible directions of the historical process as such; if one assumes, as both do, that there is such a thing as a historical process with a definable direction and a predictable end, it obviously can land us only in paradise or in hell.

It is, moreover, in the nature of the very image in which history is usually conceived, as process or stream or development, that everything comprehended by it can change into anything else, that distinctions become meaningless because they become obsolete, submerged, as it were, by the historical stream, the moment they have appeared. From this viewpoint, liberalism and conservatism present themselves as the political philosophies which correspond to the much more general and comprehensive philosophy of history of the nineteenth century. In form and content, they are the political expression of the history-consciousness of the last stage of the modern age. Their inability to distinguish, theoretically justified by the concepts of history and process, progress or doom, testifies to an age in which certain notions, clear in their distinctness to all previous centuries, have begun to lose their clarity and plausibility because they have lost their meaning in the public-political reality—without altogether losing their significance.

The second and more recent theory implicitly challenging the importance of making distinctions is, especially in the social sciences, the almost universal functionalization of all concepts and ideas. Here, as in the example previously quoted, liberalism and conservatism differ not in method, viewpoint, and approach, but only in emphasis and evaluation. A convenient instance may be provided by the wide-spread conviction in the free world today that communism is a new "religion," notwithstanding its avowed atheism, because it fulfills socially, psychologically, and "emotionally" the same function traditional religion fulfilled and still fulfills in the free world. The concern of the social sciences does not lie in what bolshevism as ideology or as form of government is, nor in what its spokesmen have to say for themselves; that is not the interest of the social sciences, and many social scientists believe they can do without the study of what the historical sciences call the sources themselves. Their concern is only with functions, and whatever fulfills the same function can, according to this view, be called the same. It is as though I had the right to call the heel of my shoe a hammer because I, like most women, use it to drive nails into the wall.

Obviously one can draw quite different conclusions from such equations. Thus it would be characteristic of conservatism to insist that after all a heel is not a hammer, but that the use of the heel as a substitute for the hammer proves that hammers are indispensable. In other words, it will find in the fact that atheism can fulfill the same function as religion the best proof that religion is necessary, and recommend the return to true religion as the only way to counter a "heresy." The argument is weak, of course; if it is only a question of function and how a thing works, the adherents of "false religion" can make as good a case for using theirs as I can for using my heel, which does not work so badly either. The liberals, on the contrary, view the same phenomena as a bad case of treason to the cause of secularism and believe that only "true secularism" can cure us of the pernicious influence of both false and true religion on politics. But these conflicting recommendations at the address of free society to return to true religion and become more religious, or to rid ourselves of institutional religion (especially of Roman Catholicism with its constant challenge to secularism) hardly conceal the opponents' agreement on one point: that whatever fulfills the function of a religion is a religion.

The same argument is frequently used with respect to authority: if violence fulfills the same function as authority—namely, makes people obey—then violence is authority. Here again we find those who counsel a return to authority because they think only a reintroduction of the order-obedience relationship can master the problems of a mass society, and those who believe that a mass society can rule itself, like any other social body. Again both parties agree on the one essential point: authority is whatever makes people obey. All those who call modern dictatorships "authoritarian," or mistake totalitarianism for an authoritarian structure, have implicitly equated violence with authority, and this includes those conservatives who explain the rise of dictatorships in our century by the need to find a surrogate for authority. The crux of the argument is always the same: everything is related to a functional context, and the use of violence is taken to demonstrate that no society can exist except in an authoritarian framework.

The dangers of these equations, as I see them, lie not only in the confusion of political issues and in the blurring of the distinctive lines which separate totalitarianism from all other forms of government. I do not believe that atheism is a substitute for or can fulfill the same function as a religion any more than I believe that violence can become a substitute for authority. But if we follow the recommendations of the conservatives, who at this particular moment have a rather good chance of being heard, I am quite convinced that we shall not find it hard to produce such substitutes, that we shall use violence and pretend to have restored authority or that our rediscovery of the functional usefulness of religion will produce a substitute-religion—as though our civilization were not already sufficiently cluttered up with all sorts of pseudo-things and nonsense.

Compared with these theories, the distinctions between tyrannical, authoritarian, and totalitarian systems which I have proposed are unhistorical, if one understands by history not the historical space in which certain forms of government appeared as recognizable entities, but the historical process in which everything can always change into something else; and they are anti-functional insofar as the content of the phenomenon is taken to determine both the nature of the political body and its function in society, and not vice-versa. Politically speaking, they have a tendency to assume that in the modern world authority has disappeared almost to the vanishing point, and this in the so-called authoritarian systems no less than in the free world, and that freedom—that is, the freedom of movement of human beings—is threatened everywhere, even in free societies, but abolished radically only in totalitarian systems, and not in tyrannies and dictatorships.

It is in the light of this present situation that I propose to raise the following questions: What were the political experiences that corresponded to the concept of authority and from which it sprang? What is the nature of a public-political world constituted by authority? Is it true that the Platonic-Aristotelian statement that every well-ordered community is constituted of those who rule and those who are ruled was always valid prior to the modern age? Or, to put it differently, what kind of world came to an end after the modern age not only challenged one or another form of authority in different spheres of life but caused the whole concept of authority to lose its validity altogether?

II

Authority as the one, if not the decisive, factor in human communities did not always exist, though it can look back on a long history, and the experiences on which this concept is based are not necessarily present in all bodies politic. The word and the concept are Roman in origin. Neither the Greek language nor the varied political experiences of Greek history shows any knowledge of authority and the kind of rule it implies.[3] This is expressed most clearly in the philosophy of Plato and Aristotle, who, in quite different ways but from the same political experiences, tried to introduce something akin to authority into the public life of the Greek polis.

There existed two kinds of rule on which they could fall back and from which they derived their political philosophy, one known to them from the public-political realm, and the other from the private sphere of Greek household and family life. To the polis, absolute rule was known as tyranny, and the chief characteristics of the tyrant were that he ruled by sheer violence, had to be protected from the people by a bodyguard, and insisted that his subjects mind their own business and leave to him the care of the public realm. The last characteristic, in Greek public opinion, signified that he destroyed the public realm of the polis altogether— "a polis belonging to one man is no polis" [4]—and thereby deprived the citizens of that political faculty which they felt was the very essence of freedom. Another political experience of the need for command and obedience might have been provided by the experience in warfare, where danger and the necessity to make and carry out decisions quickly seem to constitute an inherent reason for the establishment of authority. Neither of these political models, however, could possibly serve the purpose. The tyrant remained, for Plato as for Aristotle, the "wolf in human shape," and the military commander was too obviously connected with a temporary emergency to be able to serve as model for a permanent institution.

Because of this absence of valid political experience on which to base a claim to authoritarian rule, both Plato and Aristotle, albeit in very different ways, had to rely on examples of human relations drawn from Greek household and family life, where the head of the household ruled as a "despot," in uncontested mastery over the members of his family and the slaves of the household. The despot, unlike the king, the βασιλεύς, who had been the leader of household heads and as such *primus inter pares,* was by definition vested with the power to coerce. Yet it was precisely this characteristic that made the despot unfit for political purposes; his power to coerce was incompatible not only with the freedom of others but with his own freedom as well. Wherever he ruled there was only one relation, that between master and slaves. And the master, according to Greek common opinion (which was still blissfully unaware of Hegelian dialectics), was not free when he moved among his slaves; his freedom consisted in his ability to leave the sphere of the household altogether and to move among his equals, freemen. Hence, neither the despot nor the tyrant, the one moving among slaves, the other among subjects, could be called a free man.

Authority implies an obedience in which men retain their freedom, and Plato hoped to have found such an obedience when, in his old age, he bestowed upon the laws that quality which would make them undisputable rulers over the whole public realm. Men could at least have the illusion of being free because they did not depend upon other men. Yet the rulership of these laws was construed in an obviously despotic rather than an authoritarian manner, the clearest sign of which is that Plato was led to speak of them in terms of private household affairs, and not in political terms, and to say, probably in a variation of Pindar's νόμος βασιλεὺς πάντων ("a law is king over everything"): νόμος δεσπότης τῶν ἀρχόντων, οἱ δὲ ἄρχοντες δοῦλοι τοῦ νόμου ("the law is the *despot* of the rulers, and the rulers are the *slaves* of the law").[5] In Plato, the despotism originating in the household, and its concomitant destruction of the political realm as antiquity understood it, remained utopian. But it is interesting to note that when the destruction became a reality in the last centuries of the Roman Empire, the change was introduced by the application to public rule of the term *dominus,* which in Rome (where the family also was "organized like a monarchy")[6] had the same meaning as the Greek "despot." Caligula was the first Roman emperor who consented to be called *dominus,* that is, to be given a name "which Augustus and Tiberius still had rejected as if it were a malediction and an injury,"[7] precisely because it implied a despotism unknown in the political realm, although all too familiar in the private, household realm.

The political philosophies of Plato and Aristotle have dominated all subsequent political thought, even when their concepts have been superimposed upon such greatly different political experiences as those of the Romans. If we wish not only to comprehend the actual political experiences behind the concept of authority—which, at least in its positive aspect, is exclusively Roman—but also to understand authority as the Romans themselves already understood it theoretically and made it part of the political tradition of the West, we shall have to concern ourselves briefly with those features of Greek political philosophy which have so decisively influenced its shaping.

Nowhere else has Greek thinking so closely approached the concept of authority as in Plato's *Republic,* wherein he confronted the reality of the polis with a utopian rule of reason in the person of the philosopher-king. The motive for establishing reason as ruler in the realm of politics was exclusively political, although the consequences of expecting reason to develop into an instrument of coercion perhaps have been no less decisive for the tradition of Western philosophy than for the tradition of Western politics. The fatal resemblance between Plato's philosopher-king and the Greek tyrant, as well as the potential harm to the political realm that his rule would imply, seems to have been recognized by Aristotle; [8] but that this combination of reason and rule implied a danger to philosophy as well has been pointed out, as far as I know, only in Kant's reply to Plato: "It is not to be expected that kings philosophize or that philosophers become kings, nor is it to be desired, because the possession of power corrupts the free judgment of reason inevitably" [9]—although even this reply does not go to the root of the matter.

The reason Plato wanted the philosophers to become the rulers of the city lay in the conflict between the philosopher and the polis, or in the hostility of the polis toward philosophy, which probably had lain dormant for some time before it showed its immediate threat to the life of the philosopher in the trial and death of Socrates. Politically, Plato's philosophy shows the rebellion of the philosopher against the polis. The philosopher announces his claim to rule, but not so much for the sake of the polis and politics (although patriotic motivation cannot be denied in Plato and distinguishes his philosophy from those of his followers in antiquity) as for the sake of philosophy and the safety of the philosopher.

It was after Socrates' death that Plato began to discount persuasion as insufficient for the guidance of men and to seek for something liable to compel them without using external means of violence. Very early in his search he must have discovered that truth, namely, the truths we call self-evident, compels the mind, and that this coercion, though it needs no violence to be effective, is stronger than persuasion and argument. The trouble with coercion through reason, however, is that only the few are subject to it, so that the problem arises of how to assure that the many, the people who in their very multitude compose the body politic, can be submitted to the same truth. Here, to be sure, other means of coercion must be found, and here again coercion through violence must be avoided if political life as the Greeks understood it is not to be destroyed.[10] This is the central predicament of Plato's political philosophy and has remained a predicament of all attempts to establish a tyranny of reason. In *The Republic* the problem is solved through the concluding myth of rewards and punishments in the hereafter, a myth which Plato himself obviously neither believed nor wanted the philosophers to believe. What the allegory of the cave story in the middle of *The Republic* is for the few or for the philosopher the myth of hell at the end is for the many who are not capable of philosophical truth. In the *Laws* Plato deals with the same perplexity, but in the opposite way; here he proposes a substitute for persuasion, the introduction to the laws in which their intent and purpose are to be explained to the citizens.

In his attempts to find a legitimate principle of coercion Plato was originally guided by a great number of models of existing relations, such as that between the shepherd and his sheep, between the helmsman of a ship and the passengers, between the physician and the patient, or between the master and the slave. In all these instances either expert knowledge commands confidence so that neither force nor persuasion are necessary to obtain compliance, or the ruler and the ruled belong to two altogether different categories of beings, one of which is already by implication subject to the other, as in the cases of the shepherd and his flock or the master and his slaves. All these examples are taken from what to the Greeks was the private sphere of life, and they occur time and again in all the great political dialogues, *The Republic,* the *Statesman,* and the *Laws.* Nevertheless, it is obvious that the relation between master and slave has a special significance. The master, according to the discussion in the *Statesman,* knows what should be done and gives his orders, while the slave executes them and obeys, so that knowing what to do and actual doing become separate and mutually exclusive functions. In *The Republic* they are the political characteristics of two different classes of men. The plausibility of these examples lies in the natural inequality prevailing between the ruling and the ruled, most apparent in the example of the shepherd, where Plato himself ironically concludes that no man, only a god, could relate to human beings as the shepherd relates to his sheep. Although it is obvious that Plato himself was not satisfied with these models, for his purpose, to establish the "authority" of the philosopher over the polis, he returned to them time and again, because only in these instances of glaring inequality could rule be exerted without seizure of power and the possession of the means of violence. What he was looking for was a relationship in which the compelling element lies in the relationship itself and is prior to the actual issuance of commands; the patient became subject to the physician's authority when he fell ill, and the slave came under the command of his master when he became a slave.

It is important to bear these examples in mind in order to realize what kind of coercion Plato expected reason to exert in the hands of the king-philosopher. Here, it is true, the compelling power does not lie in the person or in inequality as such, but in the ideas which are perceived by the philosopher. These ideas can be used as measures of human behavior because they transcend the sphere of human affairs in the same way that a yardstick transcends, is outside and beyond, all things whose length it can measure. In the parable of the cave in *The Republic,* the sky of ideas stretches above the cave of human existence, and therefore can become its standard. But the philosopher who leaves the cave for the pure sky of ideas does not originally do so in order to acquire those standards and learn the "art of measurement" [11] but to contemplate the true essence of Being—βλέπειν εἰς τὸ ἀληθέστατον. The basically authoritative element of the ideas, that is, the quality which enables them to rule and compel, is therefore not at all a matter of course. The ideas become measures only after the philosopher has left the bright sky of ideas and returned to the dark cave of human existence. In this part of the story Plato touches upon the deepest reason for the conflict between the philosopher and the polis.[12] He tells of the philosopher's loss of orientation in human affairs, of the blindness striking the eyes, of the predicament of not being able to communicate what he has seen, and of the actual danger to his life which thereby arises. It is in this predicament that the philosopher resorts to what he has seen, the ideas, as standards and measures, and finally, in fear of his life, uses them as instruments of domination.

For the transformation of the ideas into measures, Plato is helped by an analogy from practical life, where it appears that all arts and crafts are also guided by "ideas," that is, by the "shapes" of objects, visualized by the inner eye of the craftsman, who then reproduces them in reality through imitation.[13] This analogy enables him to understand the transcendent character of the ideas in the same manner as he does the transcendent existence of the model, which lies beyond the fabrication process it guides and therefore can eventually become the standard for its success or failure. The ideas become the unwavering, "absolute" standards for political and moral behavior and judgment in the same sense that the "idea" of a bed in general is the standard for making and judging the fitness of all particular manufactured beds. For there is no great difference between using the ideas as models and using them, in a somewhat cruder fashion, as actual yardsticks of behavior, and Aristotle in his earliest dialogue, written under the direct influence of Plato, already compares "the most perfect law," that is, the law which is the closest possible approximation to the idea, with "the plummet, the rule, and the compass . . . [which] are outstanding among all tools." [14]

It is only in this context that the ideas relate to the varied multitude of things concrete in the same way as one yardstick relates to the varied multitude of things measurable, or as the rule of reason or common sense relates to the varied multitude of concrete events which can be subsumed under it. This aspect of Plato's doctrine of ideas had the greatest influence on the Western tradition, and even Kant, though he had a very different and considerably deeper concept of human judgment, still occasionally mentioned this capacity for subsuming as its essential function. Likewise, the essential characteristic of specifically authoritarian forms of government—that the source of their authority, which legitimates the exercise of power, must be beyond the sphere of power and, like the law of nature or the commands of God, must not be man-made—goes back to this applicability of the ideas in Plato's political philosophy.

At the same time the analogy relating to fabrication and the arts and crafts offers a welcome opportunity to justify the otherwise very dubious use of examples and instances taken from activities in which some expert knowledge and specialization are required. Here the concept of the expert enters the realm of political action for the first time, and the statesman is understood to be competent to deal with human affairs in the same sense as the carpenter is competent to make furniture or the physician to heal the sick. Closely connected with this choice of examples and analogies is the element of violence, which is so glaringly evident in Plato's utopian republic and actually constantly defeats his great concern for assuring voluntary obedience, that is, for establishing a sound foundation for what, since the Romans, we call authority. Plato solved his dilemma through rather lengthy tales about a hereafter with rewards and punishments, which he hoped would be believed literally by the many and whose usage he therefore recommended to the attention of the few at the close of most of his political dialogues. In view of the enormous influence these tales have exerted upon the images of hell in religious thought, it is of some importance to note that they were originally designed for purely political purposes. In Plato they are simply an ingenious device to enforce obedience upon those who are not subject to the compelling power of reason, without actually using external violence.

It is of greater relevance in our context, however, that an element of violence is inevitably inherent in all activities of making, fabricating, and producing, that is, in all activities by which men confront nature directly, as distinguished from such activities as action and speech, which are primarily directed toward human beings. The building of the human artifice always involves some violence done to nature—we must kill a tree in order to have lumber, and we must violate this material in order to build a table. In the few

instances where Plato shows a dangerous preference for the tyrannical form of government, he is carried to this extreme by his own
analogies. This, obviously, is most tempting when he speaks about
the right way to found new communities, because this foundation
can be easily seen in the light of another "making" process. If the
republic is to be made by somebody who is the political equivalent
of a craftsman or artist, in accordance with an established τέχνη and
the rules and measurements valid in this particular "art," the tyrant
is indeed in the best position to achieve the purpose.[15]

We have seen that, in the parable of the cave, the philosopher
leaves the cave in search of the true essence of Being without a second thought to the practical applicability of what he is going to find.
Only later, when he finds himself again confined to the darkness and
uncertainty of human affairs and encounters the hostility of his
fellow human beings, does he begin to think of his "truth" in terms
of standards applicable to the behavior of other people. This discrepancy between the ideas as true essences to be contemplated and
as measures to be applied [16] is manifest in the two entirely different
ideas which represent the highest idea, the one to which all others
owe their existence. We find in Plato either that this supreme idea
is that of the beautiful, as in the *Symposion,* where it constitutes the
topmost rung of the ladder that leads to truth,[17] and in *Phaedrus,*
where Plato speaks of the "lover of wisdom or of beauty" as though
these two actually were the same because beauty is what "shines
forth most" (the beautiful is ἐκφανέστατον) and therefore illuminates
everything else; [18] or that the highest idea is the idea of the good, as
in *The Republic.*[19] Obviously Plato's choice was based on the current ideal of the καλὸν κ'ἀγαθόν, but it is striking that the idea of the
good is found only in the strictly political context of *The Republic.*
If we were to analyze the original philosophical experiences underlying the doctrine of ideas (which we cannot do here), it would appear that the idea of the beautiful as the highest idea reflected these
experiences far more adequately than the idea of the good. Even in
the first books of *The Republic* [20] the philosopher is still defined as
a lover of beauty, not of goodness, and only in the sixth book is the
idea of good as the highest idea introduced. For the original func-

tion of the ideas was not to rule or otherwise determine the chaos of human affairs, but, in "shining brightness," to illuminate their darkness. As such, the ideas have nothing whatever to do with politics, political experience, and the problem of action, but pertain exclusively to philosophy, the experience of contemplation, and the quest for the "true being of things." It is precisely ruling, measuring, subsuming, and regulating that are entirely alien to the experiences underlying the doctrine of ideas in its original conception. It seems that Plato was the first to take exception to the political "irrelevance" of his new teaching, and he tried to modify the doctrine of ideas so that it would become useful for a theory of politics. But usefulness could be saved only by the idea of the good, since "good" in the Greek vocabulary always means "good for" or "fit." If the highest idea, in which all other ideas must partake in order to be ideas at all, is that of fitness, then the ideas are applicable by definition, and in the hands of the philosopher, the expert in ideas, they can become rules and standards or, as later in the *Laws,* they can become laws. (The difference is negligible. What in *The Republic* is still the philosopher's, the philosopher-king's, direct personal claim to rule, has become reason's impersonal claim to domination in the *Laws.*) The actual consequence of this political interpretation of the doctrine of ideas would be that neither man nor a god is the measure of all things, but the good itself—a consequence which apparently Aristotle, not Plato, drew in one of his earlier dialogues.[21]

For our purposes it is essential to remember that the element of rule, as reflected in our present concept of authority so tremendously influenced by Platonic thinking, can be traced to a conflict between philosophy and politics, but not to specifically political experiences, that is, experiences immediately derived from the realm of human affairs. One cannot understand Plato without bearing in mind both his repeated emphatic insistence on the philosophic irrelevance of this realm, which he always warned should not be taken too seriously, and the fact that he himself, in distinction to nearly all philosophers who came after him, still took human affairs so seriously that he changed the very center of his thought to make it applicable to politics. And it is this ambivalence rather than any formal exposition of his new doctrine of ideas which forms the true content of the parable of the cave in *The Republic,* which after all is told in the context of a strictly political dialogue searching for the best form of government. In the midst of this search Plato tells his parable, which turns out to be the story of the philosopher in this world, as though he had intended to write the concentrated biography of *the* philosopher. Hence, the search for the best form of government reveals itself to be the search for the best government for philosophers, which turns out to be a government in which philosophers have become the rulers of the city—a not too surprising solution for people who had witnessed the life and death of Socrates.

Still, the philosopher's rule had to be justified, and it could be justified only if the philosopher's truth possessed a validity for that very realm of human affairs which the philosopher had to turn away from in order to perceive it. Insofar as the philosopher is nothing but a philosopher, his quest ends with the contemplation of the highest truth, which, since it illuminates everything else, is also the highest beauty; but insofar as the philosopher is a man among men, a mortal among mortals, and a citizen among citizens, he must take his truth and transform it into a set of rules, by virtue of which transformation he then may claim to become an actual ruler—the king-philosopher. The lives of the many in the cave over which the philosopher has established his rule are characterized not by contemplation but by λέξις, speech, and πρᾶξις, action; it is therefore characteristic that in the parable of the cave Plato depicts the lives of the inhabitants as though they too were interested only in seeing: first the images on the screen, then the things themselves in the dim light of the fire in the cave, until finally those who want to see truth itself must leave the common world of the cave altogether and embark upon their new adventure all by themselves.

In other words, the whole realm of human affairs is seen from the viewpoint of a philosophy which assumes that even those who inhabit the cave of human affairs are human only insofar as they too want to see, though they remain deceived by shadows and images. And the rule of the philosopher-king, that is, the domination of human affairs by something outside its own realm, is justified not only by an absolute priority of seeing over doing, of contemplation over speaking and acting, but also by the assumption that what makes men human is the urge to see. Hence, the interest of the philosopher and the interest of man *qua* man coincide; both demand that human affairs, the results of speech and action, must not acquire a dignity of their own but be subjected to the domination of something outside their realm.

III

The dichotomy between seeing the truth in solitude and remoteness and being caught in the relationships and relativities of human affairs became authoritative for the tradition of political thought. It is expressed most forcefully in Plato's parable of the cave, and one is therefore somehow tempted to see its origin in the Platonic doctrine of ideas. Historically, however, it was not dependent upon an acceptance of this doctrine, but depended much more upon an attitude which Plato expressed only once, almost casually in a random remark, and which Aristotle later quoted in a famous sentence of *Metaphysics* almost verbatim, namely that the beginning of all philosophy is θαυμάζειν, the surprised wonder at everything that is as it is. More than anything else, Greek "theory" is the prolongation and Greek philosophy the articulation and conceptualization of this initial wonder. To be capable of it is what separates the few from the many, and to remain devoted to it is what alienates them from the affairs of men. Aristotle, therefore, without accepting Plato's doctrine of ideas, and even repudiating Plato's ideal state, still followed him in the main not only by separating a "theoretical way of life" (βίος θεωρητικός) from a life devoted to human affairs (βίος πολιτικός)—the first to establish such ways of life in hierarchical order had been Plato in his *Phaedrus*—but accepted as a matter of course the hierarchical order implied in it. The point in our context is not only that thought was supposed to rule over action, to prescribe principles to action so that the rules of the latter were invariably derived from experiences of the former, but that by way of the βίοι, of identifying activities with ways of life, the principle of ruler-ship was established between men as well. Historically this became the hallmark of the political philosophy of the Socratic school, and the irony of this development is probably that it was precisely this dichotomy between thought and action that Socrates had feared and tried to prevent in the polis.

Thus it is in the political philosophy of Aristotle that we find the second attempt to establish a concept of authority in terms of rulers and the ruled; it was equally important for the development of the tradition of political thought, although Aristotle took a basically different approach. For him reason has neither dictatorial nor tyran-nical features, and there is no philosopher-king to regulate human affairs once and for all. His reason for maintaining that "each body politic is composed of those who rule and those who are ruled" does not derive from the superiority of the expert over the layman, and he is too conscious of the difference between acting and making to draw his examples from the sphere of fabrication. Aristotle, as far as I can see, was the first to appeal, for the purpose of establish-ing rule in the handling of human affairs, to "nature," which "es-tablished the difference . . . between the younger and the older ones, destined the ones to be ruled and the others to rule." [22]

The simplicity of this argument is all the more deceptive since centuries of repetition have degraded it into a platitude. This may be why one usually overlooks its flagrant contradiction of Aristotle's own definition of the polis as also given in *Politics:* "The polis is a community of equals for the sake of a life which is potentially the best." [23] Obviously the notion of rule in the polis was for Aristotle himself so far from convincing that he, one of the most consistent and least self-contradictory great thinkers, did not feel particularly bound by his own argument. We therefore need not be surprised when we read at the beginning of the *Economics* (a pseudo-Aris-totelian treatise, but written by one of his closest disciples) that the essential difference between a political community (the πόλις) and a private household (the οἰκία) is that the latter constitutes a "mon-archy," a one-man rule, while the polis, on the contrary, "is com-posed of many rulers." [24] In order to understand this characterization we must remember first that the words "monarchy" and "tyranny" were used synonymously and in clear contradistinction to kingship; second, that the character of the polis as "composed of many rulers" has nothing to do with the various forms of government that usually are opposed to one-man rule, such as oligarchy, aristocracy, or democracy. The "many rulers" in this context are the household heads, who have established themselves as "monarchs" at home before they join to constitute the public-political realm of the city. Ruling itself and the distinction between rulers and ruled belong to a sphere which precedes the political realm, and what disinguishes it from the "economic" sphere of the household is that the polis is based upon the principle of equality and knows no differentiation between rulers and ruled.

In this distinction between what we would today call the private and the public spheres, Aristotle only articulates current Greek public opinion, according to which "every citizen belongs to two orders of existence," because "the polis gives each individual . . . besides his private life a sort of second life, his *bios politikos*." [25] (The latter Aristotle called the "good life," and redefined its content; only this definition, not the differentiation itself, conflicted with common Greek opinion.) Both orders were forms of human living-together, but only the household community was concerned with keeping alive as such and coping with the physical necessities (ἀναγκαῖα) involved in maintaining individual life and guaranteeing the survival of the species. In characteristic difference from the modern approach, care for the preservation of life, both of the individual and the species, belonged exclusively in the private sphere of the household, while in the polis man appeared κατ' ἀριθμόν, as an individual personality, as we would say today.[26] As living beings, concerned with the preservation of life, men are confronted with and driven by necessity. Necessity must be mastered before the political "good life" can begin, and it can be mastered only through domination. Hence the freedom of the "good life" rests on the domination of necessity.

The mastery of necessity then has as its goal the controlling of the necessities of life, which coerce men and hold them in their power. But such domination can be accomplished only by controlling and doing violence to others, who as slaves relieve free men from themselves being coerced by necessity. The free man, the citizen of a polis, is neither coerced by the physical necessities of life nor subject to the man-made domination of others. He not only must not be a slave, he must own and rule over slaves. The freedom of the political realm begins after all elementary necessities of sheer living have been mastered by rule, so that domination and subjection, command and obedience, ruling and being ruled, are preconditions for establishing the political realm precisely because they are not its content.

There can be no question that Aristotle, like Plato before him, meant to introduce a kind of authority into the handling of public affairs and the life of the polis, and no doubt for very good political reasons. Yet he too had to resort to a kind of makeshift solution in order to make plausible the introduction into the political realm of a distinction between rulers and ruled, between those who command and those who obey. And he too could take his examples and models only from a prepolitical sphere, from the private realm of the household and the experiences of a slave economy. This leads him into glaringly contradictory statements, insofar as he superimposes on the actions and life in the polis those standards which, as he explains elsewhere, are valid only for the behavior and life in the household community. The inconsistency of his enterprise is apparent even if we consider only the famous example from the *Politics* previously mentioned, in which the differentiation between rulers and ruled is derived from the natural difference between the younger and the elder. For this example is in itself eminently unsuitable to prove Aristotle's argument. The relation between old and young is educational in essence, and in this education no more is involved than the training of the future rulers by the present rulers. If rule is at all involved here, it is entirely different from political forms of rule, not only because it is limited in time and intent, but because it happens between people who are potentially equals. Yet substitution of education for rule had the most far-reaching consequences. On its grounds rulers have posed as educators and educators have been accused of ruling. Then, as well as now, nothing is more questionable than the political relevance of examples drawn from the field of education. In the political realm we deal always with adults who are past the age of education, properly speaking, and politics or the right to participate in the management of public affairs begins precisely where education has come to an end. (Adult education, individual or communal, may be of great relevance for the formation of personality, its full development or greater enrichment, but is politically irrelevant unless its purpose is to supply technical requirements, somehow not acquired in youth, needed for participation in public affairs.) In education, conversely, we always deal with people who cannot yet be admitted to politics and equality because they are being prepared for it. Aristotle's example is nevertheless of great relevance because it is true that the necessity for "authority" is more plausible and evident in child-rearing and education than anywhere else. That is why it is so characteristic of our own time to want to eradicate even this extremely limited and politically irrelevant form of authority.

Politically, authority can acquire an educational character only if we presume with the Romans that under all circumstances ancestors represent the example of greatness for each successive generation, that they are the *maiores,* the greater ones, by definition. Wherever the model of education through authority, without this fundamental conviction, was superimposed on the realm of politics (and this has happened often enough and still is a mainstay of conservative argument), it served primarily to obscure real or coveted claims to rule and pretended to educate while in reality it wanted to dominate.

The grandiose attempts of Greek philosophy to find a concept of authority which would prevent deterioration of the polis and safeguard the life of the philosopher foundered on the fact that in the realm of Greek political life there was no awareness of authority based on immediate political experience. Hence all prototypes by which subsequent generations understood the content of authority were drawn from specifically unpolitical experiences, stemming either from the sphere of "making" and the arts, where there must

be experts and where fitness is the highest criterion, or from the
private household community. It is precisely in this politically determined aspect that the philosophy of the Socratic school has exerted
its greatest impact upon our tradition. Even today we believe that
Aristotle defined man primarily as a political being endowed with
speech or reason, which he did only in a political context, or that
Plato exposed the original meaning of his doctrine of ideas in *The
Republic,* where, on the contrary, he changed it for political reasons.
In spite of the grandeur of Greek political philosophy, it may be
doubted that it would have lost its inherent utopian character if the
Romans, in their indefatigable search for tradition and authority,
had not decided to take it over and acknowledge it as their highest
authority in all matters of theory and thought. But they were able
to accomplish this integration only because both authority and tradition had already played a decisive role in the political life of the
Roman republic.

IV

At the heart of Roman politics, from the beginning of the republic
until virtually the end of the imperial era, stands the conviction of
the sacredness of foundation, in the sense that once something has
been founded it remains binding for all future generations. To be
engaged in politics meant first and foremost to preserve the founding
of the city of Rome. This is why the Romans were unable to repeat
the founding of their first polis in the settlement of colonies but
were capable of adding to the original foundation until the whole
of Italy and, eventually, the whole of the Western world were united
and administered by Rome, as though the whole world were nothing
but Roman hinterland. From beginning to end, the Romans were
bound to the specific locality of this one city, and unlike the Greeks,
they could not say in times of emergency or overpopulation, "Go
and found a new city, for wherever you are you will always be a
polis." Not the Greeks, but the Romans, were really rooted in the
soil, and the word *patria* derives its full meaning from Roman his-

tory. The foundation of a new body politic—to the Greeks an almost commonplace experience—became to the Romans the central, decisive, unrepeatable beginning of their whole history, a unique event. And the most deeply Roman divinities were Janus, the god of beginning, with whom, as it were, we still begin our year, and Minerva, the goddess of remembrance.

The founding of Rome—*tanta molis erat Romanam condere gentem* ("so great was the effort and toil to found the Roman people"), as Virgil sums up the ever-present theme of the *Aeneid,* that all wandering and suffering reach their end and their goal *dum conderet urbem* ("that he may found the city")—this foundation and the equally un-Greek experience of the sanctity of house and hearth, as though Homerically speaking the spirit of Hector had survived the fall of Troy and been resurrected on Italian soil, form the deeply political content of Roman religion. In contrast to Greece, where piety depended upon the immediate revealed presence of the gods, here religion literally meant *re-ligare:* [27] to be tied back, obligated, to the enormous, almost superhuman and hence always legendary effort to lay the foundations, to build the cornerstone, to found for eternity.[28] To be religious meant to be tied to the past, and Livy, the great recorder of past events, could therefore say, *Mihi vetustas res scribenti nescio quo pacto antiquus fit animus et quaedam religio tenet* ("While I write down these ancient events, I do not know through what connection my mind grows old and some *religio* holds [me]").[29] Thus religious and political activity could be considered as almost identical, and Cicero could say, "In no other realm does human excellence approach so closely the paths of the gods (*numen*) as it does in the founding of new and in the preservation of already founded communities." [30] The binding power of the foundation itself was religious, for the city also offered the gods of the people a permanent home—again unlike Greece, whose gods protected the cities of the mortals and occasionally dwelt in them but had their own home, far from the abode of men, on Mount Olympus.

It is in this context that word and concept of authority originally appeared. The word *auctoritas* derives from the verb *augere,* "augment," and what authority or those in authority constantly augment is the foundation. Those endowed with authority were the elders, the Senate or the *patres,* who had obtained it by descent and by transmission (tradition) from those who had laid the foundations for all things to come, the ancestors, whom the Romans therefore called the *maiores.* The authority of the living was always derivative, depending upon the *auctores imperii Romani conditoresque,* as Pliny puts it, upon the authority of the founders, who no longer were among the living. Authority, in contradistinction to power (*potestas*), had its roots in the past, but this past was no less present in the actual life of the city than the power and strength of the living. *Moribus antiquis res stat Romana virisque,* in the words of Ennius.

In order to understand more concretely what it meant to be in authority, it may be useful to notice that the word *auctores* can be used as the very opposite of the *artifices,* the actual builders and makers, and this precisely when the word *auctor* signifies the same thing as our "author." Who, asks Pliny at the occasion of a new theater, should be more admired, the maker or the author, the inventor or the invention?—meaning, of course, the latter in both instances. The author in this case is not the builder but the one who inspired the whole enterprise and whose spirit, therefore, much more than the spirit of the actual builder, is represented in the building itself. In distinction to the *artifex,* who only made it, he is the actual "author" of the building, namely its founder; with it he has become an "augmenter" of the city.

However, the relation between *auctor* and *artifex* is by no means the (Platonic) relation between the master who gives orders and the servant who executes them. The most conspicuous characteristic of those in authority is that they do not have power. *Cum potestas in populo auctoritas in senatu sit,* "while power resides in the people, authority rests with the Senate." [31] Because the "authority," the augmentation which the Senate must add to political decisions, is not power, it seems to us curiously elusive and intangible, bearing in this respect a striking resemblance to Montesquieu's judiciary branch of government, whose power he called "somehow nil" (*en quelque façon nulle*) and which nevertheless constitutes the highest authority in constitutional governments.[32] Mommsen called it "more than advice and less than a command, an advice which one may not safely ignore," whereby it is assumed that "the will and the actions of the people like those of children are exposed to error and mistakes and therefore need 'augmentation' and confirmation through the council of elders."[33] The authoritative character of the "augmentation" of the elders lies in its being a mere advice, needing neither the form of command nor external coercion to make itself heard.[34]

The binding force of this authority is closely connected with the religiously binding force of the *auspices,* which, unlike the Greek oracle, does not hint at the objective course of future events but reveals merely divine approval or disapproval of decisions made by men.[35] The gods too have authority among, rather than power over, men; they "augment" and confirm human actions but do not guide them. And just as "all *auspices* were traced back to the great sign by which the gods gave Romulus the authority to found the city,"[36] so all authority derives from this foundation, binding every act back to the sacred beginning of Roman history, adding, as it were, to every single moment the whole weight of the past. *Gravitas,* the ability to bear this weight, became the outstanding trait of the Roman character, just as the Senate, the representation of authority in the republic, could function—in the words of Plutarch ("Life of Lycurgus")—as "a central weight, like ballast in a ship, which always keeps things in a just equilibrium."

Thus precedents, the deeds of the ancestors and the usage that grew out of them, were always binding.[37] Anything that happened was transformed into an example, and the *auctoritas maiorum* became identical with authoritative models for actual behavior, with the moral political standard as such. This is also why old age, as distinguished from mere adulthood, was felt by the Romans to contain the very climax of human life; not so much because of accumulated wisdom and experience as because the old man had grown closer to the ancestors and the past. Contrary to our concept of growth, where one grows into the future, the Romans felt that growth was directed toward the past. If one wants to relate this attitude to the hierarchical order established by authority and to visualize this hierarchy in the familiar image of the pyramid, it is as though the peak of the pyramid did not reach into the height of a sky above (or, as in Christianity, beyond) the earth, but into the depth of an earthly past.

It is in this primarily political context that the past was sanctified through tradition. Tradition preserved the past by handing down from one generation to the next the testimony of the ancestors, who first had witnessed and created the sacred founding and then augmented it by their authority throughout the centuries. As long as this tradition was uninterrupted, authority was inviolate; and to act without authority and tradition, without accepted, time-honored standards and models, without the help of the wisdom of the founding fathers, was inconceivable. The notion of a spiritual tradition and of authority in matters of thought and ideas is here derived from the political realm and therefore essentially derivative—just as Plato's conception of the role of reason and ideas in politics was derived from the philosophical realm and became derivative in the realm of human affairs. But the historically all-important fact is that the Romans felt they needed founding fathers and authoritative examples in matters of thought and ideas as well, and accepted the great "ancestors" in Greece as their authorities for theory, philosophy, and poetry. The great Greek authors became authorities in the hands of the Romans, not of the Greeks. The way Plato and others before and after him treated Homer, "the educator of all Hellas," was inconceivable in Rome, nor would a Roman philosopher have dared "to raise his hand against his [spiritual] father," as Plato said of himself (in the *Sophistes*) when he broke with the teaching of Parmenides.

Just as the derivative character of the applicability of the ideas to politics did not prevent Platonic political thought from becoming the origin of Western political theory, so the derivative character of authority and tradition in spiritual matters did not prevent them from becoming the dominant features of Western philosophic thought for the longer part of our history. In both instances the political origin and the political experiences underlying the theories were forgotten, the original conflict between politics and philosophy, between the citizen and the philosopher, no less than the experience of foundation in which the Roman trinity of religion, authority, and tradition had its legitimate source. The strength of this trinity lay in the binding force of an authoritative beginning to which "religious" bonds tied men back through tradition. The Roman trinity not only survived the transformation of the republic into the empire but penetrated wherever the *pax Romana* created Western civilization on Roman foundations.

The extraordinary strength and endurance of this Roman spirit —or the extraordinary reliability of the founding principle for the creation of bodies politic—were subjected to a decisive test and proved themselves conspicuously after the decline of the Roman Empire, when Rome's political and spiritual heritage passed to the Christian Church. Confronted with this very real mundane task, the Church became so "Roman" and adapted itself so thoroughly to Roman thinking in matters of politics that it made the death and resurrection of Christ the cornerstone of a new foundation, erecting on it a new human institution of tremendous durability. Thus, after Constantine the Great had called upon the Church to secure for the declining empire the protection of the "most powerful God," the Church was eventually able to overcome the antipolitical and anti-institutional tendencies of the Christian faith, which had caused so much trouble in earlier centuries, and which are so manifest in the New Testament and in early Christian writings, and seemingly so insurmountable. The victory of the Roman spirit is really almost a miracle; in any event, it alone enabled the Church "to offer men in the membership of the Church the sense of citizenship which neither Rome nor municipality could any longer offer them." [38] Yet, just as Plato's politicalization of the ideas changed Western philosophy and determined the philosophic concept of reason, so the politicalization of the Church changed the Christian religion. The basis of the Church as a community of believers and a public institution was now no longer the Christian faith in resurrection (though this faith remained its content) or the Hebrew obedience to the commands of God, but rather the testimony of the life, of the birth, death, and resurrection, of Jesus of Nazareth as a historically recorded event.[39] As witnesses to this event the Apostles could become the "founding fathers" of the Church, from whom she would derive her own authority as long as she handed down their testimony by way of tradition from generation to generation. Only when this had happened, one is tempted to say, had the Christian faith become a "religion" not only in the post-Christian sense but in the ancient sense as well; only then, at any rate, could a whole world—as distinguished from mere groups of believers, no matter how large they might have been —become Christian. The Roman spirit could survive the catastrophe of the Roman Empire because its most powerful enemies—those who had laid, as it were, a curse on the whole realm of worldly public affairs and sworn to live in hiding—discovered in their own faith something which could be understood as a worldly event as well and could be transformed into a new mundane beginning to which the world was bound back once more (*religare*) in a curious mixture of new and old religious awe. This transformation was to a large extent accomplished by Augustine, the only great philosopher the Romans ever had. For the mainstay of his philosophy, *Sedis animi est in memoria* ("the seat of the mind is in memory"), is precisely that conceptual articulation of the specifically Roman experience which the Romans themselves, overwhelmed as they were by Greek philosophy and concepts, never achieved.

Thanks to the fact that the foundation of the city of Rome was repeated in the foundation of the Catholic Church, though, of course, with a radically different content, the Roman trinity of religion, authority, and tradition could be taken over by the Christian era. The most conspicuous sign of this continuity is perhaps that the Church, when she embarked upon her great political career in the fifth century, at once adopted the Roman distinction between authority and power, claiming for herself the old authority of the Senate and leaving the power—which in the Roman Empire was no longer in the hands of the people but had been monopolized by the imperial household—to the princes of the world. Thus, at the close of the fifth century, Pope Gelasius I could write to Emperor Anastasius I: "Two are the things by which this world is chiefly ruled; the sacred authority of the Popes and the royal power." [40] The result of the continuity of the Roman spirit in the history of the West was twofold. On one hand, the miracle of permanence repeated itself once more; for within the framework of our history the durability and continuity of the Church as a public institution can be compared only with the thousand years of Roman history in antiquity. The separation of church and state, on the other hand, far from signifying unequivocally a secularization of the political realm and, hence, its rise to the dignity of the classical period, actually implied that the political had now, for the first time since the Romans, lost its authority and with it that element which, at least in Western history, had endowed political structures with durability, continuity, and permanence.

It is true that Roman political thought at a very early date began to use Platonic concepts in order to understand and interpret the specifically Roman political experiences. Yet it seems as though it has been only in the Christian era that Plato's invisible spiritual yardsticks, by which the visible, concrete affairs of men were to be measured and judged, have unfolded their full political effectiveness. Precisely those parts of Christian doctrine which would have had great difficulty in fitting in and being assimilated to the Roman political structure—namely, the revealed commandments and truths of a genuinely transcendent authority which, unlike Plato's, did not stretch above but was beyond the earthly realm—could be integrated into the Roman foundation legend via Plato. God's revelation could now be interpreted politically as if the standards for human conduct and the principle of political communities, intuitively anticipated by Plato, had been finally revealed directly, so that, in the words of a modern Platonist, it appeared as though Plato's early "orientation toward the unseen measure was now confirmed through the revelation of the measure itself." [41] To the extent that the Catholic Church incorporated Greek philosophy into the structure of its doctrines and dogmatic beliefs, it amalgamated the Roman political concept of authority, which inevitably was based on a beginning, a founding in the past, with the Greek notion of transcending measurements and rules. General and transcendent standards under which the particular and immanent could be subsumed were now required for any political order, moral rules for all interhuman behavior, and rational measurements for the guidance of all individual judgment. There is scarcely anything that eventually was to assert itself with greater authority and more far-reaching consequences than the amalgamation itself.

Since then it has turned out, and this fact speaks for the stability of the amalgamation, that wherever one of the elements of the Roman trinity, religion or authority or tradition, was doubted or eliminated, the remaining two were no longer secure. Thus, it was Luther's error to think that his challenge of the temporal authority of the Church and his appeal to unguided individual judgment would leave tradition and religion intact. So it was the error of Hobbes and the political theorists of the seventeenth century to hope that authority and religion could be saved without tradition. So, too, was it finally the error of the humanists to think it would be possible to remain within an unbroken tradition of Western civilization without religion and without authority.

V

Politically the most momentous consequence of the amalgamation of Roman political institutions with Greek philosophic ideas was that it enabled the Church to interpret the rather vague and conflicting notions of early Christianity about life in the hereafter in the light of the Platonic political myths, and thus to elevate to the rank of dogmatic certitude an elaborate system of rewards and punishments for deeds and misdeeds that did not find their just retribution on earth. This happened not before the fifth century, when the earlier teachings of the redemption of all sinners, even of Satan himself (as taught by Origen and still held by Gregory of Nyssa), and the spiritualizing interpretation of the torments of hell as torments of conscience (also taught by Origen) were declared to be heretical; but it coincided with the downfall of Rome, the disappearance of an assured secular order, the assumption of responsibility for secular affairs by the Church, and the emergence of the papacy as a temporal power. Popular and literate notions about a hereafter with rewards and punishments were, of course, widespread then as they had been throughout antiquity, but the original Christian version of these beliefs, consistent with the "glad tidings" and the redemption from sin, was not a threat of eternal punishment and eternal suffering, but, on the contrary, the *descensus ad inferos,* Christ's mission to the underworld where he had spent the three days between his death and his resurrection in order to liquidate hell, defeat Satan, and liberate the souls of dead sinners, as he had liberated the souls of the living, from death and punishment.

We find it somewhat difficult to gauge correctly the political, non-religious origin of the doctrine of hell because the Church incorporated it, in its Platonic version, so early into the body of dogmatic beliefs. It seems only natural that this incorporation in its turn should have blurred the understanding of Plato himself to the point of identifying his strictly philosophic teaching of the immortality of the soul, which was meant for the few, with his political teaching of a hereafter with punishments and rewards, which was clearly meant for the multitude. The philosopher's concern is with the invisible which can be perceived by the soul, which itself is something invisible (ἀειδές) and hence goes to Hades, the place of invisibility (Ἀ-ίδης), after death has rid the invisible part of man of his body, the organ of sense perception.[42] This is the reason why philosophers always seem "to pursue death and dying" and why philosophy can also be called "the study of death." [43] Those who have no experience with a philosophic truth beyond the range of sense perception, of course, cannot be persuaded of the immortality of a bodyless soul; for them, Plato invented a number of tales to conclude his political dialogues, usually after the argument itself had broken down, as in *The Republic,* or it had turned out that Socrates' opponent could not be persuaded, as in the *Gorgias.*[44] Of these tales, the Er-myth of *The Republic* is the most elaborate and has exerted the greatest influence. Between Plato and the secular victory of Christianity in the fifth century, which brought with it the religious sanction of the doctrine of hell (so that from then on this became so general a feature of the Christian world that political treatises did not need to mention it specifically), there was hardly an important discussion of political problems—except in Aristotle—which did not conclude with an imitation of the Platonic myth.[45] And it is still Plato, as distinguished from the Hebrew and early Christian speculations about an afterlife, who is the true forerunner of Dante's elaborate descriptions; for in Plato we find for the first time not merely a concept of final judgment about eternal life or eternal death, about rewards and punishments, but the geographical separation of hell, purgatory, and paradise, as well as the horribly concrete notions of graduated bodily punishment.[46]

The purely political implications of Plato's myths in the last book of *The Republic,* as well as in the concluding parts of *Phaedon* and *Gorgias,* seem to be indisputable. The distinction between the philosophic conviction of the immortality of the soul and the politically desirable belief in an afterlife runs parallel to the distinction in the doctrine of ideas between the idea of the beautiful as the highest idea of the philosopher and the idea of the good as the highest idea of the statesman. Yet while Plato, when applying his philosophy of ideas to the political realm, somehow blurred the decisive distinction between the ideas of the beautiful and of the good, silently substituting the latter for the former in his discussions of politics, the same cannot be said for the distinction between an immortal, invisible, bodyless soul and an afterlife in which bodies, sensitive to pain, will receive their punishment. One of the clearest indications for the political character of these myths is indeed that they, because they imply bodily punishment, stand in flagrant contradiction to his doctrine of the mortality of the body, and of this contradiction Plato himself was by no means unaware.[47] Moreover, when he came to telling his tales, he used elaborate precautions to make sure that what followed was not truth but a possible opinion of which one better persuaded the multitude "as though it were the truth." [48] Finally, is it not rather obvious, especially in *The Republic,* that this whole concept of life after death cannot possibly make sense to those who have understood the story of the cave and know that the true underworld is life on earth?

No doubt Plato relied on popular beliefs, perhaps on Orphic and Pythagorean traditions, for his descriptions of an afterlife, just as the Church, almost a thousand years later, could choose freely which of the then prevalent beliefs and speculations she wanted to lay down as dogma and which to declare as heretical. The distinction between Plato and his predecessors, whoever they may have been, was that he was the first to become aware of the enormous, strictly political potentiality inherent in such beliefs, just as the distinction between Augustine's elaborate teachings about hell, purgatory, and paradise and the speculations of Origen or Clement of Alexandria was that he (and perhaps Tertullian before him) understood to what an extent these doctrines could be used as threats in this world, quite apart from their speculative value about a future life. Nothing, indeed, is more suggestive in this context than that it was Plato who coined the word "theology," for the passage in which the new word is used occurs again in a strictly political discussion, namely in *The Republic,* when the dialogue deals with the founding of cities.[49] This new theological god is neither a living God nor the god of the philosophers nor a pagan divinity; he is a political device, "the measurement of measurements," [50] that is, the standard according to which cities may be founded and rules of behavior laid down for the multitude. Theology, moreover, teaches how to enforce these standards absolutely, even in cases when human justice seems at a loss, that is, in the case of crimes which escape punishment as well as in the case of those for which even the death sentence would not be adequate. For "the main thing" about the hereafter is, as Plato says explicitly, that "for every wrong men had done to anyone they suffered tenfold." [51] To be sure, Plato had no inkling of theology as we understand it, as the interpretation of God's word whose sacrosanct text is the Bible; theology to him was part and parcel of "political science," and specifically that part which taught the few how to rule the many.

Whatever other historical influences may have been at work to elaborate the doctrine of hell, it continued, during antiquity, to be used for political purposes in the interest of the few to retain a moral and political control over the multitude. The point at stake was always the same: truth by its very nature is self-evident and therefore cannot be satisfactorily argued out and demonstrated.[52] Hence, belief is necessary for those who lack the eyes for what is at the same time self-evident, invisible, and beyond argument. Platonically speaking, the few cannot persuade the multitude of truth because truth cannot be the object of persuasion, and persuasion is the only way to deal with the multitude. But the multitude, carried away by the irresponsible tales of poets and storytellers, can be persuaded to believe almost anything; the appropriate tales which carry the truth of the few to the multitude are tales about rewards and punishments after death; persuading the citizens of the existence of hell will make them behave as though they knew the truth.

As long as Christianity remained without secular interests and responsibilities, it left the beliefs and speculations about a hereafter as free as they had been in antiquity. Yet when the purely religious development of the new creed had come to an end and the Church had become aware of, and willing to take over, political responsibilities, she found herself confronted with a perplexity similar to the one that had given rise to Plato's political philosophy. Again it had become a question of imposing absolute standards on a realm which is made up of human affairs and relations, whose very essence therefore seems to be relativity; and to this relativity corresponds the fact that the worst man can do to man is to kill him, that is, to bring about what one day is bound to happen to him anyhow. The "improvement" on this limitation, proposed in the hell images, is precisely that punishment can mean more than the "eternal death" which early Christianity thought to be the appropriate reward of sin, namely eternal suffering, compared to which eternal death is salvation.

The introduction of the Platonic hell into the body of Christian dogmatic beliefs strengthened religious authority to the point where it could hope to remain victorious in any contest with secular power. But the price paid for this additional strength was that the Roman concept of authority was diluted, and an element of violence was permitted to insinuate itself into both the very structure of Western religious thought and the hierarchy of the Church. How high this price actually was might be gauged by the more than embarrassing fact that men of unquestionable stature—among them Tertullian and even Thomas Aquinas—could be convinced that one of the joys in heaven would be the privilege of watching the spectacle of unspeakable sufferings in hell. Nothing perhaps in the whole development of Christianity throughout the centuries is farther removed from and more alien to the letter and spirit of the teaching of Jesus of Nazareth than the elaborate catalogue of future punishments and the enormous power of coercion through fear which only in the last stages of the modern age have lost their public, political significance. As far as religious thought is concerned, it certainly is a terrible irony that the "glad tidings" of the Gospels, "Life is everlasting," should eventually have resulted not in an increase of joy but of fear on earth, should not have made it easier but harder for man to die.

However that may be, the fact is that the most significant consequence of the secularization of the modern age may well be the elimination from public life, along with religion, of the only political element in traditional religion, the fear of hell. We who had to witness how, during the Hitler and Stalin era, an entirely new and unprecedented criminality, almost unchallenged in the respective countries, was to invade the realm of politics should be the last to underestimate its "persuasive" influence upon the functioning of conscience. And the impact of these experiences is likely to grow when we recall that, in the very age of enlightenment, the men of the French Revolution no less than the founding fathers in America insisted on making the fear of an "avenging God" and hence the belief in "a future state" part and parcel of the new body politic. For the obvious reason why the men of the revolutions of all people should be so strangely out of tune in this respect with the general climate of their age was that precisely because of the new separation of church and state they found themselves in the old Platonic predicament. When they warned against the elimination of the fear of hell from public life because this would pave the way "to make murder itself as indifferent as shooting plover, and the extermination of the Rohilla nation as innocent as the swallowing of mites on a morsel of cheese," [53] their words may sound with an almost prophetic ring in our ears; yet they were clearly spoken not out of any dogmatic faith in the "avenging God" but out of mistrust in the nature of man.

Thus the belief in a future state of rewards and punishments, consciously designed as a political device by Plato and perhaps no less consciously adopted, in its Augustinian form, by Gregory the Great, was to survive all other religious and secular elements which together had established authority in Western history. It was not during the Middle Ages, when secular life had become religious to such an extent that religion could not serve as a political instrument, but during the modern age that the usefulness of religion for secular authority was rediscovered. The true motives of this rediscovery have been somewhat overshadowed by the various more or less infamous alliances of "throne and altar" when kings, frightened at the prospect of revolution, believed that "the people must not be permitted to lose its religion" because, in Heine's words, *Wer sich von seinem Gotte reisst,/ wird endlich auch abtrünnig werden/ von seinen irdischen Behörden* ("who tears himself away from his God will end by deserting his earthly authorities as well"). The point is rather that the revolutionaries themselves preached belief in a future state, that even Robespierre ended by appealing to an "Immortal Legislator" to give sanction to the revolution, that none of the early American constitutions lacked an appropriate provision for future rewards and punishments, that men like John Adams regarded them as "the only true foundation of morality." [54]

It certainly is not surprising that all these attempts at retaining the only element of violence from the crumbling edifice of religion, authority, and tradition, and at using it as safeguard for the new, secular political order should be in vain. And it was by no means the rise of socialism or of the Marxian belief that "religion is the opiate of the people" which put an end to them. (Authentic religion in general and the Christian faith in particular—with its unrelenting stress on the individual and his own role in salvation, which led to the elaboration of a catalogue of sins greater than in any other religion—could never be used as tranquilizers. Modern ideologies, whether political or psychological or social, are far better fitted to immunize man's soul against the shocking impact of reality than any traditional religion we know. Compared with the various superstitions of the twentieth century, the pious resignation to God's will seems like a child's pocket-knife in competition with atomic weapons.) The conviction that "good morals" in civil society ultimately depended upon fear and hope for another life may still have appeared to the political men of the eighteenth century no more than good common sense; to those of the nineteenth century it appeared simply scandalous that, for instance, English courts took it for granted "that the oath is worthless of a person who does not believe in a future state," and this not only for political reasons but also because it implies "that they who do believe are only prevented from lying . . . by the fear of hell." [55]

Superficially speaking, the loss of belief in future states is politically, though certainly not spiritually, the most significant distinction between our present period and the centuries before. And this loss is definite. For no matter how religious our world may turn again, or how much authentic faith still exists in it, or how deeply our moral values may be rooted in our religious systems, the fear of hell is no longer among the motives which would prevent or stimulate the actions of a majority. This seems inevitable if secularity of the world involves separation of the religious and political realms of life; under these circumstances religion was bound to lose its political element, just as public life was bound to lose the religious sanction of transcendent authority. In this situation, it would be well to recall that Plato's device of how to persuade the multitude to follow the standards of the few had remained utopian prior to its being sanctioned by religion; its purpose, to establish rule of the few over the many, was too patent to be useful. For the same reason the beliefs in future states withered from the public realm at once when their political usefulness was blatantly exposed by the very fact that they, out of the whole body of dogmatic beliefs, were deemed worthy of preservation.

VI

One thing, however, is particularly striking in this context: while all the models, prototypes, and examples for authoritarian relationships—such as the statesman as healer and physician, as expert, as helmsman, as the master who knows, as educator, as the wise man—all Greek in origin, have been faithfully preserved and further articulated until they became empty platitudes, the one political experience which brought authority as word, concept, and reality into our history—the Roman experience of foundation—seems to have been entirely lost and forgotten. And this to such an extent that the moment we begin to talk and think about authority, after all one of the central concepts of political thought, it is as though we were caught in a maze of abstractions, metaphors, and figures of speech in which everything can be taken and mistaken for something else, because we have no reality, either in history or in everyday experience, to which we can unanimously appeal. This, among other things, indicates what could also be proved otherwise, namely that the Greek concepts, once they had been sanctified by the Romans through tradition and authority, simply eliminated from historical consciousness all political experiences which could not be fitted into their framework.

However, this statement is not entirely true. There exists in our political history one type of event for which the notion of founding is decisive, and there is in our history of thought one political thinker in whose work the concept of foundation is central, if not paramount. The events are the revolutions of the modern age, and the thinker is Machiavelli, who stood at the threshold of this age and, though he never used the word, was the first to conceive of a revolution.

Machiavelli's unique position in the history of political thought has little to do with his often praised but by no means unarguable realism, and he was certainly not the father of political science, a role now frequently attributed to him. (If one understands by political science political theory, its father certainly is Plato rather than Machiavelli. If one stresses the scientific character of political science, it is hardly possible to date its birth earlier than the rise of all modern science, that is, in the sixteenth and seventeenth centuries. In my opinion the scientific character of Machiavelli's theories is often greatly exaggerated.) His unconcern with moral judgments and his freedom from prejudice are astonishing enough, but they do not strike the core of the matter; they have contributed more to his fame than to the understanding of his works, because most of his readers, then as today, were too shocked even to read him properly. When he insists that in the public-political realm men "should learn how not to be good," [56] he of course never meant that they should learn how to be evil. After all, there is scarcely another political thinker who has spoken with such vehement contempt of "methods [by which] one may indeed gain power but not glory." [57] The truth is only that he opposed both concepts of the good which we find in our tradition: the Greek concept of the "good for" or fitness, and the Christian concept of an absolute goodness which is not of this world. Both concepts in his opinion were valid, but only in the private sphere of human life; in the public realm of politics they had no more place than their opposites, unfitness or incompetence and evil. The *virtù,* on the other hand, which according to Machiavelli is the specifically political human quality, has neither the connotation of moral character as does the Roman *virtus,* nor that of a morally neutral excellence like the Greek ἀρετή. *Virtù* is the response, summoned up by man, to the world, or rather to the constellation of *fortuna* in which the world opens up, presents and offers itself to him, to his *virtù.* There is no *virtù* without *fortuna* and no *fortuna* without *virtù;* the interplay between them indicates a harmony between man and world—playing with each other and succeeding together—which is as remote from the wisdom of the statesman as from the excellence, moral or otherwise, of the individual, and the competence of experts.

His experiences in the struggles of his time taught Machiavelli a deep contempt for all traditions, Christian and Greek, as presented, nurtured, and reinterpreted by the Church. His contempt was leveled at a corrupt Church which had corrupted the political life of Italy, but such corruption, he argued, was inevitable because of the Christian character of the Church. What he witnessed, after all, was not only corruption but also the reaction against it, the deeply religious and sincere revival emanating from the Franciscans and Dominicans, culminating in the fanaticism of Savonarola, whom he held in considerable respect. Respect for these religious forces and contempt for the Church together led him to certain conclusions about a basic discrepancy between the Christian faith and politics that are oddly reminiscent of the first centuries of our era. His point was that every contact between religion and politics must corrupt both, and that a noncorrupt Church, though considerably more respectable, would be even more destructive to the public realm than its present corruption.[58] What he did not, and perhaps in his time could not, see was the Roman influence on the Catholic Church, which, indeed, was much less noticeable than its Christian content and its Greek theoretical framework of reference.

It was more than patriotism and more than the current revival of interest in antiquity that sent Machiavelli to search for the central political experiences of the Romans as they had originally been presented, equally removed from Christian piety and Greek philosophy. The greatness of his rediscovery lies in that he could not simply revive or resort to an articulate conceptual tradition, but had himself to articulate those experiences which the Romans had not conceptualized but rather expressed in terms of Greek philosophy vulgarized for this purpose.[59] He saw that the whole of Roman history and mentality depended upon the experience of foundation, and he believed it should be possible to repeat the Roman experience through the foundation of a unified Italy which was to become the same sacred cornerstone for an "eternal" body politic for the Italian nation as the founding of the Eternal City had been for the Italic people. The fact that he was aware of the contemporary beginnings of the birth of nations and the need for a new body politic, for which he therefore used the hitherto unknown term *lo stato,* has caused him to be commonly and rightfully identified as the father of the modern nation-state and its notion of a "reason of state."

What is even more striking, though less well known, is that Machiavelli and Robespierre so often seem to speak the same language. When Robespierre justifies terror, "the despotism of liberty against tyranny," he sounds at times as if he were repeating almost word for word Machiavelli's famous statements on the necessity of violence for the founding of new political bodies and for the reforming of corrupt ones.

This resemblance is all the more startling since both Machiavelli and Robespierre in this respect go beyond what the Romans themselves had to say about foundation. To be sure, the connection between foundation and dictatorship could be learned from the Romans themselves, and Cicero, for instance, appeals explicitly to Scipio to become *dictator rei publicae constituendae,* to seize the dictatorship in order to restore the republic.[60] Like the Romans, Machiavelli and Robespierre felt founding was the central political action, the one great deed that established the public-political realm and made politics possible; but unlike the Romans, to whom this was an event of the past, they felt that for this supreme "end" all "means," and chiefly the means of violence, were justified. They understood the act of founding entirely in the image of making; the question to them was literally how to "make" a unified Italy or a French republic, and their justification of violence was guided by and received its inherent plausibility from the underlying argument: You cannot make a table without killing trees, you cannot make an omelet without breaking eggs, you cannot make a republic without killing people. In this respect, which was to become so fateful for the history of revolutions, Machiavelli and Robespierre were not Romans, and the authority to which they could have appealed would have been rather Plato, who also recommended tyranny as the government where "change is likely to be easiest and most rapid." [61]

It is precisely in this double respect, because of his rediscovery of the foundation experience and his reinterpretation of it in terms of the justification of (violent) means for a supreme end, that Machiavelli may be regarded as the ancestor of modern revolutions, all of which can be characterized by Marx's remark that the French Revolution appeared on the stage of history in Roman costume. Unless it is recognized that the Roman pathos for foundation inspired them, it seems to me that neither the grandeur nor the tragedy of Western revolutions in the modern age can be properly understood. For if I am right in suspecting that the crisis of the present world is primarily political, and that the famous "decline of the West" consists primarily in the decline of the Roman trinity of religion, tradition, and authority, with the concomitant undermining of the specifically Roman foundations of the political realm, then the revolutions of the modern age appear like gigantic attempts to repair these foundations, to renew the broken thread of tradition, and to restore, through founding new political bodies, what for so many centuries had endowed the affairs of men with some measure of dignity and greatness.

Of these attempts, only one, the American Revolution, has been successful: the founding fathers as, characteristically enough, we still call them, founded a completely new body politic without violence and with the help of a constitution. And this body politic has at least endured to the present day, in spite of the fact that the specifically modern character of the modern world has nowhere else produced such extreme expressions in all nonpolitical spheres of life as it has in the United States.

This is not the place to discuss the reasons for the surprising stability of a political structure under the onslaught of the most vehement and shattering social instability. It seems certain that the relatively nonviolent character of the American Revolution, where violence was more or less restricted to regular warfare, is an important factor in this success. It may also be that the founding fathers, because they had escaped the European development of the nation-state, had remained closer to the original Roman spirit. More important, perhaps, was that the act of foundation, namely the colonization of the American continent, had preceded the Declaration of Independence, so that the framing of the Constitution, falling back on existing charters and agreements, confirmed and legalized an already existing body politic rather than made it anew.[62] Thus the actors in the American Revolution were spared the effort of "initiating a new order of things" altogether; that is, they were spared the one action of which Machiavelli once said that "there is nothing more difficult to carry out, nor more doubtful of success, nor more dangerous to handle." [63] And Machiavelli surely must have known. for he, like Robespierre and Lenin and all the great revolutionaries whose ancestor he was, wished nothing more passionately than to initiate a new order of things.

However that may be, revolutions, which we commonly regard as radical breaks with tradition, appear in our context as events in which the actions of men are still inspired by and derive their greatest strength from the origins of this tradition. They seem to be the only salvation which this Roman-Western tradition has provided for emergencies. The fact that not only the various revolutions of the twentieth century but all revolutions since the French have gone wrong, ending in either restoration or tyranny, seems to indicate that even these last means of salvation provided by tradition have become inadequate. Authority as we once knew it, which grew out of the Roman experience of foundation and was understood in the light of Greek political philosophy, has nowhere been re-established, either through revolutions or through the even less promising means of restoration, and least of all through the conservative moods and trends which occasionally sweep public opinion. For to live in a political realm with neither authority nor the concomitant awareness that the source of authority transcends power and those who are in power, means to be confronted anew, without the religious trust in a sacred beginning and without the protection of traditional and therefore self-evident standards of behavior, by the elementary problems of human living-together.

4

WHAT IS FREEDOM?

I

To raise the question, what is freedom? seems to be a hopeless enterprise. It is as though age-old contradictions and antinomies were lying in wait to force the mind into dilemmas of logical impossibility so that, depending which horn of the dilemma you are holding on to, it becomes as impossible to conceive of freedom or its opposite as it is to realize the notion of a square circle. In its simplest form, the difficulty may be summed up as the contradiction between our consciousness and conscience, telling us that we are free and hence responsible, and our everyday experience in the outer world, in which we orient ourselves according to the principle of causality. In all practical and especially in political matters we hold human freedom to be a self-evident truth, and it is upon this axiomatic assumption that laws are laid down in human communities, that decisions are taken, that judgments are passed. In all fields of scientific and theoretical endeavor, on the contrary, we proceed according to the no less self-evident truth of *nihil ex nihilo,* of *nihil sine causa,* that is, on the assumption that even "our own lives are, in the last analysis, subject to causation" and that if

143

there should be an ultimately free ego in ourselves, it certainly never makes its unequivocal appearance in the phenomenal world, and therefore can never become the subject of theoretical ascertainment. Hence freedom turns out to be a mirage the moment psychology looks into what is supposedly its innermost domain; for "the part which force plays in nature, as the cause of motion, has its counterpart in the mental sphere in motive as the cause of conduct." [1] It is true that the test of causality—the predictability of effect if all causes are known—cannot be applied to the realm of human affairs; but this practical impredictability is no test of freedom, it signifies merely that we are in no position ever to know all causes which come into play, and this partly because of the sheer number of factors involved, but also because human motives, as distinguished from natural forces, are still hidden from all onlookers, from inspection by our fellow men as well as from introspection.

The greatest clarification in these obscure matters we owe to Kant and to his insight that freedom is no more ascertainable to the inner sense and within the field of inner experience than it is to the senses with which we know and understand the world. Whether or not causality is operative in the household of nature and the universe, it certainly is a category of the mind to bring order into all sensory data, whatever their nature may be, and thus it makes experience possible. Hence the antinomy between practical freedom and theoretical non-freedom, both equally axiomatic in their respective fields, does not merely concern a dichotomy between science and ethics, but lies in everyday life experiences from which both ethics and science take their respective points of departure. It is not scientific theory but thought itself, in its pre-scientific and pre-philosophical understanding, that seems to dissolve freedom on which our practical conduct is based into nothingness. For the moment we reflect upon an act which was undertaken under the assumption of our being a free agent, it seems to come under the sway of two kinds of causality, of the causality of inner motivation on one hand and of the causal principle which rules the outer world on the other. Kant saved freedom from this twofold assault upon it by distinguishing between a "pure" or theoretical reason and a "practical reason" whose center is free will, whereby it is important to keep in mind that the free-willing agent, who is practically all-important, never appears in the phenomenal world, neither in the outer world of our five senses nor in the field of the inner sense with which I sense myself. This solution, pitting the dictate of the will against the understanding of reason, is ingenious enough and may even suffice to establish a moral law whose logical consistency is in no way inferior to natural laws. But it does little to eliminate the greatest and most dangerous difficulty, namely, that thought itself, in its theoretical as well as its pre-theoretical form, makes freedom disappear—quite apart from the fact that it must appear strange indeed that the faculty of the will whose essential activity consists in dictate and command should be the harborer of freedom.

To the question of politics, the problem of freedom is crucial, and no political theory can afford to remain unconcerned with the fact that this problem has led into "the obscure wood wherein philosophy has lost its way." [2] It is the contention of the following considerations that the reason for this obscurity is that the phenomenon of freedom does not appear in the realm of thought at all, that neither freedom nor its opposite is experienced in the dialogue between me and myself in the course of which the great philosophic and metaphysical questions arise, and that the philosophical tradition, whose origin in this respect we shall consider later, has distorted, instead of clarifying, the very idea of freedom such as it is given in human experience by transposing it from its original field, the realm of politics and human affairs in general, to an inward domain, the will, where it would be open to self-inspection. As a first, preliminary justification of this approach, it may be pointed out that historically the problem of freedom has been the last of the time-honored great metaphysical questions—such as being, nothingness, the soul, nature, time, eternity, etc.—to become a topic of philosophic inquiry at all. There is no preoccupation with freedom in the whole history of great philosophy from the pre-Socratics up to Plotinus, the last ancient philosopher. And when freedom made its first appearance in our philosophical tradition, it was the experience of religious conversion—of Paul first and then of Augustine—which gave rise to it.

The field where freedom has always been known, not as a problem, to be sure, but as a fact of everyday life, is the political realm. And even today, whether we know it or not, the question of politics and the fact that man is a being endowed with the gift of action must always be present to our mind when we speak of the problem of freedom; for action and politics, among all the capabilities and potentialities of human life, are the only things of which we could not even conceive without at least assuming that freedom exists, and we can hardly touch a single political issue without, implicitly or explicitly, touching upon an issue of man's liberty. Freedom, moreover, is not only one among the many problems and phenomena of the political realm properly speaking, such as justice, or power, or equality; freedom, which only seldom—in times of crisis or revolution—becomes the direct aim of political action, is actually the reason that men live together in political organization at all. Without it, political life as such would be meaningless. The *raison d'être* of politics is freedom, and its field of experience is action.

This freedom which we take for granted in all political theory and which even those who praise tyranny must still take into account is the very opposite of "inner freedom," the inward space into which men may escape from external coercion and *feel* free. This inner feeling remains without outer manifestations and hence is by definition politically irrelevant. Whatever its legitimacy may be, and however eloquently it may have been described in late antiquity, it is historically a late phenomenon, and it was originally the result of an estrangement from the world in which worldly experiences were transformed into experiences within one's own self. The experiences of inner freedom are derivative in that they always presuppose a retreat from the world, where freedom was denied, into an inwardness to which no other has access. The inward space where the self is sheltered against the world must not be mistaken for the heart or the mind, both of which exist and function only in interrelationship with the world. Not the heart and not the mind, but inwardness as a place of absolute freedom within one's own self was discovered in late antiquity by those who had no place of their own in the world and hence lacked a worldly condition which, from early antiquity to almost the middle of the nineteenth century, was unanimously held to be a prerequisite for freedom.

The derivative character of this inner freedom, or of the theory that "the appropriate region of human liberty" is the "inward domain of consciousness,"[3] appears more clearly if we go back to its origins. Not the modern individual with his desire to unfold, to develop, and to expand, with his justified fear lest society get the better of his individuality, with his emphatic insistence "on the importance of genius" and originality, but the popular and popularizing sectarians of late antiquity, who have hardly more in common with philosophy than the name, are representative in this respect. Thus the most persuasive arguments for the absolute superiority of inner freedom can still be found in an essay of Epictetus, who begins by stating that free is he who lives as he wishes, a definition which oddly echoes a sentence from Aristotle's *Politics* in which the statement "Freedom means the doing what a man likes" is put in the mouths of those who do not know what freedom is.[5] Epictetus then goes on to show that a man is free if he limits himself to what is in his power, if he does not reach into a realm where he can be hindered.[6] The "science of living"[7] consists in knowing how to distinguish between the alien world over which man has no power and the self of which he may dispose as he sees fit.[8]

Historically it is interesting to note that the appearance of the problem of freedom in Augustine's philosophy was thus preceded by the conscious attempt to divorce the notion of freedom from politics, to arrive at a formulation through which one may be a slave in the world and still be free. Conceptually, however, Epictetus's freedom which consists in being free from one's own desires is no more than a reversal of the current ancient political notions, and the political background against which this whole body of popular philosophy was formulated, the obvious decline of freedom in the late Roman Empire, manifests itself still quite clearly in the role which such notions as power, domination, and property play in it. According to ancient understanding, man could liberate himself from necessity only through power over other men, and he could be free only if he owned a place, a home in the world. Epictetus transposed these worldly relationships into relationships within man's own self, whereby he discovered that no power is so absolute as that which man yields over himself, and that the inward space where man struggles and subdues himself is more entirely his own, namely, more securely shielded from outside interference, than any worldly home could ever be.

Hence, in spite of the great influence the concept of an inner, nonpolitical freedom has exerted upon the tradition of thought, it seems safe to say that man would know nothing of inner freedom if he had not first experienced a condition of being free as a worldly tangible reality. We first become aware of freedom or its opposite in our intercourse with others, not in the intercourse with ourselves. Before it became an attribute of thought or a quality of the will, freedom was understood to be the free man's status, which enabled him to move, to get away from home, to go out into the world and meet other people in deed and word. This freedom clearly was preceded by liberation: in order to be free, man must have liberated himself from the necessities of life. But the status of freedom did not follow automatically upon the act of liberation. Freedom needed, in addition to mere liberation, the company of other men who were in the same state, and it needed a common public space to meet them—a politically organized world, in other words, into which each of the free men could insert himself by word and deed.

Obviously not every form of human intercourse and not every kind of community is characterized by freedom. Where men live together but do not form a body politic—as, for example, in tribal societies or in the privacy of the household—the factors ruling their actions and conduct are not freedom but the necessities of life and concern for its preservation. Moreover, wherever the man-made world does not become the scene for action and speech—as in despotically ruled communities which banish their subjects into the narrowness of the home and thus prevent the rise of a public realm

—freedom has no worldly reality. Without a politically guaranteed public realm, freedom lacks the worldly space to make its appearance. To be sure it may still dwell in men's hearts as desire or will or hope or yearning; but the human heart, as we all know, is a very dark place, and whatever goes on in its obscurity can hardly be called a demonstrable fact. Freedom as a demonstrable fact and politics coincide and are related to each other like two sides of the same matter.

Yet it is precisely this coincidence of politics and freedom which we cannot take for granted in the light of our present political experience. The rise of totalitarianism, its claim to having subordinated all spheres of life to the demands of politics and its consistent nonrecognition of civil rights, above all the rights of privacy and the right to freedom from politics, makes us doubt not only the coincidence of politics and freedom but their very compatibility. We are inclined to believe that freedom begins where politics ends, because we have seen that freedom has disappeared when so-called political considerations overruled everything else. Was not the liberal credo, "The less politics the more freedom," right after all? Is it not true that the smaller the space occupied by the political, the larger the domain left to freedom? Indeed, do we not rightly measure the extent of freedom in any given community by the free scope it grants to apparently nonpolitical activities, free economic enterprise or freedom of teaching, of religion, of cultural and intellectual activities? Is it not true, as we all somehow believe, that politics is compatible with freedom only because and insofar as it guarantees a possible freedom *from* politics?

This definition of political liberty as a potential freedom from politics is not urged upon us merely by our most recent experiences; it has played a large part in the history of political theory. We need go no farther than the political thinkers of the seventeenth and eighteenth centuries, who more often than not simply identified political freedom with security. The highest purpose of politics, "the end of government," was the guaranty of security; security, in turn, made freedom possible, and the word "freedom" designated a quintessence of activities which occurred outside the political realm.

Even Montesquieu, though he had not only a different but a much higher opinion of the essence of politics than Hobbes or Spinoza, could still occasionally equate political freedom with security.[9] The rise of the political and social sciences in the nineteenth and twentieth centuries has even widened the breach between freedom and politics; for government, which since the beginning of the modern age had been identified with the total domain of the political, was now considered to be the appointed protector not so much of freedom as of the life process, the interests of society and its individuals. Security remained the decisive criterion, but not the individual's security against "violent death," as in Hobbes (where the condition of all liberty is freedom from fear), but a security which should permit an undisturbed development of the life process of society as a whole. This life process is not bound up with freedom but follows its own inherent necessity; and it can be called free only in the sense that we speak of a freely flowing stream. Here freedom is not even the nonpolitical aim of politics, but a marginal phenomenon—which somehow forms the boundary government should not overstep unless life itself and its immediate interests and necessities are at stake.

Thus not only we, who have reasons of our own to distrust politics for the sake of freedom, but the entire modern age has separated freedom and politics. I could descend even deeper into the past and evoke older memories and traditions. The pre-modern secular concept of freedom certainly was emphatic in its insistence on separating the subjects' freedom from any direct share in government; the people's "liberty and freedom consisted in having the government of those laws by which their life and their goods may be most their own: 'tis not for having share in government, that is nothing pertaining to them"—as Charles I summed it up in his speech from the scaffold. It was not out of a desire for freedom that people eventually demanded their share in government or admission to the political realm, but out of mistrust in those who held power over their life and goods. The Christian concept of political freedom, moreover, arose out of the early Christians' suspicion of and hostility against the public realm as such, from whose concerns they demanded to be absolved in order to be free. And this Christian freedom for the sake of salvation had been preceded, as we saw before, by the philosophers' abstention from politics as a prerequisite for the highest and freest way of life, the *vita contemplativa*.

Despite the enormous weight of this tradition and despite the perhaps even more telling urgency of our own experiences, both pressing into the same direction of a divorce of freedom from politics, I think the reader may believe he has read only an old truism when I said that the *raison d'être* of politics is freedom and that this freedom is primarily experienced in action. In the following I shall do no more than reflect on this old truism.

II

Freedom as related to politics is not a phenomenon of the will. We deal here not with the *liberum arbitrium,* a freedom of choice that arbitrates and decides between two given things, one good and one evil, and whose choice is predetermined by motive which has only to be argued to start its operation—"And therefore, since I cannot prove a lover,/ To entertain these fair well-spoken days,/ I am determined to prove a villain,/ And hate the idle pleasures of these days." Rather it is, to remain with Shakespeare, the freedom of Brutus: "That this shall be or we will fall for it," that is, the freedom to call something into being which did not exist before, which was not given, not even as an object of cognition or imagination, and which therefore, strictly speaking, could not be known. Action, to be free, must be free from motive on one side, from its intended goal as a predictable effect on the other. This is not to say that motives and aims are not important factors in every single act, but they are its determining factors, and action is free to the extent that it is able to transcend them. Action insofar as it is determined is guided by a future aim whose desirability the intellect has grasped before the will wills it, whereby the intellect calls upon the will, since only the will can dictate action—to paraphrase a characteristic description of this process by Duns Scotus.[10] The aim of action varies and depends upon the changing circumstances of the world; to recognize the aim is not a matter of freedom, but of right or wrong judgment. Will, seen as a distinct and separate human faculty, follows judgment, i.e., cognition of the right aim, and then commands its execution. The power to command, to dictate action, is not a matter of freedom but a question of strength or weakness.

Action insofar as it is free is neither under the guidance of the intellect nor under the dictate of the will—although it needs both for the execution of any particular goal—but springs from something altogether different which (following Montesquieu's famous analysis of forms of government) I shall call a principle. Principles do not operate from within the self as motives do—"mine own deformity" or my "fair proportion"—but inspire, as it were, from without; and they are much too general to prescribe particular goals, although every particular aim can be judged in the light of its principle once the act has been started. For, unlike the judgment of the intellect which precedes action, and unlike the command of the will which initiates it, the inspiring principle becomes fully manifest only in the performing act itself; yet while the merits of judgment lose their validity, and the strength of the commanding will exhausts itself, in the course of the act which they execute in cooperation, the principle which inspired it loses nothing in strength or validity through execution. In distinction from its goal, the principle of an action can be repeated time and again, it is inexhaustible, and in distinction from its motive, the validity of a principle is universal, it is not bound to any particular person or to any particular group. However, the manifestation of principles comes about only through action, they are manifest in the world as long as the action lasts, but no longer. Such principles are honor or glory, love of equality, which Montesquieu called virtue, or distinction or excellence—the Greek ἀεὶ ἀριστεύειν ("always strive to do your best and to be the best of all"), but also fear or distrust or hatred. Freedom or its opposite appears in the world whenever such principles are actualized; the appearance of freedom, like the manifestation of principles, coincides with the performing act. Men *are* free—as distinguished from their possessing the gift for freedom—as long as they act, neither before nor after; for to *be* free and to act are the same.

Freedom as inherent in action is perhaps best illustrated by Machiavelli's concept of *virtù,* the excellence with which man answers the opportunities the world opens up before him in the guise of *fortuna.* Its meaning is best rendered by "virtuosity," that is, an excellence we attribute to the performing arts (as distinguished from the creative arts of making), where the accomplishment lies in the performance itself and not in an end product which outlasts the activity that brought it into existence and becomes independent of it. The virtuoso-ship of Machiavelli's *virtù* somehow reminds us of the fact, although Machiavelli hardly knew it, that the Greeks always used such metaphors as flute-playing, dancing, healing, and seafaring to distinguish political from other activities, that is, that they drew their analogies from those arts in which virtuosity of performance is decisive.

Since all acting contains an element of virtuosity, and because virtuosity is the excellence we ascribe to the performing arts, politics has often been defined as an art. This, of course, is not a definition but a metaphor, and the metaphor becomes completely false if one falls into the common error of regarding the state or government as a work of art, as a kind of collective masterpiece. In the sense of the creative arts, which bring forth something tangible and reify human thought to such an extent that the produced thing possesses an existence of its own, politics is the exact opposite of an art—which incidentally does not mean that it is a science. Political institutions, no matter how well or how badly designed, depend for continued existence upon acting men; their conservation is achieved by the same means that brought them into being. Independent existence marks the work of art as a product of making; utter dependence upon further acts to keep it in existence marks the state as a product of action.

The point here is not whether the creative artist is free in the process of creation, but that the creative process is not displayed in public and not destined to appear in the world. Hence the element of freedom, certainly present in the creative arts, remains hidden; it is not the free creative process which finally appears and matters for the world, but the work of art itself, the end product of the process. The performing arts, on the contrary, have indeed a strong affinity with politics. Performing artists—dancers, play-actors, musicians, and the like—need an audience to show their virtuosity, just as acting men need the presence of others before whom they can appear; both need a publicly organized space for their "work," and both depend upon others for the performance itself. Such a space of appearances is not to be taken for granted wherever men live together in a community. The Greek polis once was precisely that "form of government" which provided men with a space of appearances where they could act, with a kind of theater where freedom could appear.

To use the word "political" in the sense of the Greek polis is neither arbitrary nor far-fetched. Not only etymologically and not only for the learned does the very word, which in all European languages still derives from the historically unique organization of the Greek city-state, echo the experiences of the community which first discovered the essence and the realm of the political. It is indeed difficult and even misleading to talk about politics and its innermost principles without drawing to some extent upon the experiences of Greek and Roman antiquity, and this for no other reason than that men have never, either before or after, thought so highly of political activity and bestowed so much dignity upon its realm. As regards the relation of freedom to politics, there is the additional reason that only ancient political communities were founded for the express purpose of serving the free—those who were neither slaves, subject to coercion by others, nor laborers, driven and urged on by the necessities of life. If, then, we understand the political in the sense of the polis, its end or *raison d'être* would be to establish and keep in existence a space where freedom as virtuosity can appear. This is the realm where freedom is a worldly reality, tangible in words which can be heard, in deeds which can be seen, and in events which are talked about, remembered, and turned into stories before they are finally incorporated into the great storybook of human history. Whatever occurs in this space of appearances is political by definition, even when it is not a direct product of action. What remains outside it, such as the great feats of barbarian empires, may be impressive and noteworthy, but it is not political, strictly speaking.

Every attempt to derive the concept of freedom from experiences in the political realm sounds strange and startling because all our theories in these matters are dominated by the notion that freedom is an attribute of will and thought much rather than of action. And this priority is not merely derived from the notion that every act must psychologically be preceded by a cognitive act of the intellect and a command of the will to carry out its decision, but also, and perhaps even primarily, because it is held that "perfect liberty is incompatible with the existence of society," that it can be tolerated in its perfection only outside the realm of human affairs. This current argument does not hold—what perhaps is true—that it is in the nature of thought to need more freedom than does any other activity of men, but rather that thinking in itself is not dangerous, so that only action needs to be restrained: "No one pretends that actions should be as free as opinions." [11] This, of course, belongs among the fundamental tenets of liberalism, which, its name notwithstanding, has done its share to banish the notion of liberty from the political realm. For politics, according to the same philosophy, must be concerned almost exclusively with the maintenance of life and the safeguarding of its interests. Now, where life is at stake all action is by definition under the sway of necessity, and the proper realm to take care of life's necessities is the gigantic and still increasing sphere of social and economic life whose administration has overshadowed the political realm ever since the beginning of the modern age. Only foreign affairs, because the relationships between nations still harbor hostilities and sympathies which cannot be reduced to economic factors, seem to be left as a purely political domain. And even here the prevailing tendency is to consider international power problems and rivalries as ultimately springing from economic factors and interests.

Yet just as we, despite all theories and isms, still believe that to say "Freedom is the *raison d'être* of politics" is no more than a truism, so do we, in spite of our apparently exclusive concern with life, still hold as a matter of course that courage is one of the cardinal political virtues, although—if all this were a matter of consistency, which it obviously is not—we should be the first to condemn courage as the foolish and even vicious contempt for life and its interests, that is, for the allegedly highest of all goods. Courage is a big word, and I do not mean the daring of adventure which gladly risks life for the sake of being as thoroughly and intensely alive as one can be only in the face of danger and death. Temerity is no less concerned with life than is cowardice. Courage, which we still believe to be indispensable for political action, and which Churchill once called "the first of human qualities, because it is the quality which guarantees all others," does not gratify our individual sense of vitality but is demanded of us by the very nature of the public realm. For this world of ours, because it existed before us and is meant to outlast our lives in it, simply cannot afford to give primary concern to individual lives and the interests connected with them; as such the public realm stands in the sharpest possible contrast to our private domain, where, in the protection of family and home, everything serves and must serve the security of the life process. It requires courage even to leave the protective security of our four walls and enter the public realm, not because of particular dangers which may lie in wait for us, but because we have arrived in a realm where the concern for life has lost its validity. Courage liberates men from their worry about life for the freedom of the world. Courage is indispensable because in politics not life but the world is at stake.

III

Obviously this notion of an interdependence of freedom and politics stands in contradiction to the social theories of the modern age. Unfortunately it does not follow that we need only to revert to older, pre-modern traditions and theories. Indeed, the greatest difficulty in reaching an understanding of what freedom is arises from the fact that a simple return to tradition, and especially to what we are wont to call the great tradition, does not help us. Neither the philosophical concept of freedom as it first arose in late antiquity, where freedom became a phenomenon of thought by which man could, as it were, reason himself out of the world, nor the Christian and modern notion of free will has any ground in political experience. Our philosophical tradition is almost unanimous in holding that freedom begins where men have left the realm of political life inhabited by the many, and that it is not experienced in association with others but in intercourse with one's self—whether in the form of an inner dialogue which, since Socrates, we call thinking, or in a conflict within myself, the inner strife between what I would and what I do, whose murderous dialectics disclosed first to Paul and then to Augustine the equivocalities and impotence of the human heart.

For the history of the problem of freedom, Christian tradition has indeed become the decisive factor. We almost automatically equate freedom with free will, that is, with a faculty virtually unknown to classical antiquity. For will, as Christianity discovered it, had so little in common with the well-known capacities to desire, to intend, and to aim at, that it claimed attention only after it had come into conflict with them. If freedom were actually nothing but a phenomenon of the will, we would have to conclude that the ancients did not know freedom. This, of course, is absurd, but if one wished to assert it he could argue what I have mentioned before, namely, that the idea of freedom played no role in philosophy prior to Augustine. The reason for this striking fact is that, in Greek as well as Roman antiquity, freedom was an exclusively political concept, indeed the quintessence of the city-state and of citizenship. Our philosophical tradition of political thought, beginning with Parmenides and Plato, was founded explicitly in opposition to this polis and its citizenship. The way of life chosen by the philosopher was understood in opposition to the βίος πολιτικός, the political way of life. Freedom, therefore, the very center of poli-

tics as the Greeks understood it, was an idea which almost by
definition could not enter the framework of Greek philosophy.
Only when the early Christians, and especially Paul, discovered a
kind of freedom which had no relation to politics, could the concept of freedom enter the history of philosophy. Freedom became
one of the chief problems of philosophy when it was experienced as
something occurring in the intercourse between me and myself, and
outside of the intercourse between men. Free will and freedom became synonymous notions,[12] and the presence of freedom was experienced in complete solitude, "where no man might hinder the
hot contention wherein I had engaged with myself," the deadly conflict which took place in the "inner dwelling" of the soul and the
dark "chamber of the heart." [13]

Classical antiquity was by no means inexperienced in the phenomena of solitude; it knew well enough that solitary man is no
longer one but two-in-one, that an intercourse between me and
myself begins the moment the intercourse between me and my fellow men has been interrupted for no matter what reason. In addition to this dualism which is the existential condition of thought,
classical philosophy since Plato had insisted on a dualism between
soul and body whereby the human faculty of motion had been
assigned to the soul, which was supposed to move the body as well
as itself, and it was still within the range of Platonic thought to interpret this faculty as a rulership of the soul over the body. Yet the
Augustinian solitude of "hot contention" within the soul itself was
utterly unknown, for the fight in which he had become engaged
was not between reason and passion, between understanding and
θυμός,[14] that is, between two different human faculties, but it was a
conflict within the will itself. And this duality within the self-same
faculty had been known as the characteristic of thought, as the
dialogue which I hold with myself. In other words, the two-in-one
of solitude which sets the thought process into motion has the
exactly opposite effect on the will: it paralyzes and locks it within
itself; willing in solitude is always *velle* and *nolle,* to will and not to
will at the same time.

The paralyzing effect the will seems to have upon itself comes all the more surprisingly as its very essence obviously is to command and be obeyed. Hence it appears to be a "monstrosity" that man may command himself and not be obeyed, a monstrosity which can be explained only by the simultaneous presence of an I-will and an I-will-not.[15] This, however, is already an interpretation by Augustine; the historical fact is that the phenomenon of the will originally manifested itself in the experience that what I would I do not, that there is such a thing as I-will-and-cannot. What was unknown to antiquity was not that there is a possible I-know-but-I-will-not, but that I-will and I-can are not the same—*non hoc est velle, quod posse*.[16] For the I-will-and-I-can was of course very familiar to the ancients. We need only remember how much Plato insisted that only those who knew how to rule themselves had the right to rule others and be freed from the obligation of obedience. And it is true that self-control has remained one of the specifically political virtues, if only because it is an outstanding phenomenon of virtuosity where I-will and I-can must be so well attuned that they practically coincide.

Had ancient philosophy known of a possible conflict between what I can and what I will, it would certainly have understood the phenomenon of freedom as an inherent quality of the I-can, or it might conceivably have defined it as the coincidence of I-will and I-can; it certainly would not have thought of it as an attribute of the I-will or I-would. This assertion is no empty speculation; even the Euripidean conflict between reason and θυμός, both simultaneously present in the soul, is a relatively late phenomenon. More typical, and in our context more relevant, was the conviction that passion may blind men's reason but that once reason has succeeded in making itself heard there is no passion left to prevent man from doing what he *knows* is right. This conviction still underlies Socrates' teaching that virtue is a kind of knowledge, and our amazement that anybody could ever have thought that virtue was "rational," that it could be learned and taught, arises from our acquaintance with a will which is broken in itself, which wills and wills-not at the same time, much rather than from any superior insight in the alleged powerlessness of reason.

In other words, will, will-power, and will-to-power are for us almost identical notions; the seat of power is to us the faculty of the will as known and experienced by man in his intercourse with himself. And for the sake of this will-power we have emasculated not only our reasoning and cognitive faculties but other more "practical" faculties as well. But is it not plain even to us that, in the words of Pindar, "this is the greatest grief: to stand with his feet outside the right and the beautiful one knows [forced away], by necessity"? [17] The necessity which prevents me from doing what I know and will may arise from the world, or from my own body, or from an insufficiency of talents, gifts, and qualities which are bestowed upon man by birth and over which he has hardly more power than he has over other circumstances; all these factors, the psychological ones not excluded, condition the person from the outside as far as the I-will and the I-know, that is, the ego itself, are concerned; the power that meets these circumstances, that liberates, as it were, willing and knowing from their bondage to necessity is the I-can. Only where the I-will and the I-can coincide does freedom come to pass.

There exists still another way to check our current notion of free will, born of a religious predicament and formulated in philosophical language, against the older, strictly political experiences of freedom. In the revival of political thought which accompanied the rise of the modern age, we may distinguish between those thinkers who can truly be called the fathers of political "science," since they took their cue from the new discoveries of the natural sciences—their greatest representative is Hobbes—and those who, relatively undisturbed by these typically modern developments, harkened back to the political thought of antiquity, not out of any predilection for the past as such but simply because the separation of church and state, of religion and politics, had given rise to an independent secular, political realm such as had been unknown since the fall of the Roman Empire. The greatest representative of this political secularism was Montesquieu, who, though indifferent to problems of a strictly philosophic nature, was deeply aware of the inadequacy of the Christian and the philosophers' concept of freedom for political purposes. In order to get rid of it, he expressly distinguished between philosophical and political freedom, and the difference consisted in that philosophy demands no more of freedom than the exercise of the will (*l'exercice de la volonté*), independent of circumstances and of attainment of the goals the will has set. Political freedom, on the contrary, consists in being able to do what one ought to will (*la liberté ne peut consister qu' à pouvoir faire ce que l'on doit vouloir*—the emphasis is on *pouvoir*).[18] For Montesquieu as for the ancients it was obvious that an agent could no longer be called free when he lacked the capacity to do—whereby it is irrelevant whether this failure is caused by exterior or by interior circumstances.

I chose the example of self-control because to us this is clearly a phenomenon of will and of will-power. The Greeks, more than any other people, have reflected on moderation and the necessity to tame the steeds of the soul, and yet they never became aware of the will as a distinct faculty, separate from other human capacities. Historically, men first discovered the will when they experienced its impotence and not its power, when they said with Paul: "For to will is present with me; but how to perform that which is good I find not." It is the same will of which Augustine complained that it seemed "no monstrousness [for it] partly to will, partly to nill"; and although he points out that this is "a disease of the mind," he also admits that this disease is, as it were, natural for a mind possessed of a will: "For the will commands that there be a will, it commands not something else but itself. . . . Were the will entire, it would not even command itself to be, because it would already be." [19] In other words, if man has a will at all, it must always appear as though there were two wills present in the same man, fighting with each other for power over his mind. Hence, the will is both powerful and impotent, free and unfree.

When we speak of impotence and the limits set to will-power, we usually think of man's powerlessness with respect to the surrounding world. It is, therefore, of some importance to notice that in these early testimonies the will was not defeated by some overwhelming force of nature or circumstances; the contention which its appearance raised was neither the conflict between the one against the many nor the strife between body and mind. On the contrary, the relation of mind to body was for Augustine even the outstanding example for the enormous power inherent in the will: "The mind commands the body, and the body obeys instantly; the mind commands itself, and is resisted." [20] The body represents in this context the exterior world and is by no means identical with one's self. It is within one's self, in the "interior dwelling" (*interior domus*), where Epictetus still believed man to be an absolute master, that the conflict between man and himself broke out and that the will was defeated. Christian will-power was discovered as an organ of self-liberation and immediately found wanting. It is as though the I-will immediately paralyzed the I-can, as though the moment men *willed* freedom, they lost their capacity to *be* free. In the deadly conflict with worldly desires and intentions from which will-power was supposed to liberate the self, the most willing seemed able to achieve was oppression. Because of the will's impotence, its incapacity to generate genuine power, its constant defeat in the struggle with the self, in which the power of the I-can exhausted itself, the will-to-power turned at once into a will-to-oppression. I can only hint here at the fatal consequences for political theory of this equation of freedom with the human capacity to will; it was one of the causes why even today we almost automatically equate power with oppression or, at least, with rule over others.

However that may be, what we usually understand by will and will-power has grown out of this conflict between a willing and a performing self, out of the experience of an I-will-and-can*not,* which means that the I-will, no matter what is willed, remains subject to the self, strikes back at it, spurs it on, incites it further, or is ruined by it. However far the will-to-power may reach out, and even if somebody possessed by it begins to conquer the whole world, the I-will can never rid itself of the self; it always remains bound to it and, indeed, under its bondage. This bondage to the self distinguishes the I-will from the I-think, which also is carried on between me and myself but in whose dialogue the self is not the object of the activity of thought. The fact that the I-will has become so power-thirsty, that will and will-to-power have become practically identical, is perhaps due to its having been first experienced in its impotence. Tyranny at any rate, the only form of government which arises directly out of the I-will, owes its greedy cruelty to an egotism utterly absent from the utopian tyrannies of reason with which the philosophers wished to coerce men and which they conceived on the model of the I-think.

I have said that the philosophers first began to show an interest in the problem of freedom when freedom was no longer experienced in acting and in associating with others but in willing and in the intercourse with one's self, when, briefly, freedom had become free will. Since then, freedom has been a philosophical problem of the first order; as such it was applied to the political realm and thus has become a political problem as well. Because of the philosophic shift from action to will-power, from freedom as a state of being manifest in action to the *liberum arbitrium,* the ideal of freedom ceased to be virtuosity in the sense we mentioned before and became sovereignty, the ideal of a free will, independent from others and eventually prevailing against them. The philosophic ancestry of our current political notion of freedom is still quite manifest in eighteenth-century political writers, when, for instance, Thomas Paine insisted that "to be free it is sufficient [for man] that he wills it," a word which Lafayette applied to the nation-state: *"Pour qu'une nation soit libre, il suffit qu'elle veuille l'être."*

Obviously such words echo the political philosophy of Jean-Jacques Rousseau, who has remained the most consistent representative of the theory of sovereignty, which he derived directly from the will, so that he could conceive of political power in the strict image of individual will-power. He argued against Montesquieu that power must be sovereign, that is, indivisible, because "a divided will would be inconceivable." He did not shun the consequences of this extreme individualism, and he held that in an ideal state "the citizens had no communications one with another," that in order to avoid factions "each citizen should think only his own thoughts." In reality Rousseau's theory stands refuted for the simple reason that "it is absurd for the will to bind itself for the future"; [21] a community actually founded on this sovereign will would be built not on sand but on quicksand. All political business is, and always has been, transacted within an elaborate framework of ties and bonds for the future—such as laws and constitutions, treaties and alliances—all of which derive in the last instance from the faculty to promise and to keep promises in the face of the essential uncertainties of the future. A state, moreover, in which there is no communication between the citizens and where each man thinks only his own thoughts is by definition a tyranny. That the faculty of will and will-power in and by itself, unconnected with any other faculties, is an essentially nonpolitical and even anti-political capacity is perhaps nowhere else so manifest as in the absurdities to which Rousseau was driven and in the curious cheerfulness with which he accepted them.

Politically, this identification of freedom with sovereignty is perhaps the most pernicious and dangerous consequence of the philosophical equation of freedom and free will. For it leads either to a denial of human freedom—namely, if it is realized that whatever men may be, they are never sovereign—or to the insight that the freedom of one man, or a group, or a body politic can be purchased only at the price of the freedom, i.e., the sovereignty, of all others. Within the conceptual framework of traditional philosophy, it is indeed very difficult to understand how freedom and non-sovereignty can exist together or, to put it another way, how freedom could have been given to men under the condition of non-sovereignty. Actually it is as unrealistic to deny freedom because of the fact of human non-sovereignty as it is dangerous to believe that one can be free—as an individual or as a group—only if he is sovereign. The famous sovereignty of political bodies has always been an illusion, which, moreover, can be maintained only by the instruments of violence, that is, with essentially nonpolitical means. Under human conditions, which are determined by the fact that not man but men live on the earth, freedom and sovereignty are so little identical that they cannot even exist simultaneously. Where men wish to be sovereign, as individuals or as organized groups, they must submit to the oppression of the will, be this the individual will with which I force myself, or the "general will" of an organized group. If men wish to be free, it is precisely sovereignty they must renounce.

IV

Since the whole problem of freedom arises for us in the horizon of Christian traditions on one hand, and of an originally anti-political philosophic tradition on the other, we find it difficult to realize that there may exist a freedom which is not an attribute of the will but an accessory of doing and acting. Let us therefore go back once more to antiquity, i.e., to its political and pre-philosophical traditions, certainly not for the sake of erudition and not even because of the continuity of our tradition, but merely because a freedom experienced in the process of acting and nothing else—though, of course, mankind never lost this experience altogether—has never again been articulated with the same classical clarity.

However, for reasons we mentioned before and which we cannot discuss here, this articulation is nowhere more difficult to grasp than in the writings of the philosophers. It would of course lead us too far to try to distill, as it were, adequate concepts from the body of non-philosophical literature, from poetic, dramatic, historical, and political writings, whose articulation lifts experiences into a realm of splendor which is not the realm of conceptual thought. And for our purposes this is not necessary. For whatever ancient literature, Greek as well as Latin, has to tell us about these matters is ultimately rooted in the curious fact that both the Greek and the Latin language possess two verbs to designate what we uniformly call "to act." The two Greek words are ἄρχειν: to begin, to lead, and, finally, to rule; and πράττειν: to carry something through. The corresponding Latin verbs are *agere:* to set something in motion; and *gerere,* which is hard to translate and somehow means the enduring and supporting continuation of past acts whose results are the *res gestae,* the deeds and events we call historical. In both instances action occurs in two different stages; its first stage is a beginning by which something new comes into the world. The Greek word ἄρχειν, which covers beginning, leading, ruling, that is, the outstanding qualities of the free man, bears witness to an experience in which being free and the capacity to begin something new coincided. Freedom, as we would say today, was experienced in spontaneity. The manifold meaning of ἄρχειν indicates the following: only those could begin something new who were already rulers (i.e., household heads who ruled over slaves and family) and had thus liberated themselves from the necessities of life for enterprises in distant lands or citizenship in the polis; in either case, they no longer ruled, but were rulers among rulers, moving among their peers, whose help they enlisted as leaders in order to begin something new, to start a new enterprise; for only with the help of others could the ἄρχων, the ruler, beginner and leader, really act, πράττειν, carry through whatever he had started to do.

In Latin, to be free and to begin are also interconnected, though in a different way. Roman freedom was a legacy bequeathed by the founders of Rome to the Roman people; their freedom was tied to the beginning their forefathers had established by founding the city, whose affairs the descendants had to manage, whose consequences they had to bear, and whose foundations they had to "augment." All these together are the *res gestae* of the Roman republic. Roman historiography therefore, essentially as political as Greek historiography, never was content with the mere narration of great deeds and events; unlike Thucydides or Herodotus, the Roman historians always felt bound to the beginning of Roman history, because this beginning contained the authentic element of Roman freedom and thus made their history political; whatever they had to relate, they started *ab urbe condita,* with the foundation of the city, the guaranty of Roman freedom.

I have already mentioned that the ancient concept of freedom played no role in Greek philosophy precisely because of its exclusively political origin. Roman writers, it is true, rebelled occasionally against the anti-political tendencies of the Socratic school. but their strange lack of philosophic talent apparently prevented their finding a theoretical concept of freedom which could have been adequate to their own experiences and to the great institutions of liberty present in the Roman *res publica*. If the history of ideas were as consistent as its historians sometimes imagine, we should have even less hope of finding a valid political idea of freedom in Augustine, the great Christian thinker who in fact introduced Paul's free will, along with its perplexities, into the history of philosophy. Yet we find in Augustine not only the discussion of freedom as *liberum arbitrium,* though this discussion became decisive for the tradition, but also an entirely differently conceived notion which characteristically appears in his only political treatise, in *De Civitate Dei.* In the *City of God* Augustine, as is only natural, speaks more from the background of specifically Roman experiences than in any of his other writings, and freedom is conceived there not as an inner human disposition but as a character of human existence in the world. Man does not possess freedom so much as he, or better his coming into the world, is equated with the appearance of freedom in the universe; man is free because he is a beginning and was so created after the universe had already come into existence: [*Initium*] *ut esset, creatus est homo, ante quem nemo fuit.*[22] In the birth of each man this initial beginning is reaffirmed, because in each instance something new comes into an already existing world which will continue to exist after each individual's death. Because he *is* a beginning, man can begin; to be human and to be free are one and the same. God created man in order to introduce into the world the faculty of beginning: freedom.

The strong anti-political tendencies of early Christianity are so familiar that the notion of a Christian thinker's having been the first to formulate the philosophical implications of the ancient political idea of freedom strikes us as almost paradoxical. The only explanation that comes to mind is that Augustine was a Roman as well as a Christian, and that in this part of his work he formulated the central political experience of Roman antiquity, which was that freedom *qua* beginning became manifest in the act of foundation. Yet I am convinced that this impression would considerably change if the sayings of Jesus of Nazareth were taken more seriously in their philosophic implications. We find in these parts of the New Testament an extraordinary understanding of freedom, and particularly of the power inherent in human freedom; but the human capacity which corresponds to this power, which, in the words of the Gospel, is capable of removing mountains, is not will but faith. The work of faith, actually its product, is what the gospels called "miracles," a word with many meanings in the New Testament and difficult to understand. We can neglect the difficulties here and refer only to those passages where miracles are clearly not supernatural events but only what all miracles, those performed by men no less than those performed by a divine agent, always must be, namely, interruptions of some natural series of events, of some automatic process, in whose context they constitute the wholly unexpected.

No doubt human life, placed on the earth, is surrounded by automatic processes—by the natural processes of the earth, which, in turn, are surrounded by cosmic processes, and we ourselves are driven by similar forces insofar as we too are a part of organic nature. Our political life, moreover, despite its being the realm of action, also takes place in the midst of processes which we call historical and which tend to become as automatic as natural or cosmic processes, although they were started by men. The truth is that automatism is inherent in all processes, no matter what their origin may be—which is why no single act, and no single event, can ever, once and for all, deliver and save a man, or a nation, or mankind. It is in the nature of the automatic processes to which man is subject, but within and against which he can assert himself through action, that they can only spell ruin to human life. Once man-made, historical processes have become automatic, they are no less ruinous than the natural life process that drives our organism and which in its own terms, that is, biologically, leads from being to non-being, from birth to death. The historical sciences know only too well such cases of petrified and hopelessly declining civilizations where doom seems foreordained, like a biological necessity, and since such historical processes of stagnation can last and creep on for centuries, they even occupy by far the largest space in recorded history; the periods of being free have always been relatively short in the history of mankind.

What usually remains intact in the epochs of petrification and foreordained doom is the faculty of freedom itself, the sheer capacity to begin, which animates and inspires all human activities and is the hidden source of production of all great and beautiful things. But so long as this source remains hidden, freedom is not a worldly, tangible reality; that is, it is not political. Because the source of freedom remains present even when political life has become petrified and political action impotent to interrupt automatic processes, freedom can so easily be mistaken for an essentially nonpolitical phenomenon; in such circumstances, freedom is not experienced as a mode of being with its own kind of "virtue" and virtuosity, but as a supreme gift which only man, of all earthly creatures, seems to have received, of which we can find traces and signs in almost all his activities, but which, nevertheless, develops fully only when action has created its own worldly space where it can come out of hiding, as it were, and make its appearance.

Every act, seen from the perspective not of the agent but of the process in whose framework it occurs and whose automatism it interrupts, is a "miracle"—that is, something which could not be expected. If it is true that action and beginning are essentially the same, it follows that a capacity for performing miracles must likewise be within the range of human faculties. This sounds stranger than it actually is. It is in the very nature of every new beginning that it breaks into the world as an "infinite improbability," and yet it is precisely this infinitely improbable which actually constitutes the very texture of everything we call real. Our whole existence rests, after all, on a chain of miracles, as it were—the coming into being of the earth, the development of organic life on it, the evolution of mankind out of the animal species. For from the viewpoint of the processes in the universe and in nature, and their statistically overwhelming probabilities, the coming into being of the earth out of cosmic processes, the formation of organic life out of inorganic processes, the evolution of man, finally, out of the processes of organic life are all "infinite improbabilities," they are "miracles" in everyday language. It is because of this element of the "miraculous" present in all reality that events, no matter how well anticipated in fear or hope, strike us with a shock of surprise once they have come to pass. The very impact of an event is never wholly explicable; its factuality transcends in principle all anticipation. The experience which tells us that events are miracles is neither arbitrary nor sophisticated; it is, on the contrary, most natural and, indeed, in ordinary life almost commonplace. Without this commonplace experience, the part assigned by religion to supernatural miracles would be well-nigh incomprehensible.

I chose the example of natural processes which are interrupted by the advent of some "infinite improbability" in order to illustrate that what we call real in ordinary experience has mostly come into existence through coincidences which are stranger than fiction. Of course the example has its limitations and cannot be simply applied to the realm of human affairs. It would be sheer superstition to hope for miracles, for the "infinitely improbable," in the context of automatic historical or political processes, although even this can never be completely excluded. History, in contradistinction to nature, is full of events; here the miracle of accident and infinite improbability occurs so frequently that it seems strange to speak of miracles at all. But the reason for this frequency is merely that historical processes are created and constantly interrupted by human initiative, by the *initium* man is insofar as he is an acting being. Hence it is not in the least superstitious, it is even a counsel of realism, to look for the unforeseeable and unpredictable, to be prepared for and to expect "miracles" in the political realm. And the more heavily the scales are weighted in favor of disaster, the more miraculous will the deed done in freedom appear; for it is disaster, not salvation, which always happens automatically and therefore always must appear to be irresistible.

Objectively, that is, seen from the outside and without taking into account that man is a beginning and a beginner, the chances that tomorrow will be like yesterday are always overwhelming. Not quite so overwhelming, to be sure, but very nearly so as the chances were that *no* earth would ever rise out of cosmic occurrences, that *no* life would develop out of inorganic processes, and that *no* man would emerge out of the evolution of animal life. The decisive difference between the "infinite improbabilities" on which the reality of our earthly life rests and the miraculous character inherent in those events which establish historical reality is that, in the realm of human affairs, we know the author of the "miracles." It is men who perform them—men who because they have received the twofold gift of freedom and action can establish a reality of their own.

5

THE CRISIS IN
EDUCATION

I

THE general crisis that has overtaken the modern world everywhere and in almost every sphere of life manifests itself differently in each country, involving different areas and taking on different forms. In America, one of its most characteristic and suggestive aspects is the recurring crisis in education that, during the last decade at least, has become a political problem of the first magnitude, reported on almost daily in the newspapers. To be sure, no great imagination is required to detect the dangers of a constantly progressing decline of elementary standards throughout the entire school system, and the seriousness of the trouble has been properly underlined by the countless unavailing efforts of the educational authorities to stem the tide. Still, if one compares this crisis in education with the political experiences of other countries in the twentieth century, with the revolutionary turmoil after the First World War, with concentration and extermination camps, or even with the profound malaise which, appearances of prosperity to the contrary notwithstanding, has spread throughout Europe ever since the end of the Second World War, it is somewhat difficult to take a crisis in education as seriously as it deserves. It is tempting indeed to regard it as a local phenomenon, unconnected with the larger issues of the century, to be blamed on certain peculiarities of life in the United States which are not likely to find a counterpart in other parts of the world.

Yet, if this were true, the crisis in our school system would not have become a political issue and the educational authorities would not have been unable to deal with it in time. Certainly more is involved here than the puzzling question of why Johnny can't read. Moreover, there is always a temptation to believe that we are dealing with specific problems confined within historical and national boundaries and of importance only to those immediately affected. It is precisely this belief that in our time has consistently proved false. One can take it as a general rule in this century that whatever is possible in one country may in the foreseeable future be equally possible in almost any other.

Aside from these general reasons that would make it seem advisable for the layman to be concerned with trouble in fields about which, in the specialist's sense, he may know nothing (and this, since I am not a professional educator, is of course my case when I deal with a crisis in education), there is another even more cogent reason for his concerning himself with a critical situation in which he is not immediately involved. And that is the opportunity, provided by the very fact of crisis—which tears away façades and obliterates prejudices—to explore and inquire into whatever has been laid bare of the essence of the matter, and the essence of education is natality, the fact that human beings are *born* into the world. The disappearance of prejudices simply means that we have lost the answers on which we ordinarily rely without even realizing they were originally answers to questions. A crisis forces us back to the questions themselves and requires from us either new or old answers, but in any case direct judgments. A crisis becomes a disaster only when we respond to it with preformed judgments, that is, with prejudices. Such an attitude not only sharpens the crisis but makes us forfeit the experience of reality and the opportunity for reflection it provides.

However clearly a general problem may present itself in a crisis, it is nevertheless impossible ever to isolate completely the universal element from the concrete and specific circumstances in which it makes its appearance. Though the crisis in education may affect the whole world, it is characteristic that we find its most extreme form in America, the reason being that perhaps only in America could a crisis in education actually become a factor in politics. In America, as a matter of fact, education plays a different and, politically, incomparably more important role than in other countries. Technically, of course, the explanation lies in the fact that America has always been a land of immigrants; it is obvious that the enormously difficult melting together of the most diverse ethnic groups—never fully successful but continuously succeeding beyond expectation—can only be accomplished through the schooling, education, and Americanization of the immigrants' children. Since for most of these children English is not their mother tongue but has to be learned in school, schools must obviously assume functions which in a nation-state would be performed as a matter of course in the home.

More decisive, however, for our considerations is the role that continuous immigration plays in the country's political consciousness and frame of mind. America is not simply a colonial country in need of immigrants to populate the land, though independent of them in its political structure. For America the determining factor has always been the motto printed on every dollar bill: *Novus Ordo Seclorum,* A New Order of the World. The immigrants, the newcomers, are a guarantee to the country that it represents the new order. The meaning of this new order, this founding of a new world against the old, was and is the doing away with poverty and oppression. But at the same time its magnificence consists in the fact that from the beginning this new order did not shut itself off from the outside world—as has elsewhere been the custom in the founding of utopias—in order to confront it with a perfect model, nor was its purpose to enforce imperial claims or to be preached as an evangel to others. Rather its relation to the outside world has been characterized from the start by the fact that this republic, which planned to abolish poverty and slavery, welcomed all the poor and enslaved of the earth. In the words spoken by John Adams in 1765—that is, before the Declaration of Independence—"I always consider the settlement of America as the opening of a grand scheme and design in Providence for the illumination and emancipation of the slavish part of mankind all over the earth." This is the basic intent or the basic law in accordance with which America began her historical and political existence.

The extraordinary enthusiasm for what is new, which is shown in almost every aspect of American daily life, and the concomitant trust in an "indefinite perfectibility"—which Tocqueville noted as the credo of the common "uninstructed man" and which as such antedates by almost a hundred years the development in other countries of the West—would presumably have resulted in any case in greater attention paid and greater significance ascribed to the newcomers by birth, that is, the children, whom, when they had outgrown their childhood and were about to enter the community of adults as young people, the Greeks simply called οἱ νέοι, the new ones. There is the additional fact, however, a fact that has become decisive for the meaning of education, that this pathos of the new, though it is considerably older than the eighteenth century, only developed conceptually and politically in that century. From this source there was derived at the start an educational ideal, tinged with Rousseauism and in fact directly influenced by Rousseau, in which education became an instrument of politics, and political activity itself was conceived of as a form of education.

The role played by education in all political utopias from ancient times onward shows how natural it seems to start a new world with those who are by birth and nature new. So far as politics is concerned, this involves of course a serious misconception: instead of joining with one's equals in assuming the effort of persuasion and running the risk of failure, there is dictatorial intervention, based upon the absolute superiority of the adult, and the attempt to produce the new as a *fait accompli,* that is, as though the new already existed. For this reason, in Europe, the belief that one must begin with the children if one wishes to produce new conditions has remained principally the monopoly of revolutionary movements of tyrannical cast which, when they came to power, took the children away from their parents and simply indoctrinated them. Education can play no part in politics, because in politics we always have to deal with those who are already educated. Whoever wants to educate adults really wants to act as their guardian and prevent them from political activity. Since one cannot educate adults, the word "education" has an evil sound in politics; there is a pretense of education, when the real purpose is coercion without the use of force. He who seriously wants to create a new political order through education, that is, neither through force and constraint nor through persuasion, must draw the dreadful Platonic conclusion: the banishment of all older people from the state that is to be founded. But even the children one wishes to educate to be citizens of a utopian morrow are actually denied their own future role in the body politic, for, from the standpoint of the new ones, whatever new the adult world may propose is necessarily older than they themselves. It is in the very nature of the human condition that each new generation grows into an old world, so that to prepare a new generation for a new world can only mean that one wishes to strike from the newcomers' hands their own chance at the new.

All this is by no means the case in America, and it is exactly this fact that makes it so hard to judge these questions correctly here. The political role that education actually plays in a land of immigrants, the fact that the schools not only serve to Americanize the children but affect their parents as well, that here in fact one helps to shed an old world and to enter into a new one, encourages the illusion that a new world is being built through the education of the children. Of course the true situation is not this at all. The world into which children are introduced, even in America, is an old world, that is, a pre-existing world, constructed by the living and the dead, and it is new only for those who have newly entered it by immigration. But here illusion is stronger than reality because it springs directly from a basic American experience, the experience that a new order can be founded, and what is more, founded with full consciousness of a historical continuum, for the phrase "New World" gains its meaning from the Old World, which, however admirable on other scores, was rejected because it could find no solution for poverty and oppression.

Now in respect to education itself the illusion arising from the pathos of the new has produced its most serious consequences only in our own century. It has first of all made it possible for that complex of modern educational theories which originated in Middle Europe and consists of an astounding hodgepodge of sense and nonsense to accomplish, under the banner of progressive education, a most radical revolution in the whole system of education. What in Europe has remained an experiment, tested out here and there in single schools and isolated educational institutions and then gradually extending its influences in certain quarters, in America about twenty-five years ago completely overthrew, as though from one day to the next, all traditions and all the established methods of teaching and learning. I shall not go into details, and I leave out of account private schools and especially the Roman Catholic parochial school system. The significant fact is that for the sake of certain theories, good or bad, all the rules of sound human reason were thrust aside. Such a procedure is always of great and pernicious significance, especially in a country that relies so extensively on common sense in its political life. Whenever in political questions sound human reason fails or gives up the attempt to supply answers we are faced by a crisis; for this kind of reason is really that common sense by virtue of which we and our five individual senses are fitted into a single world common to us all and by the aid of which we move about in it. The disappearance of common sense in the present day is the surest sign of the present-day crisis. In every crisis a piece of the world, something common to us all, is destroyed. The failure of common sense, like a divining rod, points to the place where such a cave-in has occurred.

In any case the answer to the question of why Johnny can't read or to the more general question of why the scholastic standards of the average American school lag so very far behind the average standards in actually all the countries of Europe is not, unfortunately, simply that this country is young and has not yet caught up with the standards of the Old World but, on the contrary, that this country in this particular field is the most "advanced" and most modern in the world. And this is true in a double sense: nowhere have the education problems of a mass society become so acute, and nowhere else have the most modern theories in the realm of pedagogy been so uncritically and slavishly accepted. Thus the crisis in American education, on the one hand, announces the bankruptcy of progressive education and, on the other, presents a problem of immense difficulty because it has arisen under the conditions and in response to the demands of a mass society.

In this connection we must bear in mind another more general factor which did not, to be sure, cause the crisis but which has aggravated it to a remarkable degree, and this is the unique role the concept of equality plays and always has played in American life. Much more is involved in this than equality before the law, more too than the leveling of class distinctions, more even than what is expressed in the phrase "equality of opportunity," though that has a greater significance in this connection because in the American view a right to education is one of the inalienable civic rights. This last has been decisive for the structure of the public-school system in that secondary schools in the European sense exist only as exceptions. Since compulsory school attendance extends to the age of sixteen, every child must enter high school, and the high school therefore is basically a kind of continuation of primary school. As a result of this lack of a secondary school the preparation for the college course has to be supplied by the colleges themselves, whose curricula therefore suffer from a chronic overload. which in turn affects the quality of the work done there.

At first glance one might perhaps think that this anomaly lies in the very nature of a mass society in which education is no longer a privilege of the wealthy classes. A glance at England, where, as everyone knows, secondary education has also been made available in recent years to all classes of the population, will show that this is not the case. For there at the end of primary school, with students

at the age of eleven, has been instituted the dreaded examination
that weeds out all but some ten per cent of the scholars suited for
higher education. The rigor of this selection was not accepted even
in England without protest; in America it would have been simply
impossible. What is aimed at in England is "meritocracy," which is
clearly once more the establishment of an oligarchy, this time not
of wealth or of birth but of talent. But this means, even though people in England may not be altogether clear about it, that the country even under a socialist government will continue to be governed
as it has been from time out of mind, that is, neither as a monarchy
nor as a democracy but as an oligarchy or aristocracy—the latter
in case one takes the view that the most gifted are also the best,
which is by no means a certainty. In America such an almost physical division of the children into gifted and ungifted would be considered intolerable. Meritocracy contradicts the principle of equality, of an equalitarian democracy, no less than any other oligarchy.

Thus what makes the educational crisis in American so especially
acute is the political temper of the country, which of itself struggles
to equalize or to erase as far as possible the difference between
young and old, between the gifted and the ungifted, finally between
children and adults, particularly between pupils and teachers. It is
obvious that such an equalization can actually be accomplished only
at the cost of the teacher's authority and at the expense of the gifted
among the students. However, it is equally obvious, at least to
anyone who has ever come in contact with the American educational system, that this difficulty, rooted in the political attitude of
the country, also has great advantages, not simply of a human kind
but educationally speaking as well; in any case these general factors
cannot explain the crisis in which we presently find ourselves nor
justify the measures through which that crisis has been precipitated.

II

These ruinous measures can be schematically traced back to
three basic assumptions, all of which are only too familiar. The

first is that there exist a child's world and a society formed among children that are autonomous and must insofar as possible be left to them to govern. Adults are only there to help with this government. The authority that tells the individual child what to do and what not to do rests with the child group itself—and this produces, among other consequences, a situation in which the adult stands helpless before the individual child and out of contact with him. He can only tell him to do what he likes and then prevent the worst from happening. The real and normal relations between children and adults, arising from the fact that people of all ages are always simultaneously together in the world, are thus broken off. And so it is of the essence of this first basic assumption that it takes into account only the group and not the individual child.

As for the child in the group, he is of course rather worse off than before. For the authority of a group, even a child group, is always considerably stronger and more tyrannical than the severest authority of an individual person can ever be. If one looks at it from the standpoint of the individual child, his chances to rebel or to do anything on his own hook are practically nil; he no longer finds himself in a very unequal contest with a person who has, to be sure, absolute superiority over him but in contest with whom he can nevertheless count on the solidarity of other children, that is, of his own kind; rather he is in the position, hopeless by definition, of a minority of one confronted by the absolute majority of all the others. There are very few grown people who can endure such a situation, even when it is not supported by external means of compulsion; children are simply and utterly incapable of it.

Therefore by being emancipated from the authority of adults the child has not been freed but has been subjected to a much more terrifying and truly tyrannical authority, the tyranny of the majority. In any case the result is that the children have been so to speak banished from the world of grown-ups. They are either thrown back upon themselves or handed over to the tyranny of their own group, against which, because of its numerical superiority, they cannot rebel, with which, because they are children, they cannot reason, and out of which they cannot flee to any other world because the world of adults is barred to them. The reaction of the children to this pressure tends to be either conformism or juvenile delinquency, and is frequently a mixture of both.

The *second* basic assumption which has come into question in the present crisis has to do with teaching. Under the influence of modern psychology and the tenets of pragmatism, pedagogy has developed into a science of teaching in general in such a way as to be wholly emancipated from the actual material to be taught. A teacher, so it was thought, is a man who can simply teach anything; his training is in teaching, not in the mastery of any particular subject. This attitude, as we shall presently see, is naturally very closely connected with a basic assumption about learning. Moreover, it has resulted in recent decades in a most serious neglect of the training of teachers in their own subjects, especially in the public high schools. Since the teacher does not need to know his own subject, it not infrequently happens that he is just one hour ahead of his class in knowledge. This in turn means not only that the students are actually left to their own resources but that the most legitimate source of the teacher's authority as the person who, turn it whatever way one will, still knows more and can do more than oneself is no longer effective. Thus the non-authoritarian teacher, who would like to abstain from all methods of compulsion because he is able to rely on his own authority, can no longer exist.

But this pernicious role that pedagogy and the teachers' colleges are playing in the present crisis was only possible because of a modern theory about learning. This was, quite simply, the logical application of the *third* basic assumption in our context, an assumption which the modern world has held for centuries and which found its systematic conceptual expression in pragmatism. This basic assumption is that you can know and understand only what you have done yourself, and its application to education is as primitive as it is obvious: to substitute, insofar as possible, doing for learning. The reason that no importance was attached to the teacher's mastering his own subject was the wish to compel him to the exercise of the continuous activity of learning so that he would not, as they said, pass on "dead knowledge" but, instead, would constantly demonstrate how it is produced. The conscious intention was not to teach knowledge but to inculcate a skill, and the result was a kind of transformation of institutes for learning into vocational institutions which have been as successful in teaching how to drive a car or how to use a typewriter or, even more important for the "art" of living, how to get along with other people and to be popular, as they have been unable to make the children acquire the normal prerequisites of a standard curriculum.

However, this description is at fault, not only because it obviously exaggerates in order to drive home a point, but because it fails to take into account how in this process special importance was attached to obliterating as far as possible the distinction between play and work—in favor of the former. Play was looked upon as the liveliest and most appropriate way for the child to behave in the world, as the only form of activity that evolves spontaneously from his existence as a child. Only what can be learned through play does justice to this liveliness. The child's characteristic activity, so it was thought, lies in play; learning in the old sense, by forcing a child into an attitude of passivity, compelled him to give up his own playful initiative.

The close connection between these two things—the substitution of doing for learning and of playing for working—is directly illustrated by the teaching of languages: the child is to learn by speaking, that is by doing, not by studying grammar and syntax; in other words he is to learn a foreign language in the same way that as an infant he learned his own language: as though at play and in the uninterrupted continuity of simple existence. Quite apart from the question of whether this is possible or not—it is possible, to a limited degree, only when one can keep the child all day long in the foreign-speaking environment—it is perfectly clear that this procedure consciously attempts to keep the older child as far as possible at the infant level. The very thing that should prepare the child for the world of adults, the gradually acquired habit of work and of not-playing, is done away with in favor of the autonomy of the world of childhood.

Whatever may be the connection between doing and knowing, or whatever the validity of the pragmatic formula, its application to education, that is, to the way the child learns, tends to make absolute the world of childhood in just the same way that we noted in the case of the first basic assumption. Here, too, under the pretext of respecting the child's independence, he is debarred from the world of grown-ups and artificially kept in his own, so far as that can be called a world. This holding back of the child is artificial because it breaks off the natural relationship between grown-ups and children, which consists among other things in teaching and learning, and because at the same time it belies the fact that the child is a developing human being, that childhood is a temporary stage, a preparation for adulthood.

The present crisis in America results from the recognition of the destructiveness of these basic assumptions and a desperate attempt to reform the entire educational system, that is, to transform it completely. In doing this what is actually being attempted—except for the plans for an immense increase in the facilities for training in the physical sciences and in technology—is nothing but restoration: teaching will once more be conducted with authority; play is to stop in school hours, and serious work is once more to be done; emphasis will shift from extracurricular skills to knowledge prescribed by the curriculum; finally there is even talk of transforming the present curricula for teachers so that the teachers themselves will have to learn something before being turned loose on the children.

These proposed reforms, which are still in the discussion stage and are of purely American interest, need not concern us here. Nor can I discuss the more technical, yet in the long run perhaps even more important question of how to reform the curricula of elementary and secondary schools in all countries so as to bring them up to the entirely new requirements of the present world. What is of importance to our argument is a twofold question. Which aspects of the modern world and its crisis have actually revealed themselves in the educational crisis, that is, what are the true reasons that for decades things could be said and done in such glaring contradiction to common sense? And, second, what can we learn from this crisis for the essence of education—not in the sense that one can always learn from mistakes what ought not to be done, but rather by reflecting on the role that education plays in every civilization, that is on the obligation that the existence of children entails for every human society. We shall begin with the second question.

III

A crisis in education would at any time give rise to serious concern even if it did not reflect, as in the present instance it does, a more general crisis and instability in modern society. For education belongs among the most elementary and necessary activities of human society, which never remains as it is but continuously renews itself through birth, through the arrival of new human beings. These newcomers, moreover, are not finished but in a state of becoming. Thus the child, the subject of education, has for the educator a double aspect: he is new in a world that is strange to him and he is in process of becoming, he is a new human being and he is a becoming human being. This double aspect is by no means self-evident and it does not apply to the animal forms of life; it corresponds to a double relationship, the relationship to the world on the one hand and to life on the other. The child shares the state of becoming with all living things; in respect to life and its development, the child is a human being in process of becoming, just as a kitten is a cat in process of becoming. But the child is new only in relation to a world that was there before him, that will continue after his death, and in which he is to spend his life. If the child were not a newcomer in this human world but simply a not yet finished living creature, education would be just a function of life and would need to consist in nothing save that concern for the sustenance of life and that training and practice in living that all animals assume in respect to their young.

Human parents, however, have not only summoned their children into life through conception and birth, they have simultaneously introduced them into a world. In education they assume responsibility for both, for the life and development of the child and for the continuance of the world. These two responsibilities do not by any means coincide; they may indeed come into conflict with each other. The responsibility for the development of the child turns in a certain sense against the world: the child requires special protection and care so that nothing destructive may happen to him from the world. But the world, too, needs protection to keep it from being overrun and destroyed by the onslaught of the new that bursts upon it with each new generation.

Because the child must be protected against the world, his traditional place is in the family, whose adult members daily return back from the outside world and withdraw into the security of private life within four walls. These four walls, within which people's private family life is lived, constitute a shield against the world and specifically against the public aspect of the world. They enclose a secure place, without which no living thing can thrive. This holds good not only for the life of childhood but for human life in general. Wherever the latter is consistently exposed to the world without the protection of privacy and security its vital quality is destroyed. In the public world, common to all, persons count, and so does work, that is, the work of our hands that each of us contributes to our common world; but life *qua* life does not matter there. The world cannot be regardful of it, and it has to be hidden and protected from the world.

Everything that lives, not vegetative life alone, emerges from darkness and, however strong its natural tendency to thrust itself into the light, it nevertheless needs the security of darkness to grow at all. This may indeed be the reason that children of famous parents so often turn out badly. Fame penetrates the four walls, invades their private space, bringing with it, especially in present-day conditions, the merciless glare of the public realm, which floods everything in the private lives of those concerned, so that the children no longer have a place of security where they can grow. But exactly the same destruction of the real living space occurs wherever the attempt is made to turn the children themselves into a kind of world. Among these peer groups then arises public life of a sort and, quite apart from the fact that it is not a real one and that the whole attempt is a sort of fraud, the damaging fact remains that children —that is, human beings in process of becoming but not yet complete—are thereby forced to expose themselves to the light of a public existence.

That modern education, insofar as it attempts to establish a world of children, destroys the necessary conditions for vital development and growth seems obvious. But that such harm to the developing child should be the result of modern education strikes one as strange indeed, for this education maintained that its exclusive aim was to serve the child and rebelled against the methods of the past because these had not sufficiently taken into account the child's inner nature and his needs. "The Century of the Child," as we may recall, was going to emancipate the child and free him from the standards derived from the adult world. Then how could it happen that the most elementary conditions of life necessary for the growth and development of the child were overlooked or simply not recognized? How could it happen that the child was exposed to what more than anything else characterized the adult world, its public aspect, after the decision had just been reached that the mistake in all past education had been to see the child as nothing but an undersized grown-up?

The reason for this strange state of affairs has nothing directly to do with education; it is rather to be found in the judgments and prejudices about the nature of private life and public world and their relation to each other which have been characteristic of modern society since the beginning of modern times and which educators, when they finally began, relatively late, to modernize education, accepted as self-evident assumptions without being aware of the consequences they must necessarily have for the life of the child. It is the peculiarity of modern society, and by no means a matter of course, that it regards life, that is, the earthly life of the individual as well as the family, as the highest good; and for this reason, in contrast to all previous centuries, emancipated this life and all the activities that have to do with its preservation and enrichment from the concealment of privacy and exposed tnem to the light of the public world. This is the real meaning of the emancipation of workers and women, not as persons, to be sure, but insofar as they fulfill a necessary function in the life-process of society.

The last to be affected by this process of emancipation were the children, and the very thing that had meant a true liberation for the workers and the women—because they were not only workers and women but persons as well, who therefore had a claim on the public world, that is, a right to see and be seen in it, to speak and be heard—was an abandonment and betrayal in the case of the children, who are still at the stage where the simple fact of life and growth outweighs the factor of personality. The more completely modern society discards the distinction between what is private and what is public, between what can thrive only in concealment and what needs to be shown to all in the full light of the public world, the more, that is, it introduces between the private and the public a social sphere in which the private is made public and vice versa, the harder it makes things for its children, who by nature require the security of concealment in order to mature undisturbed.

However serious these infringements of the conditions for vital growth may be, it is certain that they were entirely unintentional; the central aim of all modern education efforts has been the welfare of the child, a fact that is, of course, no less true even if the efforts made have not always succeeded in promoting the child's welfare in the way that was hoped. The situation is entirely different in the sphere of educational tasks directed no longer toward the child but toward the young person, the newcomer and stranger, who has been born into an already existing world which he does not know. These tasks are primarily, but not exclusively, the responsibility of the schools; they have to do with teaching and learning; the failure in this field is the most urgent problem in America today. What lies at the bottom of it?

Normally the child is first introduced to the world in school. Now school is by no means the world and must not pretend to be; it is rather the institution that we interpose between the private domain of home and the world in order to make the transition from the family to the world possible at all. Attendance there is required not by the family but by the state, that is by the public world, and so, in relation to the child, school in a sense represents the world, although it is not yet actually the world. At this stage of education adults, to be sure, once more assume a responsibility for the child, but by now it is not so much responsibility for the vital welfare of a growing thing as for what we generally call the free development of characteristic qualities and talents. This, from the general and essential point of view, is the uniqueness that distinguishes every human being from every other, the quality by virtue of which he is not only a stranger in the world but something that has never been here before.

Insofar as the child is not yet acquainted with the world, he must be gradually introduced to it; insofar as he is new, care must be taken that this new thing comes to fruition in relation to the world as it is. In any case, however, the educators here stand in relation to the young as representatives of a world for which they must assume responsibility although they themselves did not make it, and even though they may, secretly or openly, wish it were other than it is. This responsibility is not arbitrarily imposed upon educators; it is implicit in the fact that the young are introduced by adults into a continuously changing world. Anyone who refuses to assume joint responsibility for the world should not have children and must not be allowed to take part in educating them.

In education this responsibility for the world takes the form of authority. The authority of the educator and the qualifications of the teacher are not the same thing. Although a measure of qualification is indispensable for authority, the highest possible qualification can never by itself beget authority. The teacher's qualification consists in knowing the world and being able to instruct others about it, but his authority rests on his assumption of responsibility for that world. Vis-à-vis the child it is as though he were a representative of all adult inhabitants, pointing out the details and saying to the child: This is our world.

Now we all know how things stand today in respect to authority. Whatever one's attitude toward this problem may be, it is obvious that in public and political life authority either plays no role at all —for the violence and terror exercised by the totalitarian countries have, of course, nothing to do with authority—or at most plays a highly contested role. This, however, simply means, in essence, that people do not wish to require of anyone or to entrust to anyone the assumption of responsibility for everything else, for wherever true authority existed it was joined with responsibility for the course of things in the world. If we remove authority from political and public life, it may mean that from now on an equal responsibility for the course of the world is to be required of everyone. But it may also mean that the claims of the world and the requirements of order in it are being consciously or unconsciously repudiated; all responsibility for the world is being rejected, the responsibility for giving orders no less than for obeying them. There is no doubt that in the modern loss of authority both intentions play a part and have often been simultaneously and inextricably at work together.

In education, on the contrary, there can be no such ambiguity in regard to the present-day loss of authority. Children cannot throw off educational authority, as though they were in a position of oppression by an adult majority—though even this absurdity of treating children as an oppressed minority in need of liberation has actually been tried out in modern educational practice. Authority has been discarded by the adults, and this can mean only one thing: that the adults refuse to assume responsibility for the world into which they have brought the children.

There is of course a connection between the loss of authority in public and political life and in the private pre-political realms of the family and the school. The more radical the distrust of authority becomes in the public sphere, the greater the probability naturally becomes that the private sphere will not remain inviolate. There is this additional fact, and it is very likely the decisive one, that from time out of mind we have been accustomed in our tradition of political thought to regard the authority of parents over children, of teachers over pupils, as the model by which to understand political authority. It is just this model, which can be found as early as

Plato and Aristotle, that makes the concept of authority in politics so extraordinarily ambiguous. It is based, first of all, on an absolute superiority such as can never exist among adults and which, from the point of view of human dignity, must never exist. In the second place, following the model of the nursery, it is based on a purely temporary superiority and therefore becomes self-contradictory if it is applied to relations that are not temporary by nature —such as the relations of the rulers and the ruled. Thus it lies in the nature of the matter—that is, both in the nature of the present crisis in authority and in the nature of our traditional political thought—that the loss of authority which began in the political sphere should end in the private one; and it is naturally no accident that the place where political authority was first undermined, that is, in America, should be the place where the modern crisis in education makes itself most strongly felt.

The general loss of authority could, in fact, hardly find more radical expression than by its intrusion into the pre-political sphere, where authority seemed dictated by nature itself and independent of all historical changes and political conditions. On the other hand, modern man could find no clearer expression for his dissatisfaction with the world, for his disgust with things as they are, than by his refusal to assume, in respect to his children, responsibility for all this. It is as though parents daily said: "In this world even we are not very securely at home; how to move about in it, what to know, what skills to master, are mysteries to us too. You must try to make out as best you can; in any case you are not entitled to call us to account. We are innocent, we wash our hands of you."

This attitude has, of course, nothing to do with that revolutionary desire for a new order in the world—*Novus Ordo Seclorum*—which once animated America; it is rather a symptom of that modern estrangement from the world which can be seen everywhere but which presents itself in especially radical and desperate form under the conditions of a mass society. It is true that modern educational experiments, not in America alone, have struck very revolutionary poses, and this has, to a certain degree, increased the difficulty of clearly recognizing the situation and caused a certain

degree of confusion in the discussion of the problem; for in contradiction to all such behavior stands the unquestionable fact that
so long as America was really animated by that spirit she never
dreamed of initiating the new order with education but, on the contrary, remained conservative in educational matters.

To avoid misunderstanding: it seems to me that conservatism, in
the sense of conservation, is of the essence of the educational
activity, whose task is always to cherish and protect something—
the child against the world, the world against the child, the new
against the old, the old against the new. Even the comprehensive
responsibility for the world that is thereby assumed implies, of
course, a conservative attitude. But this holds good only for the
realm of education, or rather for the relations between grown-ups
and children, and not for the realm of politics, where we act among
and with adults and equals. In politics this conservative attitude—
which accepts the world as it is, striving only to preserve the
status quo—can only lead to destruction, because the world, in
gross and in detail, is irrevocably delivered up to the ruin of time
unless human beings are determined to intervene, to alter, to create
what is new. Hamlet's words, "The time is out of joint. O cursed
spite that ever I was born to set it right," are more or less true for
every new generation, although since the beginning of our century
they have perhaps acquired a more persuasive validity than before.

Basically we are always educating for a world that is or is becoming out of joint, for this is the basic human situation, in which
the world is created by mortal hands to serve mortals for a limited
time as home. Because the world is made by mortals it wears out;
and because it continuously changes its inhabitants it runs the risk
of becoming as mortal as they. To preserve the world against the
mortality of its creators and inhabitants it must be constantly set
right anew. The problem is simply to educate in such a way that a
setting-right remains actually possible, even though it can, of
course, never be assured. Our hope always hangs on the new
which every generation brings; but precisely because we can base
our hope only on this, we destroy everything if we so try to control
the new that we, the old, can dictate how it will look. Exactly for

the sake of what is new and revolutionary in every child, education must be conservative; it must preserve this newness and introduce it as a new thing into an old world, which, however revolutionary its actions may be, is always, from the standpoint of the next generation, superannuated and close to destruction.

IV

The real difficulty in modern education lies in the fact that, despite all the fashionable talk about a new conservatism, even that minimum of conservation and the conserving attitude without which education is simply not possible is in our time extraordinarily hard to achieve. There are very good reasons for this. The crisis of authority in education is most closely connected with the crisis of tradition, that is with the crisis in our attitude toward the realm of the past. This aspect of the modern crisis is especially hard for the educator to bear, because it is his task to mediate between the old and the new, so that his very profession requires of him an extraordinary respect for the past. Through long centuries, i.e., throughout the combined period of Roman-Christian civilization, there was no need for him to become aware of this special quality in himself because reverence for the past was an essential part of the Roman frame of mind, and this was not altered or ended by Christianity, but simply shifted onto different foundations.

It was of the essence of the Roman attitude (though this was by no means true of every civilization or even of the Western tradition taken as a whole) to consider the past *qua* past as a model, ancestors, in every instance, as guiding examples for their descendants; to believe that all greatness lies in what has been, and therefore that the most fitting human age is old age, the man grown old, who, because he is already almost an ancestor, may serve as a model for the living. All this stands in contradiction not only to our world and to the modern age from the Renaissance on, but, for example, to the Greek attitude toward life as well. When Goethe said that growing old is "the gradual withdrawal from the world of appearances," his was a comment made in the spirit of the Greeks, for whom being and appearing coincide. The Roman attitude would have been that precisely in growing old and slowly disappearing from the community of mortals man reaches his most characteristic form of being, even though, in respect to the world of appearances, he is in the process of disappearing; for only now can he approach the existence in which he will be an authority for others.

With the undisturbed background of such a tradition, in which education has a political function (and this was a unique case), it is in fact comparatively easy to do the right thing in matters of education without even pausing to consider what one is really doing, so completely is the specific ethos of the educational principle in accord with the basic ethical and moral convictions of society at large. To educate, in the words of Polybius, was simply "to let you see that you are altogether worthy of your ancestors," and in this business the educator could be a "fellow-contestant" and a "fellow-workman" because he too, though on a different level, went through life with his eyes glued to the past. Fellowship and authority were in this case indeed but the two sides of the same matter, and the teacher's authority was firmly grounded in the encompassing authority of the past as such. Today, however, we are no longer in that position; and it makes little sense to act as though we still were and had only, as it were, accidentally strayed from the right path and were free at any moment to find our way back to it. This means that wherever the crisis has occurred in the modern world, one cannot simply go on nor yet simply turn back. Such a reversal will never bring us anywhere except to the same situation out of which the crisis has just arisen. The return would simply be a repeat performance—though perhaps different in form, since there are no limits to the possibilities of nonsense and capricious notions that can be decked out as the last word in science. On the other hand, simple, unreflective perseverance, whether it be pressing forward in the crisis or adhering to the routine that blandly believes the crisis will not engulf its particular sphere of life, can only, because it surrenders to the course of time, lead to ruin; it can only, to be more precise, increase that estrangement from the world by which we are already threatened on all sides. Consideration of the principles of education must take into account this process of estrangement from the world; it can even admit that we are here presumably confronted by an automatic process, provided only that it does not forget that it lies within the power of human thought and action to interrupt and arrest such processes.

The problem of education in the modern world lies in the fact that by its very nature it cannot forgo either authority or tradition, and yet must proceed in a world that is neither structured by authority nor held together by tradition. That means, however, that not just teachers and educators, but all of us, insofar as we live in one world together with our children and with young people, must take toward them an attitude radically different from the one we take toward one another. We must decisively divorce the realm of education from the others, most of all from the realm of public, political life, in order to apply to it alone a concept of authority and an attitude toward the past which are appropriate to it but have no general validity and must not claim a general validity in the world of grown-ups.

In practice the first consequence of this would be a clear understanding that the function of the school is to teach children what the world is like and not to instruct them in the art of living. Since the world is old, always older than they themselves, learning inevitably turns toward the past, no matter how much living will spend itself in the present. Second, the line drawn between children and adults should signify that one can neither educate adults nor treat children as though they were grown up; but this line should never be permitted to grow into a wall separating children from the adult community as though they were not living in the same world and as though childhood were an autonomous human state, capable of living by its own laws. Where the line between childhood and adulthood falls in each instance cannot be determined by a general rule; it changes often, in respect to age, from country to country, from one civilization to another, and also from individual to individual. But education, as distinguished from learning, must have a predictable end. In our civilization this end probably coincides with graduation from college rather than with graduation from high school, for the professional training in universities or technical schools, though it always has something to do with education, is nevertheless in itself a kind of specialization. It no longer aims to introduce the young person to the world as a whole, but rather to a particular, limited segment of it. One cannot educate without at the same time teaching; an education without learning is empty and therefore degenerates with great ease into moral-emotional rhetoric. But one can quite easily teach without educating, and one can go on learning to the end of one's days without for that reason becoming educated. All these are particulars, however, that must really be left to the experts and the pedagogues.

What concerns us all and cannot therefore be turned over to the special science of pedagogy is the relation between grown-ups and children in general or, putting it in even more general and exact terms, our attitude toward the fact of natality: the fact that we have all come into the world by being born and that this world is constantly renewed through birth. Education is the point at which we decide whether we love the world enough to assume responsibility for it and by the same token save it from that ruin which, except for renewal, except for the coming of the new and young, would be inevitable. And education, too, is where we decide whether we love our children enough not to expel them from our world and leave them to their own devices, nor to strike from their hands their chance of undertaking something new, something unforeseen by us, but to prepare them in advance for the task of renewing a common world.

6

THE CRISIS IN CULTURE:

Its Social and Its Political Significance

I

FOR more than ten years now, we have witnessed a still growing concern among intellectuals with the relatively new phenomenon of mass culture. The term itself clearly derives from the not much older term "mass society"; the tacit assumption, underlying all discussions of the matter, is that mass culture, logically and inevitably, is the culture of mass society. The most significant fact about the short history of both terms is that, while even a few years ago they were still used with a strong sense of reprobation—implying that mass society was a depraved form of society and mass culture a contradiction in terms—they now have become respectable, the subject of innumerable studies and research projects whose chief effect, as Harold Rosenberg pointed out, is "to add to kitsch an intellectual dimension." This "intellectualization of kitsch" is justified on the grounds that mass society, whether we like it or not, is going to stay with us into the foreseeable future; hence its "culture," "popular culture [cannot] be left to the populace." [1] However, the question is whether what is true for mass society is true for mass culture also, or, to put it another way, whether the relationship between mass society and culture will be, *mutatis mutandis,* the same as the relation of society toward culture which preceded it.

The question of mass culture raises first of all another and more fundamental problem, namely, the highly problematic relationship of society and culture. One needs only to recall to what an extent the entire movement of modern art started with a vehement rebellion of the artist against society as such (and not against a still unknown mass society) in order to become aware how much this earlier relationship must have left to be desired and thus to beware of the facile yearning of so many critics of mass culture for a Golden Age of good and genteel society. This yearning is much more widespread today in America than it is in Europe for the simple reason that America, though only too well acquainted with the barbarian philistinism of the nouveaux-riches, has only a nodding acquaintance with the equally annoying cultural and educated philistinism of European society, where culture has acquired snob-value, where it has become a matter of status to be educated enough to appreciate culture; this lack of experience may even explain why American literature and painting has suddenly come to play such a decisive role in the development of modern art and why it can make its influence felt in countries whose intellectual and artistic vanguard has adopted outspoken anti-American attitudes. It has, however, the unfortunate consequence that the profound malaise which the very word "culture" is likely to evoke precisely among those who are its foremost representatives may go unnoticed or not be understood in its symptomatic significance.

Yet whether or not any particular country has actually passed through all stages in which society developed since the rise of the modern age, mass society clearly comes about when "the mass of the population has become incorporated into society." [2] And since society in the sense of "good society" comprehended those parts of the population which disposed not only of wealth but of leisure time, that is, of time to be devoted to "culture," mass society does indeed indicate a new state of affairs in which the mass of the population has been so far liberated from the burden of physically exhausting labor that it too disposes of enough leisure for "culture." Hence, mass society and mass culture seem to be interrelated phenomena, but their common denominator is not the mass but rather the society into which the masses too have been incorporated. Historically as well as conceptually, mass society was preceded by society, and society is no more a generic term than mass society; it too can be dated and described historically; it is older, to be sure, than mass society, but not older than the modern age. In fact, all the traits that crowd psychology has meanwhile discovered in mass man: nis loneliness—and loneliness is neither isolation nor solitude—regardless of his adaptability; his excitability and lack of standards; his capacity for consumption, accompanied by inability to judge, or even to distinguish; above all, his egocentricity and that fateful alienation from the world which since Rousseau is mistaken for self-alienation—all these traits first appeared in good society, where there was no question of masses, numerically speaking.

Good society, as we know it from the eighteenth and nineteenth centuries, probably had its origin in the European courts of the age of absolutism, especially the court society of Louis XIV, who knew so well how to reduce French nobility to political insignificance by the simple means of gathering them at Versailles, transforming them into courtiers, and making them entertain one another through the intrigues, cabals, and endless gossip which this perpetual party inevitably engendered. Thus the true forerunner of the novel, this entirely modern art form, is not so much the picaresque romance of adventurers and knights as the *Mémoires* of Saint-Simon, while the novel itself clearly anticipated the rise of the social sciences as well as of psychology, both of which are still centered around conflicts between society and the "individual." The true forerunner of modern mass man is this individual, who was defined and indeed discovered by those who, like Rousseau in the eighteenth century or John Stuart Mill in the nineteenth century, found themselves in open rebellion against society. Since then, the story of a conflict between society and its individuals has repeated itself time and again in reality no less than in fiction; the modern, and no longer so modern, individual forms part and parcel of the society against which he tries to assert himself and which always gets the better of him.

There is, however, an important difference between the earlier stages of society and mass society with respect to the situation of the individual. As long as society itself was restricted to certain classes of the population, the individual's chances for survival against its pressures were rather good; they lay in the simultaneous presence within the population of other non-society strata into which the individual could escape, and one reason why these individuals so frequently ended by joining revolutionary parties was that they discovered in those who were not admitted to society certain traits of humanity which had become extinct in society. This again found its expression in the novel, in the well-known glorifications of the workers and proletarians, but also, more subtly, in the role assigned to homosexuals (for instance in Proust) or to Jews, that is, to groups which society had never quite absorbed. The fact that the revolutionary élan throughout the nineteenth and twentieth centuries was so much more violently directed against society than against states and governments is not only due to the predominance of the social question in the sense of the twofold predicament of misery and exploitation. We need only to read the record of the French Revolution, and to recall to what an extent the very concept of *le peuple* received its connotations from an outrage of the "heart"—as Rousseau and even Robespierre would have said—against the corruption and hypocrisy of the salons, to realize what the true role of society was throughout the nineteenth century. A good part of the despair of individuals under the conditions of mass society is due to the fact that these avenues of escape are now closed because society has incorporated all strata of the population.

Here we are not concerned with the conflict between the individual and society, however, although it is of some importance to note that the last individual left in a mass society seems to be the artist. Our concern is with culture, or rather with what happens to culture under the different conditions of society and of mass society, and our interest in the artist, therefore, does not so much concern his subjective individualism as the fact that he is, after all, the authentic producer of those objects which every civilization leaves behind as the quintessence and the lasting testimony of the spirit which animated it. That precisely the producers of the highest cultural objects, namely works of art, should turn against society, that the whole development of modern art—which together with the scientific development will probably remain the greatest achievement of our age—should have started from and remained committed to this hostility against society demonstrates an existing antagonism between society and culture prior to the rise of mass society.

The charge the artist, as distinguished from the political revolutionary, has laid to society was summed up quite early, at the turn of the eighteenth century, in the one word which has since been repeated and reinterpreted by one generation after the other. The word is "philistinism." Its origin, slightly older than its specific use, is of no great significance; it was first used in German student slang to distinguish between town and gown, whereby, however, the Biblical association indicated already an enemy superior in numbers into whose hands one may fall. When first used as a term —I think by the German writer Clemens von Brentano, who wrote a satire on the philistine *bevor, in und nach der Geschichte*—it designated a mentality which judged everything in terms of immediate usefulness and "material values" and hence had no regard for such useless objects and occupations as are implied in culture and art. All this sounds fairly familiar even today, and it is not without interest to note that even such current slang terms as "square" can already be found in Brentano's early pamphlet.

If matters had rested there, if the chief reproach leveled against society had remained its lack of culture and of interest in art, the phenomenon with which we deal here would be considerably less complicated than it actually is; by the same token, it would be all but incomprehensible why modern art rebelled against "culture" instead of fighting simply and openly for its own "cultural" interests. The point of the matter is that this sort of philistinism, which simply consisted in being "uncultured" and commonplace, was very quickly succeeded by another development in which, on the contrary, society began to be only too interested in all these so-called cultural values. Society began to monopolize "culture" for its own purposes, such as social position and status. This had much to do with the socially inferior position of Europe's middle classes, which found themselves—as soon as they acquired the necessary wealth and leisure—in an uphill fight against the aristocracy and its contempt for the vulgarity of sheer moneymaking. In this fight for social position, culture began to play an enormous role as one of the weapons, if not the best-suited one, to advance oneself socially, and to "educate oneself" out of the lower regions, where supposedly reality was located, up into the higher, non-real regions, where beauty and the spirit supposedly were at home. This escape from reality by means of art and culture is important, not only because it gave the physiognomy of the cultural or educated philistine its most distinctive marks, but also because it probably was the decisive factor in the rebellion of the artists against their newly found patrons; they smelled the danger of being expelled from reality into a sphere of refined talk where what they did would lose all meaning. It was a rather dubious compliment to be recognized by a society which had grown so "polite" that, for instance, during the Irish potato famine, it would not debase itself or risk being associated with so unpleasant a reality by normal usage of the word, but would henceforth refer to that much eaten vegetable by saying "that root." This ancedote contains as in a nutshell the definition of the cultured philistine.[3]

No doubt what is at stake here is much more than the psychological state of the artists; it is the objective status of the cultural world, which, insofar as it contains tangible things—books and paintings, statues, buildings, and music—comprehends, and gives testimony to, the entire recorded past of countries, nations, and ultimately mankind. As such, the only nonsocial and authentic criterion for judging these specifically cultural things is their relative permanence and even eventual immortality. Only what will last through the centuries can ultimately claim to be a cultural object. The point or the matter is that, as soon as the immortal works of the past became the object of social and individual refinement and the status accorded to it, they lost their most important and elemental quality, which is to grasp and move the reader or the spectator over the centuries. The very word "culture" became suspect precisely because it indicated that "pursuit of perfection" which to Matthew Arnold was identical with the "pursuit of sweetness and light." The great works of art are no less misused when they serve purposes of self-education or self-perfection than when they serve any other purposes; it may be as useful and legitimate to look at a picture in order to perfect one's knowledge of a given period as it is useful and legitimate to use a painting in order to hide a hole in the wall. In both instances the art object has been used for ulterior purposes. All is well as long as one remains aware that these usages, legitimate or not, do not constitute the proper intercourse with art. The trouble with the educated philistine was not that he read the classics but that he did so prompted by the ulterior motive of self-perfection, remaining quite unaware of the fact that Shakespeare or Plato might have to tell him more important things than how to educate himself; the trouble was that he fled into a region of "pure poetry" in order to keep reality out of his life—for instance, such "prosaic" things as a potato famine—or to look at it through a veil of "sweetness and light."

We all know the rather deplorable art products which this attitude inspired and upon which it fed, in short the kitsch of the nineteenth century, whose historically so interesting lack of sense for form and style is closely connected with the severance of the arts from reality. The astounding recovery of the creative arts in our own century, and a perhaps less apparent but no less real recovery of the greatness of the past, began to assert itself when genteel society had lost its monopolizing grip on culture, together with its dominant position in the population as a whole. What had happened before and, to an extent, continued, of course, to happen even after the first appearance of modern art, was actually a disintegration of culture whose "lasting monuments" are the neo-Classic, neo-Gothic, neo-Renaissance structures that are strewn all over Europe. In this disintegration, culture, more even than other realities, had become what only then people began to call "value," i.e., a social commodity which could be circulated and cashed in in exchange for all kinds of other values, social and individual.

In other words, cultural objects were first despised as useless by the philistine until the cultural philistine seized upon them as a currency by which he bought a higher position in society or acquired a higher degree of self-esteem—higher, that is, than in his own opinion he deserved either by nature or by birth. In this process, cultural values were treated like any other values, they were what values always have been, exchange values; and in passing from hand to hand they were worn down like old coins. They lost the faculty which is originally peculiar to all cultural things, the faculty of arresting our attention and moving us. When this had come about, people began to talk of the "devaluation of values" and the end of the whole process came with the "bargain sale of values" (*Ausverkauf der Werte*) during the twenties and thirties in Germany, the forties and fifties in France, when cultural and moral "values" were sold out together.

Since then cultural philistinism has been a matter of the past in Europe, and while one may see in the "bargain sale of values" the melancholy end of the great Western tradition, it is still an open question whether it is more difficult to discover the great authors of the past without the help of any tradition than it is to rescue them from the rubbish of educated philistinism. And the task of preserving the past without the help of tradition, and often even against traditional standards and interpretations, is the same for the whole of Western civilization. Intellectually, though not socially, America and Europe are in the same situation: the thread of tradition is broken, and we must discover the past for ourselves— that is, read its authors as though nobody had ever read them before. In this task mass society is much less in our way than good and educated society, and I suspect that this kind of reading was not uncommon in nineteenth-century America precisely because this country was still that "unstoried wilderness" from which so many American writers and artists tried to escape. That American

fiction and poetry have so richly come into their own ever since
Whitman and Melville may have something to do with this. It would
be unfortunate indeed if out of the dilemmas and distractions of
mass culture and mass society there should arise an altogether un-
warranted and idle yearning for a state of affairs which is not better
but only a bit more old-fashioned.

Perhaps the chief difference between society and mass society is
that society wanted culture, evaluated and devaluated cultural
things into social commodities, used and abused them for its own
selfish purposes, but did not "consume" them. Even in their most
worn-out shapes these things remained things and retained a certain objective character; they disintegrated until they looked like a
heap of rubble, but they did not disappear. Mass society, on the
contrary, wants not culture but entertainment, and the wares
offered by the entertainment industry are indeed consumed by
society just like any other consumer goods. The products needed
for entertainment serve the life process of society, even though they
may not be as necessary for this life as bread and meat. They serve,
as the phrase is, to while away time, and the vacant time which is
whiled away is not leisure time, strictly speaking—time, that is,
in which we are free *from* all cares and activities necessitated by the
life process and therefore free *for* the world and its culture—it is
rather left-over time, which still is biological in nature, left over
after labor and sleep have received their due. Vacant time which
entertainment is supposed to fill is a hiatus in the biologically conditioned cycle of labor—in the "metabolism of man with nature,"
as Marx used to say.

Under modern conditions, this hiatus is constantly growing;
there is more and more time freed that must be filled with entertainment, but this enormous increase in vacant time does not
change the nature of the time. Entertainment, like labor and sleep,
is irrevocably part of the biological life process. And biological life
is always, whether laboring or at rest, whether engaged in consumption or in the passive reception of amusement, a metabolism feeding on things by devouring them. The commodities the entertainment industry offers are not "things," cultural objects, whose ex-

cellence is measured by their ability to withstand the life process and become permanent appurtenances of the world, and they should not be judged according to these standards; nor are they values which exist to be used and exchanged; they are consumer goods, destined to be used up, just like any other consumer goods.

Panis et circenses truly belong together; both are necessary for life, for its preservation and recuperation, and both vanish in the course of the life process—that is, both must constantly be produced anew and offered anew, lest this process cease entirely. The standards by which both should be judged are freshness and novelty, and the extent to which we use these standards today to judge cultural and artistic objects as well, things which are supposed to remain in the world even after we have left it, indicates clearly the extent to which the need for entertainment has begun to threaten the cultural world. Yet the trouble does not really stem from mass society or the entertainment industry which caters to its needs. On the contrary, mass society, since it does not want culture but only entertainment, is probably less of a threat to culture than the philistinism of good society; despite the often described malaise of artists and intellectuals—partly perhaps due to their inability to penetrate the noisy futility of mass entertainment—it is precisely the arts and sciences, in contradistinction to all political matters, which continue to flourish. At any event, as long as the entertainment industry produces its own consumer goods, we can no more reproach it for the non-durability of its articles than we can reproach a bakery because it produces goods which, if they are not to spoil, must be consumed as soon as they are made. It has always been the mark of educated philistinism to despise entertainment and amusement, because no "value" could be derived from it. The truth is we all stand in need of entertainment and amusement in some form or other, because we are all subject to life's great cycle, and it is sheer hypocrisy or social snobbery to deny that we can be amused and entertained by exactly the same things which amuse and entertain the masses of our fellow men. As far as the survival of culture is concerned, it certainly is less threatened by those who fill vacant time with entertainment than by those who fill it with some haphazard educational gadgets in order to improve their social standing. And as far as artistic productivity is concerned, it should not be more difficult to withstand the massive temptations of mass culture, or to keep from being thrown out of gear by the noise and humbug of mass society, than it was to avoid the more sophisticated temptations and the more insidious noises of the cultural snobs in refined society.

Unhappily, the case is not that simple. The entertainment industry is confronted with gargantuan appetites, and since its wares disappear in consumption, it must constantly offer new commodities. In this predicament those who produce for the mass media ransack the entire range of past and present culture in the hope of finding suitable material. This material, moreover, cannot be offered as it is; it must be altered in order to become entertaining, it must be prepared to be easily consumed.

Mass culture comes into being when mass society seizes upon cultural objects, and its danger is that the life process of society (which like all biological processes insatiably draws everything available into the cycle of its metabolism) will literally consume the cultural objects, eat them up and destroy them. Of course, I am not referring to mass distribution. When books or pictures in reproduction are thrown on the market cheaply and attain huge sales, this does not affect the nature of the objects in question. But their nature is affected when these objects themselves are changed—rewritten, condensed, digested, reduced to kitsch in reproduction, or in preparation for the movies. This does not mean that culture spreads to the masses, but that culture is being destroyed in order to yield entertainment. The result of this is not disintegration but decay, and those who actively promote it are not the Tin Pan Alley composers but a special kind of intellectuals, often well read and well informed, whose sole function is to organize, disseminate, and change cultural objects in order to persuade the masses that *Hamlet* can be as entertaining as *My Fair Lady,* and perhaps educational as well. There are many great authors of the past who have survived centuries of oblivion and neglect, but it is still an open question whether they will be able to survive an entertaining version of what they have to say.

Culture relates to objects and is a phenomenon of the world; entertainment relates to people and is a phenomenon of life. An object is cultural to the extent that it can endure; its durability is the very opposite of functionality, which is the quality which makes it disappear again from the phenomenal world by being used and used up. The great user and consumer of objects is life itself, the life of the individual and the life of society as a whole. Life is indifferent to the thingness of an object; it insists that every thing must be functional, fulfill some needs. Culture is being threatened when all worldly objects and things, produced by the present or the past, are treated as mere functions for the life process of society, as though they are there only to fulfill some need, and for this functionalization it is almost irrelevant whether the needs in question are of a high or a low order. That the arts must be functional, that cathedrals fulfill a religious need of society, that a picture is born from the need for self-expression in the individual painter and that it is looked at because of a desire for self-perfection in the spectator, all these notions are so unconnected with art and historically so new that one is tempted simply to dismiss them as modern prejudices. The cathedrals were built *ad maiorem gloriam Dei;* while they as buildings certainly served the needs of the community, their elaborate beauty can never be explained by these needs, which could have been served quite as well by any nondescript building. Their beauty transcended all needs and made them last through the centuries; but while beauty, the beauty of a cathedral like the beauty of any secular building, transcends needs and functions, it never transcends the world, even if the content of the work happens to be religious. On the contrary, it is the very beauty of religious art which transforms religious and other-worldly contents and concerns into tangible worldly realities; in this sense all art is secular, and the distinction of religious art is merely that it "secularizes"—reifies and transforms into an "objective," tangible, worldly presence—what had existed before outside the world, whereby it is irrelevant whether we follow traditional religion and localize this "outside" in the beyond of a hereafter, or follow modern explanations and localize it in the innermost recesses of the human heart.

Every thing, whether it is a use object, a consumer good, or a work of art, possesses a shape through which it appears, and only to the extent that something has a shape can we say that it is a thing at all. Among the things which do not occur in nature but only in the man-made world, we distinguish between use objects and art works, both of which possess a certain permanence ranging from ordinary durability to potential immortality in the case of works of art. As such, they are distinguished from consumer goods on one hand, whose duration in the world scarcely exceeds the time necessary to prepare them, and, on the other hand, from the products of action, such as events, deeds, and words, all of which are in themselves so transitory that they would hardly survive the hour or day they appeared in the world, if they were not preserved first by man's memory, which weaves them into stories, and then through his fabricating abilities. From the viewpoint of sheer durability, art works clearly are superior to all other things; since they stay longer in the world than anything else, they are the worldliest of all things. Moreover, they are the only things without any function in the life process of society; strictly speaking, they are fabricated not for men, but for the world which is meant to outlast the life-span of mortals, the coming and going of the generations. Not only are they not consumed like consumer goods and not used up like use objects; they are deliberately removed from the processes of consumption and usage and isolated against the sphere of human life necessities. This removal can be achieved in a great variety of ways; and only where it is done does culture, in the specific sense, come into being.

The question here is not whether worldliness, the capacity to fabricate and create a world, is part and parcel of human "nature." We know of the existence of worldless people as we know unworldly men; human life as such requires a world only insofar as it needs a home on earth for the duration of its stay here. Certainly every arrangement men make to provide shelter and put a roof over their heads—even the tents of nomadic tribes—can serve as a home on earth for those who happen to be alive at the time; but this by no means implies that such arrangements beget a world, let alone a culture. This earthly home becomes a world in the proper sense of the word only when the totality of fabricated things is so organized that it can resist the consuming life process of the people dwelling in it, and thus outlast them. Only where such survival is assured do we speak of culture, and only where we are confronted with things which exist independently of all utilitarian and functional references, and whose quality remains always the same, do we speak of works of art.

For these reasons any discussion of culture must somehow take as its starting point the phenomenon of art. While the thingness of all things by which we surround ourselves lies in their having a shape through which they appear, only works of art are made for the sole purpose of appearance. The proper criterion by which to judge appearances is beauty; if we wanted to judge objects, even ordinary use-objects, by their use-value alone and not also by their appearance—that is, by whether they are beautiful or ugly or something in between—we would have to pluck out our eyes. But in order to become aware of appearances we first must be free to establish a certain distance between ourselves and the object, and the more important the sheer appearance of a thing is, the more distance it requires for its proper appreciation. This distance cannot arise unless we are in a position to forget ourselves, the cares and interests and urges of our lives, so that we will not seize what we admire but let it be as it is, in its appearance. This attitude of disinterested joy (to use the Kantian term, *uninteressiertes Wohlgefallen*) can be experienced only after the needs of the living organism have been provided for, so that, released from life's necessity, men may be free for the world.

The trouble with society in its earlier stages was that its members, even when they had acquired release from life's necessity, could not free themselves from concerns which had much to do with themselves, their status and position in society and the re flection of this upon their individual selves, but bore no relation whatsoever to the world of objects and objectivity they moved in. The relatively new trouble with mass society is perhaps even more serious, but not because of the masses themselves, but because this society is essentially a consumers' society where leisure time is used no longer for self-perfection or acquisition of more social status, but for more and more consumption and more and more entertainment. And since there are not enough consumer goods around to satisfy the growing appetites of a life process whose vital energy, no longer spent in the toil and trouble of a laboring body, must be used up by consumption, it is as though life itself reached out and helped itself to things which were never meant for it. The result is, of course, not mass culture which, strictly speaking, does not exist, but mass entertainment, feeding on the cultural objects of the world. To believe that such a society will become more "cultured" as time goes on and education has done its work, is, I think, a fatal mistake. The point is that a consumers' society cannot possibly know how to take care of a world and the things which belong exclusively to the space of worldly appearances, because its central attitude toward all objects, the attitude of consumption, spells ruin to everything it touches.

II

I said before that a discussion of culture is bound to take the phenomenon of art as its starting point because art works are cultural objects par excellence. Yet while culture and art are closely interrelated, they are by no means the same. The distinction between them is of no great importance for the question of what happens to culture under the conditions of society and mass society; it is relevant, however, for the problem of what culture is and in what relationship it stands to the political realm.

Culture, word and concept, is Roman in origin. The word "culture" derives from *colere*—to cultivate, to dwell, to take care, to tend and preserve—and it relates primarily to the intercourse of man with nature in the sense of cultivating and tending nature until it becomes fit for human habitation. As such, it indicates an attitude of loving care and stands in sharp contrast to all efforts to subject nature to the domination of man.[4] Hence it does not only apply to tilling the soil but can also designate the "cult" of the gods, the taking care of what properly belongs to them. It seems it was Cicero who first used the word for matters of spirit and mind. He speaks of *excolere animum,* of cultivating the mind, and of *cultura animi* in the same sense in which we speak even today of a cultured mind, only that we are no longer aware of the full metaphorical content of this usage.[5] For as far as Roman usage is concerned, the chief point always was the connection of culture with nature; culture originally meant agriculture, which was held in very high regard in Rome in opposition to the poetic and fabricating arts. Even Cicero's *cultura animi,* the result of training in philosophy and therefore perhaps coined, as has been suggested, to translate the Greek παιδεία,[6] meant the very opposite of being a fabricator or creator of art works. It was in the midst of a primarily agricultural people that the concept of culture first appeared, and the artistic connotations which might have been connected with this culture concerned the incomparably close relationship of the Latin people to nature, the creation of the famous Italian landscape. According to the Romans, art was supposed to rise as naturally as the countryside; it ought to be tended nature; and the spring of all poetry was seen in "the song which the leaves sing to themselves in the green solitude of the woods."[7] But though this may be an eminently poetic thought, it is not likely that great art would ever have sprung from it. It is hardly the mentality of gardeners which produces art.

The great Roman art and poetry came into being under the impact of the Greek heritage, which the Romans, but never the Greeks, knew how to take care of and how to preserve. The reason why there is no Greek equivalent to the Roman concept of culture lies in the predominance of the fabricating arts in Greek civilization. While the Romans tended to regard even art as a kind of agriculture, of cultivating nature, the Greeks tended to consider even agriculture as part and parcel of fabrication, as belonging to the cunning, skillful, "technical" devices with which man, more awe-inspiring than all that is, tames and rules nature. What we, still under the spell of the Roman heritage, consider to be the most natural and the most peaceful of man's activities, the tilling of the soil, the Greeks understood as a daring, violent enterprise in which, year in year out, the earth, inexhaustible and indefatigable, is disturbed and violated.[8] The Greeks did not know what culture is because they did not cultivate nature but rather tore from the womb of the earth the fruits which the gods had hidden from men (Hesiod); and closely connected with this was that the great Roman reverence for the testimony of the past as such, to which we owe not merely the preservation of the Greek heritage but the very continuity of our tradition, was quite alien to them. Both together, culture in the sense of developing nature into a dwelling place for a people as well as in the sense of taking care of the monuments of the past, determine even today the content and the meaning we have in mind when we speak of culture.

Yet the meaning of the word "culture" is hardly exhausted by these strictly Roman elements. Even Cicero's *cultura animi* is suggestive of something like taste and, generally, sensitivity to beauty, not in those who fabricate beautiful things, that is, in the artists themselves, but in the spectators, in those who move among them. And this love for beauty the Greeks possessed, of course, to an extraordinary degree. In this sense we understand by culture the attitude toward, or, better, the mode of intercourse prescribed by civilizations with respect to the least useful and most worldly of things, the works of artists, poets, musicians, philosophers, and so forth. If we mean by culture the mode of intercourse of man with the things of the world, then we may try to understand Greek culture (as distinguished from Greek art) by recalling a much quoted saying, reported by Thucydides and attributed to Pericles, which reads as follows: φιλοκαλοῦμεν γὰρ μετ' εὐτελείας καὶ φιλοσοφοῦμεν ἄνευ μαλακίας.[9] The sentence, utterly simple, almost defies translation. What we understand as states or qualities, such as love of beauty or love of wisdom (called philosophy) is described here as an activity, as though to "love beautiful things" is no less an activity than to make them. Our translation of the qualifying words, furthermore, "accuracy of aim" and "effeminacy," fails to convey that both terms were strictly political, effeminacy being a barbarian vice and accuracy of aim the virtue of the man who knows how to act. Pericles therefore is saying something like this: "We love beauty within the limits of political judgment, and we philosophize without the barbarian vice of effeminacy."

Once the meaning of these words, which are so difficult to liberate from their hackneyed translation, begins to dawn upon us, there is much to be surprised at. First, we are told distinctly that it is the polis, the realm of politics, which sets limits to the love of wisdom and of beauty, and since we know that the Greeks thought it was the polis and "politics" (and by no means superior artistic achievements) which distinguished them from the barbarians, we must conclude that this difference was a "cultural" difference as well, a difference in their mode of intercourse with "cultural" things, a different attitude toward beauty and wisdom, which could be loved only within the limits set by the institution of the polis. In other words, it was a kind of over-refinement, an indiscriminate sensitivity which did not know how to choose that was deemed to be barbarian—and neither any primitive lack of culture as we understand it nor any specific quality in the cultural things themselves. Even more surprising perhaps is that the lack of virility, the vice of effeminacy, which we would associate with too great a love of beauty or aestheticism, is mentioned here as the specific danger of philosophy; and the knowledge of how to aim or, as we said, of how to judge, which we would have expected to be a qualification of philosophy, which must know how to aim at truth, is considered here to be necessary for the intercourse with the beautiful.

Could it be that philosophy in the Greek sense—which begins with "wonder," with θαυμάζειν, and ends (at least in Plato and Aristotle) in the speechless beholding of some unveiled truth—is more likely to lead into inactivity than love of beauty? Could it be, on the other hand, that love of beauty remains barbarous unless it is accompanied by εὐτελεία, by the faculty to take aim in judgment, discernment, and discrimination, in brief, by that curious and ill-defined capacity we commonly call taste? And finally, could it be that this right love of beauty, the proper kind of intercourse with beautiful things—the *cultura animi* which makes man fit to take care of the things of the world and which Cicero, in contradistinction to the Greeks, ascribed to philosophy—has something to do with politics? Could it be that taste belongs among the political faculties?

To understand the problems which these questions raise it is important to keep in mind that culture and art are not the same. One way to remain aware of the difference between them is to recall that the same men who praised love of the beautiful and the culture of the mind shared the deep ancient distrust of those artists and artisans who actually fabricated the things which then were displayed and admired. The Greeks, though not the Romans, had a word for philistinism, and this word, curiously enough, derives from a word for artists and artisans, βάναυσος; to be a philistine, a man of banausic spirit, indicated, then as today, an exclusively utilitarian mentality, an inability to think and to judge a thing apart from its function or utility. But the artist himself, being a βάναυσος, was by no means excluded from the reproach of philistinism; on the contrary, philistinism was considered to be a vice most likely to occur in those who had mastered a τέχνη, in fabricators and artists. To Greek understanding, there was no contradiction between praise of φιλοκαλεῖν, the love of the beautiful, and contempt for those who actually produced the beautiful. The mistrust and actual contempt of the artists arose from political considerations: fabrication of things, including the production of art, is not within the range of political activities; it even stands in opposition to them. The chief reason of the distrust of fabrication in all forms is that it is utilitarian by its very nature. Fabrication, but not action or speech, always involves means and ends; in fact, the category of means and ends derives its legitimacy from the sphere of making and fabricating where a clearly recognizable end, the final product, determines and organizes everything that plays a part in the process—the material, the tools, the activity itself, and even the persons participating in it; they all become mere means toward the end and they are justified as such. Fabricators cannot help regarding all things as means to their ends or, as the case may be, judging all things by their specific utility. The moment this point of view is generalized and extended to other realms than that of fabrication it will produce the banausic mentality. And the Greeks rightly suspected that this philistinism threatens not only the political realm, as it obviously does because it will judge action by the same standards of utility which are valid for fabrication, demand that action obtain a predetermined end and that it be permitted to seize on all means likely to further this end; it also threatens the cultural realm itself because it leads to a devaluation of things as things which, if the mentality that brought them into being is permitted to prevail, will again be judged according to the standard of utility and thereby lose their intrinsic, independent worth, and finally degenerate into mere means. In other words, the greatest threat to the existence of the finished work arises precisely from the mentality which brought it into being. From which it follows that the standards and rules which must necessarily prevail in erecting and building and decorating the world of things in which we move, lose their validity and become positively dangerous when they are applied to the finished world itself.

This, to be sure, does not tell the whole story of the relation between politics and art. Rome in her early period was so convinced that artists and poets pursued a childish game which did not accord with the *gravitas,* the seriousness and dignity, proper to a Roman citizen, that she simply suppressed whatever artistic talents might have flourished in the republic prior to Greek influence. Athens, on the contrary, never settled the conflict between politics and art unequivocally in favor of one or the other—which incidentally may be one of the reasons for the extraordinary display of artistic genius in classical Greece—and she kept the conflict alive and did not level it out to indifference of the two realms with regard to each other. The Greeks, so to speak, could say in one and the same breath: "He who has not seen the Zeus of Phidias at Olympia has lived in vain" *and:* "People like Phidias, namely sculptors, are unfit for citizenship." And Pericles, in the same oration in which he praises the right φιλοσοφεῖν and φιλοκαλεῖν, the active intercourse with wisdom and beauty, boasts that Athens will know how to put "Homer and his ilk" in their place, that the glory of her deeds will be so great that the city will be able to dispense with the professional fabricators of glory, the poets and artists who reify the living word and the living deed, transforming and converting them into things permanent enough to carry greatness into the immortality of fame.

We today are more likely to suspect that the realm of politics and active participation in public business give rise to philistinism and prevent the development of a cultivated mind which can regard things in their true worth without reflection upon their function and utility. One of the reasons for this shift of emphasis is, of course, that—for reasons outside these considerations—the mentality of fabrication has invaded the political realm to such an extent that we take it for granted that action, even more than fabrication, is determined by the category of means and ends. This situation, however, has the advantage that the fabricators and artists have been able to give vent to their own view of these matters and to articulate their hostility against the men of action. There is more behind this hostility than competition for the public eye. The trouble is that *Homo faber* does not stand in the same relationship to the public realm and its publicity as the things he makes, with their appearance, configuration, and form. In order to be in a position to add constantly new things to the already existing world, he himself must be isolated from the public, must be sheltered and concealed from it. Truly political activities, on the other hand, acting and speaking, cannot be performed at all without the presence of others, without the public, without a space constituted by the many. The activity of the artist and of the craftsman is therefore subject to conditions very different from those surrounding political activities, and it is quite understandable that the artist, as soon as he begins to speak his mind on things political, should feel the same distrust for the specifically political realm and its publicity as did the polis for the mentality and conditions of fabrication. This is the true malaise of the artist, not in society but in politics, and his scruples and distrust of political activity are no less legitimate than the mistrust of men of action against the mentality of *Homo faber*. At this point the conflict between art and politics arises, and this conflict cannot and must not be solved.

However, the point of the matter is that the conflict, dividing the statesman and the artist in their respective activities, no longer applies when we turn our attention from the making of art to its products, to the things themselves which must find their place in the world. These things obviously share with political "products," words and deeds, the quality that they are in need of some public space where they can appear and be seen; they can fulfill their own being, which is appearance, only in a world which is common to all; in the concealment of private life and private possession, art objects cannot attain their own inherent validity, they must, on the contrary, be protected against the possessiveness of individuals— whereby it does not matter whether this protection takes the form of their being set up in holy places, in temples and churches, or placed in the care of museums and the keepers of monuments, although the place where we put them is characteristic of our "culture," that is, of the mode of our intercourse with them. Generally speaking, culture indicates that the public realm, which is rendered politically secure by men of action, offers its space of display to those things whose essence it is to appear and to be beautiful. In other words, culture indicates that art and politics, their conflicts and tensions notwithstanding, are interrelated and even mutually dependent. Seen against the background of political experiences and of activities which, if left to themselves, come and go without leaving any trace in the world, beauty is the very manifestation of imperishability. The fleeting greatness of word and deed can endure in the world to the extent that beauty is bestowed upon it. Without the beauty, that is, the radiant glory in which potential immortality is made manifest in the human world, all human life would be futile and no greatness could endure.

The common element connecting art and politics is that they both are phenomena of the public world. What mediates the conflict between the artist and the man of action is the *cultura animi,* that is, a mind so trained and cultivated that it can be trusted to tend and take care of a world of appearances whose criterion is beauty. The reason Cicero ascribed this culture to a training in philosophy was that to him only philosophers, the lovers of wisdom, approached things as mere "spectators" without any wish to acquire something for themselves, so that he could liken the philosophers to those who, coming to the great games and festivals, sought neither "to win the glorious distinction of a crown" nor to make "gain by buying or selling" but were attracted by the "spectacle and closely watched what was done and how it was done." They were, as we would say today, completely disinterested and for this very reason those best qualified to judge, but also those who were most fascinated by the spectacle itself. Cicero calls them *maxime ingenuum,* the most noble group of the free-born men, for what they were doing: to look for the sake of seeing only was the freest, *liberalissimum,* of all pursuits.[10]

For lack of a better word that would indicate the discriminating, discerning, judging elements of an active love of beauty—that φιλοκαλεῖν μετ᾽ εὐτελείας of which Pericles speaks—I used the word "taste," and in order to justify this usage and, at the same time, to point out the one activity in which, I think, culture as such expresses itself, I should like to draw upon the first part of Kant's *Critique of Judgment,* which, as "Critique of Esthetic Judgment," contains perhaps the greatest and most original aspect of Kant's political philosophy. At any rate, it contains an analytic of the beautiful primarily from the viewpoint of the judging spectator, as even the title indicates, and it takes its starting point from the phenomenon of taste, understood as an active relationship to what is beautiful.

In order to see the faculty of judgment in its proper perspective and to understand that it implies a political rather than a merely theoretical activity, we must shortly recall what is usually considered to be Kant's political philosophy, namely, the *Critique of Practical Reason,* which deals with the lawgiving faculty of reason. The principle of lawgiving, as laid down in the "categorical imperative"—"always act in such a manner that the principle of your action can become a general law"—is based upon the necessity for rational thought to agree with itself. The thief, for instance, is actually contradicting himself, for he cannot wish that the principle of his action, stealing other people's property, should become a general law; such a law would immediately deprive him of his own acquisition. This principle of agreement with oneself is very old; it was actually discovered by Socrates, whose central tenet, as formulated by Plato, is contained in the sentence: "Since I am one, it is better for me to disagree with the whole world than to be in disagreement with myself." [11] From this sentence both Occidental ethics, with its stress upon being in agreement with one's own conscience, and Occidental logic, with its emphasis upon the axiom of contradiction, took their starting point.

In the *Critique of Judgement,* however, Kant insisted upon a different way of thinking, for which it would not be enough to be in agreement with one's own self, but which consisted of being able to "think in the place of everybody else" and which he therefore called an "enlarged mentality" (*eine erweiterte Denkungsart*).[12] The power of judgment rests on a potential agreement with others, and the thinking process which is active in judging something is not, like the thought process of pure reasoning, a dialogue between me and myself, but finds itself always and primarily, even if I am quite alone in making up my mind, in an anticipated communication with others with whom I know I must finally come to some agreement. From this potential agreement judgment derives its specific validity. This means, on the one hand, that such judgment must liberate itself from the "subjective private conditions," that is, from the idiosyncrasies which naturally determine the outlook of each individual in his privacy and are legitimate as long as they are only privately held opinions, but which are not fit to enter the market place, and lack all validity in the public realm. And this enlarged way of thinking, which as judgment knows how to transcend its own individual limitations, on the other hand, cannot function in strict isolation or solitude; it needs the presence of others "in whose place" it must think, whose perspectives it must take into consideration, and without whom it never has the opportunity to operate at all. As logic, to be sound, depends on the presence of the self, so judgment, to be valid, depends on the presence of others. Hence judgment is endowed with a certain specific validity but is never universally valid. Its claims to validity can never extend further than the others in whose place the judging person has put himself for his considerations. Judgment, Kant says, is valid "for every single judging person," [13] but the emphasis in the sentence is on "judging"; it is not valid for those who do not judge or for those who are not members of the public realm where the objects of judgment appear.

That the capacity to judge is a specifically political ability in exactly the sense denoted by Kant, namely, the ability to see things not only from one's own point of view but in the perspective of all those who happen to be present; even that judgment may be one of the fundamental abilities of man as a political being insofar as it enables him to orient himself in the public realm, in the common world—these are insights that are virtually as old as articulated political experience. The Greeks called this ability φρόνησις, or insight, and they considered it the principal virtue or excellence of the statesman in distinction from the wisdom of the philosopher.[14] The difference between this judging insight and speculative thought lies in that the former has its roots in what we usually call common sense, which the latter constantly transcends. Common sense— which the French so suggestively call the "good sense," *le bon sens* —discloses to us the nature of the world insofar as it is a common world; we owe to it the fact that our strictly private and "subjective" five senses and their sensory data can adjust themselves to a nonsubjective and "objective" world which we have in common and share with others. Judging is one, if not the most, important activity in which this sharing-the-world-with-others comes to pass.

What, however, is quite new and even startlingly new in Kant's propositions in the *Critique of Judgment* is that he discovered this phenomenon in all its grandeur precisely when he was examining the phenomenon of taste and hence the only kind of judgments which, since they concern merely aesthetic matters, have always been supposed to lie outside the political realm as well as the domain of reason. Kant was disturbed by the alleged arbitrariness and sub-jectivity of *de gustibus non disputandum est* (which, no doubt, is entirely true for private idiosyncrasies), for this arbitrariness of-fended his political and not his aesthetic sense. Kant, who certainly was not oversensitive to beautiful things, was highly conscious of the public quality of beauty; and it was because of their public rele-vance that he insisted, in opposition to the commonplace adage, that taste judgments are open to discussion because "we hope that the same pleasure is shared by others," that taste can be subject to dispute, because it "expects agreement from everyone else." [15] Therefore taste, insofar as it, like any other judgment, appeals to common sense, is the very opposite of "private feelings." In aes-thetic no less than in political judgments, a decision is made, and al-though this decision is always determined by a certain subjectivity, by the simple fact that each person occupies a place of his own from which he looks upon and judges the world, it also derives from the fact that the world itself is an objective datum, something com-mon to all its inhabitants. The activity of taste decides how this world, independent of its utility and our vital interests in it, is to look and sound, what men will see and what they will hear in it. Taste judges the world in its appearance and in its worldliness; its interest in the world is purely "disinterested," and that means that neither the life interests of the individual nor the moral interests of the self are involved here. For judgments of taste, the world is the primary thing, not man, neither man's life nor his self.

Taste judgments, furthermore, are currently held to be arbitrary because they do not compel in the sense in which demonstrable facts or truth proved by argument compel agreement. They share with political opinions that they are persuasive; the judging person —as Kant says quite beautifully—can only "woo the consent of everyone else" in the hope of coming to an agreement with him eventually.[16] This "wooing" or persuading corresponds closely to what the Greeks called πείθειν, the convincing and persuading speech which they regarded as the typically political form of peo-ple talking with one another. Persuasion ruled the intercourse of the citizens of the polis because it excluded physical violence; but the philosophers knew that it was also distinguished from another non-violent form of coercion, the coercion by truth. Persuasion appears in Aristotle as the opposite to διαλέγεσθαι, the philosophical form of speaking, precisely because this type of dialogue was concerned with knowledge and the finding of truth and therefore demanded a process of compelling proof. Culture and politics, then, belong together because it is not knowledge or truth which is at stake, but rather judgment and decision, the judicious exchange of opinion about the sphere of public life and the common world, and the decision what manner of action is to be taken in it, as well as to how it is to look henceforth, what kind of things are to appear in it.

To classify taste, the chief cultural activity, among man's political abilities sounds so strange that I may add another much more familiar but theoretically little-regarded fact to these considerations. We all know very well how quickly people recognize each other, and how unequivocally they can feel that they belong to each other, when they discover a kinship in questions of what pleases and displeases. From the viewpoint of this common experience, it is as though taste decides not only how the world is to look, but also who belongs together in it. If we think of this sense of belonging in political terms, we are tempted to regard taste as an essentially aristocratic principle of organization. But its political significance is perhaps more far-reaching and at the same time more profound. Wherever people judge the things of the world that are common to them, there is more implied in their judgments than these things. By his manner of judging, the person discloses to an extent also himself, what kind of person he is, and this disclosure, which is involuntary, gains in validity to the degree that it has liberated itself from merely individual idiosyncrasies. Now, it is precisely the realm of acting and speaking, that is, the political domain in terms of activities, in which this personal quality comes to the fore in public, in which the "who one is" becomes manifest rather than the qualities and individual talents he may possess. In this respect, the political realm is again opposed to the domain in which the artist and fabricator live and do their work and in which ultimately it is always quality that counts, the talents of the maker and the quality of the thing he makes. Taste, however, does not simply judge this quality. On the contrary, quality is beyond dispute, it is no less compellingly evident than truth and stands beyond the decisions of judgment, beyond the need of persuasion and wooing agreement, although there are times of artistic and cultural decay when only few are left who are still receptive to the self-evidence of quality. Taste as the activity of a truly cultivated mind—*cultura animi*—comes into play only where quality-consciousness is widely disseminated, the truly beautiful easily recognized; for taste discriminates and decides among qualities. As such, taste and its ever-alert judgment of things of the world sets its own limits to an indiscriminate, immoderate love of the merely beautiful; into the realm of fabrication and of quality it introduces the personal factor, that is, gives it a humanistic meaning. Taste debarbarizes the world of the beautiful by not being overwhelmed by it; it takes care of the beautiful in its own "personal" way and thus produces a "culture."

Humanism, like culture, is of course of Roman origin; there is again no word in the Greek language corresponding to the Latin *humanitas*.[17] It will not be inappropriate, therefore, if—to conclude these remarks—I choose a Roman example to illustrate the sense in which taste is the political capacity that truly humanizes the beautiful and creates a culture. There exists an odd statement of Cicero which sounds as though it were deliberately framed to counter the then current Roman commonplace: *Amicus Socrates, amicus Plato, sed magis aestimanda veritas*. This old adage, whether one agrees with it or not, must have offended the Roman sense of *humanitas,* of the integrity of the person as person; for human worth and personal rank, together with friendship, are sacrificed here to the primacy of an absolute truth. Nothing, at any rate, could be further from the ideal of absolute, compelling truth than what Cicero has to say: *Errare mehercule malo cum Platone . . . quam cum istis* (*sc. Pythagoraeis*) *vera sentire*—"I prefer before heaven to go astray with Plato rather than hold true views with his opponents."[18] The English translation blurs a certain ambiguity of the text; the sentence can mean: I would rather go astray with Platonic rationality than "feel" (*sentire*) the truth with Pythagorean irrationality, but this interpretation is unlikely in view of the answer given in the dialogue: "I should not myself be unwilling to go astray with such a man" (*Ego enim ipse cum eodem isto non invitus erraverim*), where the stress again is on the person with whom one goes astray. Thus, it seems safe to follow the English translation, and then the sentence clearly says: It is a matter of taste to prefer Plato's company and the company of his thoughts even if this should lead us astray from truth. Certainly a very bold, even an outrageously bold statement, especially because it concerns truth; obviously the same could be said and decided with respect to beauty, which for those who have trained their senses as much as most of us have trained our minds is no less compelling than truth. What Cicero in fact says is that for the true humanist neither the verities of the scientist nor the truth of the philosopher nor the beauty of the artist can be absolutes; the humanist, because he is not a specialist, exerts a faculty of judgment and taste which is beyond the coercion which each specialty imposes upon us. This Roman *humanitas* applied to men who were free in every respect, for whom the question of freedom, of not being coerced, was the decisive one—even in philosophy, even in science, even in the arts. Cicero says: In what concerns my association with men and things, I refuse to be coerced even by truth, even by beauty.[19]

This humanism is the result of the *cultura animi,* of an attitude that knows how to take care and preserve and admire the things of the world. As such, it has the task of arbitrating and mediating between the purely political and the purely fabricating activities, which are opposed to each other in many ways. As humanists, we can rise above these conflicts between the statesman and the artist as we can rise in freedom above the specialties which we all must learn and pursue. We can rise above specialization and philistinism of all sorts to the extent that we learn how to exercise our taste freely. Then we shall know how to reply to those who so frequently tell us that Plato or some other great author of the past has been superseded; we shall be able to understand that even if all criticism of Plato is right, Plato may still be better company than his critics. At any rate, we may remember what the Romans—the first people that took culture seriously the way we do—thought a cultivated person ought to be: one who knows how to choose his company among men, among things, among thoughts, in the present as well as in the past.

7

TRUTH AND POLITICS*

I

THE subject of these reflections is a commonplace. No one has ever doubted that truth and politics are on rather bad terms with each other, and no one, as far as I know, has ever counted truthfulness among the political virtues. Lies have always been regarded as necessary and justifiable tools not only of the politician's or the demagogue's but also of the statesman's trade. Why is that so? And what does it mean for the nature and the dignity of the political realm, on one side, and for the nature and the dignity of

* This essay was caused by the so-called controversy after the publication of *Eichmann in Jerusalem*. Its aim is to clarify two different, though interconnected, issues of which I had not been aware before and whose importance seemed to transcend the occasion. The first concerns the question of whether it is always legitimate to tell the truth—did I believe without qualification in *"Fiat veritas, et pereat mundus"*? The second arose through the amazing amount of lies used in the "controversy"—lies about what I had written, on one hand, and about the facts I had reported, on the other. The following reflections try to come to grips with both issues. They may also serve as an example of what happens to a highly topical subject when it is drawn into that gap between past and future which is perhaps the proper habitat of all reflections. The reader will find a brief and preliminary consideration of this gap in the Preface.

truth and truthfulness, on the other? Is it of the very essence of truth to be impotent and of the very essence of power to be deceitful? And what kind of reality does truth possess if it is powerless in the public realm, which more than any other sphere of human life guarantees reality of existence to natal and mortal men—that is, to beings who know they have appeared out of non-being and will, after a short while, again disappear into it? Finally, is not impotent truth just as despicable as power that gives no heed to truth? These are uncomfortable questions, but they arise necessarily out of our current convictions in this matter.

What lends this commonplace its high plausibility can still be summed up in the old Latin adage *"Fiat iustitia, et pereat mundus"* ("Let justice be done though the world may perish"). Apart from its probable author in the sixteenth century (Ferdinand I, successor to Charles V), no one has used it except as a rhetorical question: Should justice be done if the world's survival is at stake? And the only great thinker who dared to go against the grain of the question was Immanuel Kant, who boldly explained that the "proverbial saying . . . means in simple language: 'Justice shall prevail, even though all the rascals in the world should perish as a result.' " Since men would not find it worth while to live in a world utterly deprived of justice, this "human right must be held sacred, regardless of how much sacrifice is required of the powers that be . . . regardless of what might be the physical consequences thereof." [1] But isn't this answer absurd? Doesn't the care for existence clearly precede everything else—every virtue and every principle? Is it not obvious that they become mere chimeras if the world, where alone they can be manifested, is in jeopardy? Wasn't the seventeenth century right when it almost unanimously declared that every commonwealth was duty bound to recognize, in Spinoza's words, "no higher law than the safety of [its] own realm"? [2] For surely every principle that transcends sheer existence can be put in the place of justice, and if we put truth in its place—*"Fiat veritas, et pereat mundus"*—the old saying sounds even more plausible. If we understand political action in terms of the means-end category, we may even come to the only seemingly paradoxical conclusion that lying can very well serve to establish or safeguard the conditions for the search after truth—as Hobbes, whose relentless logic never fails to carry arguments to those extremes where their absurdity becomes obvious, pointed out long ago.[3] And lies, since they are often used as substitutes for more violent means, are apt to be considered relatively harmless tools in the arsenal of political action.

Reconsidering the old Latin saying, it will therefore come as something of a surprise that the sacrifice of truth for the survival of the world would be more futile than the sacrifice of any other principle or virtue. For while we may refuse even to ask ourselves whether life would still be worth living in a world deprived of such notions as justice and freedom, the same, curiously, is not possible with respect to the seemingly so much less political idea of truth. What is at stake is survival, the perseverance in existence (*in suo esse perseverare*), and no human world destined to outlast the short life span of mortals within it will ever be able to survive without men willing to do what Herodotus was the first to undertake consciously—namely, λέγειν τα ἐόντα, to say what is. No permanence, no perseverance in existence, can even be conceived of without men willing to testify to what is and appears to them because it is.

The story of the conflict between truth and politics is an old and complicated one, and nothing would be gained by simplification or moral denunciation. Throughout history, the truth-seekers and truthtellers have been aware of the risks of their business; as long as they did not interfere with the course of the world, they were covered with ridicule, but he who forced his fellow-citizens to take him seriously by trying to set them free from falsehood and illusion was in danger of his life: "If they could lay hands on [such a] man . . . they would kill him," Plato says in the last sentence of the cave allegory. The Platonic conflict between truthteller and citizens cannot be explained by the Latin adage, or any of the later theories that, implicitly or explicitly, justify lying, among other transgressions, if the survival of the city is at stake. No enemy is mentioned in Plato's story; the many live peacefully in their cave among themselves, mere spectators of images, involved in no action and hence threatened by nobody. The members of this community have no reason whatever to regard truth and truthtellers as their worst enemies, and Plato offers no explanation of their perverse love of deception and falsehood. If we could confront him with one of his later colleagues in political philosophy—namely, with Hobbes, who held that only "such truth, as opposeth no man's profit, nor pleasure, is to all men welcome" (an obvious statement, which, however, he thought important enough to end his *Leviathan* with)—he might agree about profit and pleasure but not with the assertion that there existed any kind of truth welcome to all men. Hobbes, but not Plato, consoled himself with the existence of indifferent truth, with "subjects" about which "men care not"—e.g., with mathematical truth, "the doctrine of lines and figures" that "crosses no man's ambition, profit or lust." For, Hobbes wrote, "I doubt not, but if it had been a thing contrary to any man's right of dominion, or to the interest of men that have dominion, that the three angles of a triangle should be equal to two angles of a square; that doctrine should have been, if not disputed, yet by the burning of all books of geometry, suppressed, as far as he whom it concerned was able." [4]

No doubt, there is a decisive difference between Hobbes' mathematical axiom and the true standard for human conduct that Plato's philosopher is supposed to bring back from his journey into the sky of ideas, although Plato, who believed that mathematical truth opened the eyes of the mind to all truths, was not aware of it. Hobbes' example strikes us as relatively harmless; we are inclined to assume that the human mind will always be able to reproduce such axiomatic statements as "the three angles of a triangle should be equal to two angles of a square," and we conclude that "the burning of all books of geometry" would not be radically effective. The danger would be considerably greater with respect to scientific statements; had history taken a different turn, the whole modern scientific development from Galileo to Einstein might not have come to pass. And certainly the most vulnerable truth of this kind would be those highly differentiated and always unique thought trains—of which Plato's doctrine of ideas is an eminent example—whereby men, since time immemorial, have tried to think rationally beyond the limits of human knowledge.

The modern age, which believes that truth is neither given to nor disclosed to but produced by the human mind, has assigned, since Leibniz, mathematical, scientific, and philosophical truths to the common species of rational truth as distinguished from factual truth. I shall use this distinction for the sake of convenience without discussing its intrinsic legitimacy. Wanting to find out what injury political power is capable of inflicting upon truth, we look into these matters for political rather than philosophical reasons, and hence can afford to disregard the question of what truth is, and be content to take the word in the sense in which men commonly understand it. And if we now think of factual truths—of such modest verities as the role during the Russian Revolution of a man by the name of Trotsky, who appears in none of the Soviet Russian history books—we at once become aware of how much more vulnerable they are than all the kinds of rational truth taken together. Moreover, since facts and events—the invariable outcome of men living and acting together—constitute the very texture of the political realm, it is, of course, factual truth that we are most concerned with here. Dominion (to speak Hobbes' language) when it attacks rational truth oversteps, as it were, its domain, while it gives battle on its own ground when it falsifies or lies away facts. The chances of factual truth surviving the onslaught of power are very slim indeed; it is always in danger of being maneuvered out of the world not only for a time but, potentially, forever. Facts and events are infinitely more fragile things than axioms, discoveries, theories—even the most wildly speculative ones—produced by the human mind; they occur in the field of the ever-changing affairs of men, in whose flux there is nothing more permanent than the admittedly relative permanence of the human mind's structure. Once they are lost, no rational effort will ever bring them back. Perhaps the chances that Euclidean mathematics or Einstein's theory of relativity—let alone Plato's philosophy—would have been reproduced in time if their authors had been prevented from handing them down to posterity are not very good either, yet they are infinitely better than the chances that a fact of importance, forgotten or, more likely, lied away, will one day be rediscovered.

II

Although the politically most relevant truths are factual, the conflict between truth and politics was first discovered and articulated with respect to rational truth. The opposite of a rationally true statement is either error and ignorance, as in the sciences, or illusion and opinion, as in philosophy. Deliberate falsehood, the plain lie, plays its role only in the domain of factual statements, and it seems significant, and rather odd, that in the long debate about this antagonism of truth and politics, from Plato to Hobbes, no one, apparently, ever believed that organized lying, as we know it today, could be an adequate weapon against truth. In Plato, the truth-teller is in danger of his life, and in Hobbes, where he has become an author, he is threatened with the burning of his books; mere mendacity is not an issue. It is the sophist and the ignoramus rather than the liar who occupy Plato's thought, and where he distinguishes between error and lie—that is, between "involuntary and voluntary $\psi\epsilon\hat{v}\delta o\varsigma$"—he is, characteristically, much harsher on people 'wallowing in swinish ignorance" than on liars.[5] Is this because organized lying, dominating the public realm, as distinguished from the private liar who tries his luck on his own hook, was still unknown? Or has this something to do with the striking fact that, except for Zoroastrianism, none of the major religions included lying as such, as distinguished from "bearing false witness," in their catalogues of grave sins? Only with the rise of Puritan morality, coinciding with the rise of organized science, whose progress had to be assured on the firm ground of the absolute veracity and reliability of every scientist, were lies considered serious offenses.

However that may be, historically the conflict between truth and politics arose out of two diametrically opposed ways of life—the life of the philosopher, as interpreted first by Parmenides and then by Plato, and the way of life of the citizen. To the citizens' ever-changing opinions about human affairs, which themselves were in a state of constant flux, the philosopher opposed the truth about those things which in their very nature were everlasting and from which, therefore, principles could be derived to stabilize human affairs. Hence the opposite to truth was mere opinion, which was equated with illusion, and it was this degrading of opinion that gave the conflict its political poignancy; for opinion, and not truth, belongs among the indispensable prerequisites of all power. "All governments rest on opinion," James Madison said, and not even the most autocratic ruler or tyrant could ever rise to power, let alone keep it, without the support of those who are like-minded. By the same token, every claim in the sphere of human affairs to an absolute truth, whose validity needs no support from the side of opinion, strikes at the very roots of all politics and all governments. This antagonism between truth and opinion was further elaborated by Plato (especially in the *Gorgias*) as the antagonism between communicating in the form of "dialogue," which is the adequate speech for philosophical truth, and in the form of "rhetoric," by which the demagogue, as we would say today, persuades the mul-titude.

Traces of this original conflict can still be found in the earlier stages of the modern age, though hardly in the world we live in. In Hobbes, for instance, we still read of an opposition of two "con-trary faculties": "solid reasoning" and "powerful eloquence," the former being "grounded upon principles of truth, the other upon opinions . . . and the passions and interests of men, which are different and mutable." [6] More than a century later, in the Age of Enlightenment, these traces have almost but not quite disappeared, and where the ancient antagonism still survives, the emphasis has shifted. In terms of pre-modern philosophy, Lessing's magnificent *"Sage jeder, was ihm Wahrheit dünkt, und die Wahrheit selbst sei Gott empfohlen"* ("Let each man say what he deems truth, and let truth itself be commended unto God") would have plainly signified, Man is not capable of truth, all his truths, alas, are δόξαι, mere opinions, whereas for Lessing it meant, on the contrary, Let us thank God that we don't know *the* truth. Even where the note of jubilation—the insight that for men, living in company, the inexhaustible richness of human discourse is infinitely more significant and meaningful than any One Truth could ever be—is absent, the awareness of the frailty of human reason has prevailed since the eighteenth century without giving rise to complaint or lamentation. We can find it in Kant's grandiose *Critique of Pure Reason*, in which reason is led to recognize its own limitations, as we hear it in the words of Madison, who more than once stressed that "the reason of man, like man himself, is timid and cautious when left alone, and acquires firmness and confidence in proportion to the number with which it is associated." [7] Considerations of this kind, much more than notions about the individual's right to self-expression, played a decisive part in the finally more or less successful struggle to obtain freedom of thought for the spoken and the printed word.

Thus Spinoza, who still believed in the infallibility of human reason and is often wrongly praised as a champion of free thought and speech, held that "every man is by indefeasible natural right the master of his own thoughts," that "every man's understanding is his own, and that brains are as diverse as palates," from which he concluded that "it is best to grant what cannot be abolished" and that laws prohibiting free thought can only result in "men thinking one thing and saying another," hence in "the corruption of good faith" and "the fostering of . . . perfidy." However, Spinoza nowhere demands freedom of speech, and the argument that human reason needs communication with others and therefore publicity for its own sake is conspicuous by its absence. He even counts man's need for communication, his inability to hide his thoughts and keep silent, among the "common failings" that the philosopher does not share. [8] Kant, on the contrary, stated that "the external power that deprives man of the freedom to communicate his thoughts publicly, *deprives him at the same time of his freedom to think*" (italics added), and that the only guarantee for "the correctness" of our thinking lies in that "we think, as it were, in community with others to whom we communicate our thoughts as they communicate theirs to us." Man's reason, being fallible, can function only if he can make "public use" of it, and this is equally true for those who, still in a state of "tutelage," are unable to use their minds "without the guidance of somebody else" and for the "scholar," who needs "the entire reading public" to examine and control his results.[9]

In this context, the question of numbers, mentioned by Madison, is of special importance. The shift from rational truth to opinion implies a shift from man in the singular to men in the plural, and this means a shift from a domain where, Madison says, nothing counts except the "solid reasoning" of one mind to a realm where "strength of opinion" is determined by the individual's reliance upon "the number which he supposes to have entertained the same opinions"—a number, incidentally, that is not necessarily limited to one's contemporaries. Madison still distinguishes this life in the plural, which is the life of the citizen, from the life of the philosopher, by whom such considerations "ought to be disregarded," but this distinction has no practical consequence, for "a nation of philosophers is as little to be expected as the philosophical race of kings wished for by Plato."[10] We may note in passing that the very notion of "a nation of philosophers" would have been a contradiction in terms for Plato, whose whole political philosophy, including its outspoken tyrannical traits, rests on the conviction that truth can be neither gained nor communicated among the many.

In the world we live in, the last traces of this ancient antagonism between the philosopher's truth and the opinions in the market place have disappeared. Neither the truth of revealed religion, which the political thinkers of the seventeenth century still treated as a major nuisance, nor the truth of the philosopher, disclosed to man in solitude, interferes any longer with the affairs of the world. In respect to the former, the separation of church and state has given us peace, and as to the latter, it ceased long ago to claim dominion—unless one takes the modern ideologies seriously as philosophies, which is difficult indeed since their adherents openly proclaim them to be political weapons and consider the whole question of truth and truthfulness irrelevant. Thinking in terms of the tradition, one may feel entitled to conclude from this state of affairs that the old conflict has finally been settled, and especially that its original cause, the clash of rational truth and opinion, has disappeared.

Strangely, however, this is not the case, for the clash of factual truth and politics, which we witness today on such a large scale, has—in some respects, at least—very similar traits. While probably no former time tolerated so many diverse opinions on religious or philosophical matters, factual truth, if it happens to oppose a given group's profit or pleasure, is greeted today with greater hostility than ever before. To be sure, state secrets have always existed; every government must classify certain information, withhold it from public notice, and he who reveals authentic secrets has always been treated as a traitor. With this I am not concerned here. The facts I have in mind are publicly known, and yet the same public that knows them can successfully, and often spontaneously, taboo their public discussion and treat them as though they were what they are not—namely, secrets. That their assertion then should prove as dangerous as, for instance, preaching atheism or some other heresy proved in former times seems a curious phenomenon, and its significance is enhanced when we find it also in countries that are ruled tyrannically by an ideological government. (Even in Hitler's Germany and Stalin's Russia it was more dangerous to talk about concentration and extermination camps, whose existence was no secret, than to hold and to utter "heretical" views on anti-Semitism, racism, and Communism.) What seems even more disturbing is that to the extent to which unwelcome factual truths are tolerated in free countries they are often, consciously or unconsciously, transformed into opinions—as though the fact of Germany's support of Hitler or of France's collapse before the German armies in 1940 or of Vatican policies during the Second World War were not a matter of historical record but a matter of opinion. Since such factual truths concern issues of immediate political relevance, there is more at stake here than the perhaps inevitable tension between two ways of life within the framework of a common and commonly recognized reality. What is at stake here is this common and factual reality itself, and this is indeed a political problem of the first order. And since factual truth, though it is so much less open to argument than philosophical truth, and so obviously within the grasp of everybody, seems often to suffer a similar fate when it is exposed in the market place—namely, to be countered not by lies and deliberate falsehoods but by opinion—it may be worth while to reopen the old and apparently obsolete question of truth versus opinion.

For, seen from the viewpoint of the truthteller, the tendency to transform fact into opinion, to blur the dividing line between them, is no less perplexing than the truthteller's older predicament, so vividly expressed in the cave allegory, in which the philosopher, upon his return from his solitary journey to the sky of everlasting ideas, tries to communicate his truth to the multitude, with the result that it disappears in the diversity of views, which to him are illusions, and is brought down to the uncertain level of opinion, so that now, back in the cave, truth itself appears in the guise of the δοκεῖ μοι ("it seems to me")—the very δόξαι he had hoped to leave behind once and for all. However, the reporter of factual truth is even worse off. He does not return from any journey into regions beyond the realm of human affairs, and he cannot console himself with the thought that he has become a stranger in this world. Similarly, we have no right to console ourselves with the notion that his truth, if truth it should be, is not of this world. If his simple factual statements are not accepted—truths seen and witnessed with the eyes of the body, and not the eyes of the mind—the suspicion arises that it may be in the nature of the political realm to deny or pervert truth of every kind, as though men were unable to come to terms with its unyielding, blatant, unpersuasive stubbornness. If this should be the case, things would look even more desperate than Plato assumed, for Plato's truth, found and actualized in solitude, transcends, by definition, the realm of the many, the world of human affairs. (One can understand that the philosopher, in his isolation, yields to the temptation to use his truth as a standard to be imposed upon human affairs; that is, to equate the transcendence inherent in philosophical truth with the altogether different kind of "transcendence" by which yardsticks and other standards of measurement are separated from the multitude of objects they are to measure, and one can equally well understand that the multitude will resist this standard, since it is actually derived from a sphere that is foreign to the realm of human affairs and whose connection with it can be justified only by a confusion.) Philosophical truth, when it enters the market place, changes its nature and becomes opinion, because a veritable μετάβασις εἰς ἄλλο γένος, a shifting not merely from one kind of reasoning to another but from one way of human existence to another, has taken place.

Factual truth, on the contrary, is always related to other people: it concerns events and circumstances in which many are involved; it is established by witnesses and depends upon testimony; it exists only to the extent that it is spoken about, even if it occurs in the domain of privacy. It is political by nature. Facts and opinions, though they must be kept apart, are not antagonistic to each other; they belong to the same realm. Facts inform opinions, and opinions, inspired by different interests and passions, can differ widely and still be legitimate as long as they respect factual truth. Freedom of opinion is a farce unless factual information is guaranteed and the facts themselves are not in dispute. In other words, factual truth informs political thought just as rational truth informs philosophical speculation.

But do facts, independent of opinion and interpretation, exist at all? Have not generations of historians and philosophers of history demonstrated the impossibility of ascertaining facts without interpretation, since they must first be picked out of a chaos of sheer happenings (and the principles of choice are surely not factual data) and then be fitted into a story that can be told only in a certain perspective, which has nothing to do with the original occurrence? No doubt these and a great many more perplexities inherent in the historical sciences are real, but they are no argument against the existence of factual matter, nor can they serve as a justification for blurring the dividing lines between fact, opinion, and interpretation, or as an excuse for the historian to manipulate facts as he pleases. Even if we admit that every generation has the right to write its own history, we admit no more than that it has the right to rearrange the facts in accordance with its own perspective; we don't admit the right to touch the factual matter itself. To illustrate this point, and as an excuse for not pursuing this issue any further: During the twenties, so a story goes, Clemenceau, shortly before his death, found himself engaged in a friendly talk with a representative of the Weimar Republic on the question of guilt for the outbreak of the First World War. "What, in your opinion," Clemenceau was asked, "will future historians think of this troublesome and controversial issue?" He replied, "This I don't know. But I know for certain that they will not say Belgium invaded Germany." We are concerned here with brutally elementary data of this kind, whose indestructibility has been taken for granted even by the most extreme and most sophisticated believers in historicism.

It is true, considerably more than the whims of historians would be needed to eliminate from the record the fact that on the night of August 4, 1914, German troops crossed the frontier of Belgium; it would require no less than a power monopoly over the entire civilized world. But such a power monopoly is far from being inconceivable, and it is not difficult to imagine what the fate of factual truth would be if power interests, national or social, had the last say in these matters. Which brings us back to our suspicion that it may be in the nature of the political realm to be at war with truth in all its forms, and hence to the question of why a commitment even to factual truth is felt to be an anti-political attitude.

III

When I said that factual, as opposed to rational, truth is not antagonistic to opinion, I stated a half-truth. All truths—not only the various kinds of rational truth but also factual truth—are opposed to opinion in their *mode of asserting validity*. Truth carries within itself an element of coercion, and the frequently tyrannical tendencies so deplorably obvious among professional truthtellers may be caused less by a failing of character than by the strain of habitually living under a kind of compulsion. Statements such as "The three angles of a triangle are equal to two angles of a square," "The earth moves around the sun," "It is better to suffer wrong than to do wrong," "In August 1914 Germany invaded Belgium" are very different in the way they are arrived at, but, once perceived as true and pronounced to be so, they have in common that they are beyond agreement, dispute, opinion, or consent. For those who accept them, they are not changed by the numbers or lack of numbers who entertain the same proposition; persuasion or dissuasion is useless, for the content of the statement is not of a persuasive nature but of a coercive one. (Thus Plato, in the *Timaeus,* draws a line between men capable of perceiving the truth and those who happen to hold right opinions. In the former, the organ for the perception of truth [*νοῦς*] is awakened through instruction, which of course implies inequality and can be said to be a mild form of coercion, whereas the latter had merely been persuaded. The views of the former, says Plato, are immovable, while the latter can always be persuaded to change their minds.[11]) What Mercier de la Rivière once remarked about mathematical truth applies to all kinds of truth: *"Euclide est un véritable despote; et les vérités géométriques qu'il nous a transmises, sont des lois véritablement despotiques."* In much the same vein, Grotius, about a hundred years earlier, had insisted—when he wished to limit the power of the absolute prince—that "even God cannot cause two times two not to make four." He was invoking the compelling force of truth against political power; he was not interested in the implied limitation of divine omnipotence. These two remarks illustrate how truth looks in the purely political perspective, from the viewpoint of power, and the question is whether power could and should be checked not only by a constitution, a bill of rights, and by a multiplicity of powers, as in the system of checks and balances, in which, in Montesquieu's words, *"le pouvoir arrête le pouvoir"*— that is, by factors that arise out of and belong to the political realm proper—but by something that arises from without, has its source outside the political realm, and is as independent of the wishes and desires of the citizens as is the will of the worst tyrant.

Seen from the viewpoint of politics, truth has a despotic character. It is therefore hated by tyrants, who rightly fear the competition of a coercive force they cannot monopolize, and it enjoys a rather precarious status in the eyes of governments that rest on consent and abhor coercion. Facts are beyond agreement and consent, and all talk about them—all exchanges of opinion based on correct information—will contribute nothing to their establishment. Unwelcome opinion can be argued with, rejected, or compromised upon, but unwelcome facts possess an infuriating stubbornness that nothing can move except plain lies. The trouble is that factual truth, like all other truth, peremptorily claims to be acknowledged and precludes debate, and debate constitutes the very essence of political life. The modes of thought and communication that deal with truth, if seen from the political perspective, are necessarily domineering; they don't take into account other people's opinions, and taking these into account is the hallmark of all strictly political thinking.

Political thought is representative. I form an opinion by considering a given issue from different viewpoints, by making present to my mind the standpoints of those who are absent; that is, I represent them. This process of representation does not blindly adopt the actual views of those who stand somewhere else, and hence look upon the world from a different perspective; this is a question neither of empathy, as though I tried to be or to feel like somebody else, nor of counting noses and joining a majority but of being and thinking in my own identity where actually I am not. The more people's standpoints I have present in my mind while I am pondering a given issue, and the better I can imagine how I would feel and think if I were in their place, the stronger will be my capacity for representative thinking and the more valid my final conclusions, my opinion. (It is this capacity for an "enlarged mentality" that enables men to judge; as such, it was discovered by Kant in the first part of his *Critique of Judgment,* though he did not recognize the political and moral implications of his discovery.) The very process of opinion formation is determined by those in whose places somebody thinks and uses his own mind, and the only condition for this exertion of the imagination is disinterested-ness, the liberation from one's own private interests. Hence, even if I shun all company or am completely isolated while forming an opinion, I am not simply together only with myself in the solitude of philosophical thought; I remain in this world of universal inter-dependence, where I can make myself the representative of every-body else. Of course, I can refuse to do this and form an opinion that takes only my own interests, or the interests of the group to which I belong, into account; nothing, indeed, is more common, even among highly sophisticated people, than the blind obstinacy that becomes manifest in lack of imagination and failure to judge. But the very quality of an opinion, as of a judgment, depends upon the degree of its impartiality.

No opinion is self-evident. In matters of opinion, but not in matters of truth, our thinking is truly discursive, running, as it were, from place to place, from one part of the world to another, through all kinds of conflicting views, until it finally ascends from these particularities to some impartial generality. Compared to this process, in which a particular issue is forced into the open that it may show itself from all sides, in every possible perspective, until it is flooded and made transparent by the full light of human com-prehension, a statement of truth possesses a peculiar opaqueness. Rational truth enlightens human understanding, and factual truth must inform opinions, but these truths, though they are never ob-scure, are not transparent either, and it is in their very nature to withstand further elucidation, as it is in the nature of light to with-stand enlightenment.

Nowhere, moreover, is this opacity more patent and more irri-tating than where we are confronted with facts and factual truth, for facts have no conclusive reason whatever for being what they are; they could always have been otherwise, and this annoying con-tingency is literally unlimited. It is because of the haphazardness of facts that pre-modern philosophy refused to take seriously the realm of human affairs, which is permeated by factuality, or to believe that any meaningful truth could ever be discovered in the "melancholy haphazardness" (Kant) of a sequence of events which constitutes the course of this world. Nor has any modern philosophy of history been able to make its peace with the intractable, unreasonable stubbornness of sheer factuality; modern philosophers have conjured up all kinds of necessity, from the dialectical necessity of a world spirit or of material conditions to the necessities of an allegedly unchangeable and known human nature, in order to cleanse the last vestiges of that apparently arbitrary "it might have been otherwise" (which is the price of freedom) from the only realm where men are truly free. It is true that in retrospect—that is, in historical perspective—every sequence of events looks as though it could not have happened otherwise, but this is an optical, or, rather, an existential, illusion: nothing could ever happen if reality did not kill, by definition, all the other potentialities originally inherent in any given situation.

In other words, factual truth is no more self-evident than opinion, and this may be among the reasons that opinion-holders find it relatively easy to discredit factual truth as just another opinion. Factual evidence, moreover, is established through testimony by eyewitnesses—notoriously unreliable—and by records, documents, and monuments, all of which can be suspected as forgeries. In the event of a dispute, only other witnesses but no third and higher instance can be invoked, and settlement is usually arrived at by way of a majority; that is, in the same way as the settlement of opinion disputes—a wholly unsatisfactory procedure, since there is nothing to prevent a majority of witnesses from being false witnesses. On the contrary, under certain circumstances the feeling of belonging to a majority may even encourage false testimony. In other words, to the extent that factual truth is exposed to the hostility of opinion-holders, it is at least as vulnerable as rational philosophical truth.

I observed before that in some respects the teller of factual truth is worse off than Plato's philosopher—that his truth has no transcendent origin and possesses not even the relatively transcendent qualities of such political principles as freedom, justice, honor, and courage, all of which may inspire, and then become manifest in, human action. We shall now see that this disadvantage has more serious consequences than we had thought; namely, consequences that concern not only the person of the truthteller but—more important—the chances for his truth to survive. Inspiration of and manifestation in human action may not be able to compete with the compelling evidence of truth, but they can compete, as we shall see, with the persuasiveness inherent in opinion. I took the Socratic proposition "It is better to suffer wrong than to do wrong" as an example of a philosophical statement that concerns human conduct, and hence has political implications. My reason was partly that this sentence has become the beginning of Western ethical thought, and partly that, as far as I know, it has remained the only ethical proposition that can be derived directly from the specifically philosophical experience. (Kant's categorical imperative, the only competitor in the field, could be stripped of its Judaeo-Christian ingredients, which account for its formulation as an imperative instead of a simple proposition. Its underlying principle is the axiom of non-contradiction—the thief contradicts himself because he wants to keep the stolen goods as his property—and this axiom owes its validity to the conditions of thought that Socrates was the first to discover.)

The Platonic dialogues tell us time and again how paradoxical the Socratic statement (a proposition, and not an imperative) sounded, how easily it stood refuted in the market place where opinion stands against opinion, and how incapable Socrates was of proving and demonstrating it to the satisfaction not of his adversaries alone but also of his friends and disciples. (The most dramatic of these passages can be found in the beginning of the *Republic*.[12] Socrates, having tried in vain to convince his adversary Thrasymachus that justice is better than injustice, is told by his disciples, Glaukon and Adeimantus, that his proof was far from convincing. Socrates admires their speeches: "There must indeed be some divine quality in your nature, if you can plead the cause of injustice so eloquently and still not be convinced yourselves that it is better than justice." In other words, they were convinced before the argument started, and all that was said to uphold the truth of the proposition not only failed to persuade the non-

convinced but had not even the force to confirm their convictions.)
Everything that can be said in its defense we find in the various
Platonic dialogues. The chief argument states that for man, *being
one,* it is better to be at odds with the whole world than to be at
odds with and contradicted by himself [13]—an argument that is
compelling indeed for the philosopher, whose thinking is characterized by Plato as a silent dialogue with himself, and whose existence therefore depends upon a constantly articulated intercourse
with himself, a splitting-into-two of the one he nevertheless *is;* for
a basic contradiction between the two partners who carry on the
thinking dialogue would destroy the very conditions of philosophizing.[14] In other words, since man contains within himself a partner
from whom he can never win release, he will be better off not to
live in company with a murderer or a liar. Or, since thought is the
silent dialogue carried on between me and myself, I must be careful to keep the integrity of this partner intact; for otherwise I shall
surely lose the capacity for thought altogether.

To the philosopher—or, rather, to man insofar as he is a thinking being—this ethical proposition about doing and suffering wrong
is no less compelling than mathematical truth. But to man insofar
as he is a citizen, an acting being concerned with the world and the
public welfare rather than with his own well-being—including, for
instance, his "immortal soul" whose "health" should have precedence over the needs of a perishable body—the Socratic statement
is not true at all. The disastrous consequences for any community
that began in all earnest to follow ethical precepts derived from
man in the singular—be they Socratic or Platonic or Christian—
have been frequently pointed out. Long before Machiavelli recommended protecting the political realm against the undiluted principles of the Christian faith (those who refuse to resist evil permit
the wicked "to do as much evil as they please"), Aristotle warned
against giving philosophers any say in political matters. (Men who
for professional reasons must be so unconcerned with "what is good
for themselves" cannot very well be trusted with what is good for
others, and least of all with the "common good," the down-to-earth
interests of the community.)[15]

Since philosophical truth concerns man in his singularity, it is unpolitical by nature. If the philosopher nevertheless wishes his truth to prevail over the opinions of the multitude, he will suffer defeat, and he is likely to conclude from this defeat that truth is impotent—a truism that is just as meaningful as if the mathematician, unable to square the circle, should deplore the fact that a circle is not a square. He may then be tempted, like Plato, to win the ear of some philosophically inclined tyrant, and in the fortunately highly unlikely case of success he might erect one of those tyrannies of "truth" which we know chiefly from the various political utopias, and which, of course, politically speaking, are as tyrannical as other forms of despotism. In the slightly less unlikely event that his truth should prevail without the help of violence, simply because men happen to concur in it, he would have won a Pyrrhic victory. For truth would then owe its prevalence not to its own compelling quality but to the agreement of the many, who might change their minds tomorrow and agree on something else; what had been philosophical truth would have become mere opinion.

Since, however, philosophical truth carries within itself an element of coercion, it may tempt the statesman under certain conditions, no less than the power of opinion may tempt the philosopher. Thus, in the Declaration of Independence, Jefferson declared certain "truths to be self-evident," because he wished to put the basic consent among the men of the Revolution beyond dispute and argument; like mathematical axioms, they should express "beliefs of men" that "depend not on their own will, but follow involuntarily the evidence proposed to their minds." [16] Yet by saying "*We hold* these truths to be self-evident," he conceded, albeit without becoming aware of it, that the statement "All men are created equal" is not self-evident but stands in need of agreement and consent—that equality, if it is to be politically relevant, is a matter of opinion, and not "the truth." There exist, on the other hand, philosophical or religious statements that correspond to this opinion—such as that all men are equal before God, or before death, or insofar as they all belong to the same species of *animal rationale*—but none of them was ever of any political or practical consequence, because the equalizer, whether God, or death, or nature, transcended and remained outside the realm in which human intercourse takes place. Such "truths" are not between men but above them, and nothing of the sort lies behind the modern or the ancient —especially the Greek—consent to equality. That all men are created equal is not self-evident nor can it be proved. We hold this opinion because freedom is possible only among equals, and we believe that the joys and gratifications of free company are to be preferred to the doubtful pleasures of holding dominion. Such preferences are politically of the greatest importance, and there are few things by which men are so profoundly distinguished from each other as by these. Their human quality, one is tempted to say, and certainly the quality of every kind of intercourse with them, depends upon such choices. Still, these are matters of opinion and not of truth—as Jefferson, much against his will, admitted. Their validity depends upon free agreement and consent; they are arrived at by discursive, representative thinking; and they are communicated by means of persuasion and dissuasion.

The Socratic proposition "It is better to suffer wrong than to do wrong" is not an opinion but claims to be truth, and though one may doubt that it ever had a direct political consequence, its impact upon practical conduct as an ethical precept is undeniable; only religious commandments, which are absolutely binding for the community of believers, can claim greater recognition. Does this fact not stand in clear contradiction to the generally accepted impotence of philosophical truth? And since we know from the Platonic dialogues how unpersuasive Socrates' statement remained for friend and foe alike whenever he tried to prove it, we must ask ourselves how it could ever have obtained its high degree of validity. Obviously, this has been due to a rather unusual kind of persuasion; Socrates decided to stake his life on this truth—to set an example, not when he appeared before the Athenian tribunal but when he refused to escape the death sentence. And this teaching by example is, indeed, the only form of "persuasion" that philosophical truth is capable of without perversion or distortion;[17] by the same token, philosophical truth can become "practical" and inspire action without violating the rules of the political realm only when it manages to become manifest in the guise of an example. This is the only chance for an ethical principle to be verified as well as validated. Thus, to verify, for instance, the notion of courage we may recall the example of Achilles, and to verify the notion of goodness we are inclined to think of Jesus of Nazareth or of St. Francis; these examples teach or persuade by inspiration, so that whenever we try to perform a deed of courage or of goodness it is as though we imitated someone else—the *imitatio Christi,* or whatever the case may be. It has often been remarked that, as Jefferson said, "a lively and lasting sense of filial duty is more effectually impressed on the mind of a son or daughter by reading *King Lear* than by all the dry volumes of ethics and divinity that ever were written," [18] and that, as Kant said, "general precepts learned at the feet either of priests or philosophers, or even drawn from one's own resources, are never so efficacious as an example of virtue or holiness." [19] The reason, as Kant explains, is that we always need "intuitions . . . to verify the reality of our concepts." "If they are pure concepts of the understanding," such as the concept of the triangle, "the intuitions go by the name of schemata," such as the ideal triangle, perceived only by the eyes of the mind and yet indispensable to the recognition of all real triangles; if, however, the concepts are practical, relating to conduct, "the intuitions are called *examples*." [20] And, unlike the schemata, which our mind produces of its own accord by means of the imagination, these examples derive from history and poetry, through which, as Jefferson pointed out, an altogether different "field of imagination is laid open to our use."

This transformation of a theoretical or speculative statement into exemplary truth—a transformation of which only moral philosophy is capable—is a borderline experience for the philosopher: by setting an example and "persuading" the multitude in the only way open to him, he has begun to act. Today, when hardly any philosophical statement, no matter how daring, will be taken seriously enough to endanger the philosopher's life, even this rare chance of having a philosophical truth politically validated has disappeared.

In our context, however, it is important to notice that such a possibility does exist for the teller of rational truth; for it does not exist under any circumstances for the teller of factual truth, who in this respect, as in other respects, is worse off. Not only do factual statements contain no principles upon which men might act and which thus could become manifest in the world; their very content defies this kind of verification. A teller of factual truth, in the unlikely event that he wished to stake his life on a particular fact, would achieve a kind of miscarriage. What would become manifest in his act would be his courage or, perhaps, his stubbornness but neither the truth of what he had to say nor even his own truthfulness. For why shouldn't a liar stick to his lies with great courage, especially in politics, where he might be motivated by patriotism or some other kind of legitimate group partiality?

IV

The hallmark of factual truth is that its opposite is neither error nor illusion nor opinion, no one of which reflects upon personal truthfulness, but the deliberate falsehood, or lie. Error, of course, is possible, and even common, with respect to factual truth, in which case this kind of truth is in no way different from scientific or rational truth. But the point is that with respect to facts there exists another alternative, and this alternative, the deliberate falsehood, does not belong to the same species as propositions that, whether right or mistaken, intend no more than to say what is, or how something that is appears to me. A factual statement—Germany invaded Belgium in August 1914—acquires political implications only by being put in an interpretative context. But the opposite proposition, which Clemenceau, still unacquainted with the art of rewriting history, thought absurd, needs no context to be of political significance. It is clearly an attempt to change the record, and as such, it is a form of *action*. The same is true when the liar, lacking the power to make his falsehood stick, does not insist on the gospel truth of his statement but pretends that this is his "opinion," to which he claims his constitutional right. This is frequently done by subversive groups, and in a politically immature public the resulting confusion can be considerable. The blurring of the dividing line between factual truth and opinion belongs among the many forms that lying can assume, all of which are forms of action.

While the liar is a man of action, the truthteller, whether he tells rational or factual truth, most emphatically is not. If the teller of factual truth wants to play a political role, and therefore to be persuasive, he will, more often than not, go to considerable lengths to explain why his particular truth serves the best interests of some group. And, just as the philosopher wins a Pyrrhic victory when his truth becomes a dominant opinion among opinion-holders, the teller of factual truth, when he enters the political realm and identifies himself with some partial interest and power formation, compromises on the only quality that could have made his truth appear plausible, namely, his personal truthfulness, guaranteed by impartiality, integrity, independence. There is hardly a political figure more likely to arouse justified suspicion than the professional truthteller who has discovered some happy coincidence between truth and interest. The liar, on the contrary, needs no such doubtful accommodation to appear on the political scene; he has the great advantage that he always is, so to speak, already in the midst of it. He is an actor by nature; he says what is not so because he wants things to be different from what they are—that is, he wants to change the world. He takes advantage of the undeniable affinity of our capacity for action, for changing reality, with this mysterious faculty of ours that enables us to *say*, "The sun is shining," when it is raining cats and dogs. If we were as thoroughly conditioned in our behavior as some philosophies have wished us to be, we would never be able to accomplish this little miracle. In other words, our ability to lie—but not necessarily our ability to tell the truth—belongs among the few obvious, demonstrable data that confirm human freedom. That we can change the circumstances under which we live at all is because we are relatively free from them, and it is this freedom that is abused and perverted through mendacity. If it is the well-nigh irresistible temptation of the professional historian to fall into the trap of necessity and implicitly deny freedom of action, it is the almost equally irresistible temptation of the professional politician to overestimate the possibilities of this freedom and implicitly condone the lying denial, or distortion of facts.

To be sure, as far as action is concerned, organized lying is a marginal phenomenon, but the trouble is that its opposite, the mere telling of facts, leads to no action whatever; it even tends, under normal circumstances, toward the acceptance of things as they are. (This, of course, is not to deny that the disclosure of facts may be legitimately used by political organizations or that, under certain circumstances, factual matters brought to public attention will considerably encourage and strengthen the claims of ethnic and social groups.) Truthfulness has never been counted among the political virtues, because it has little indeed to contribute to that change of the world and of circumstances which is among the most legitimate political activities. Only where a community has embarked upon organized lying on principle, and not only with respect to particulars, can truthfulness as such, unsupported by the distorting forces of power and interest, become a political factor of the first order. Where everybody lies about everything of importance, the truthteller, whether he knows it or not, has begun to act; he, too, has engaged himself in political business, for, in the unlikely event that he survives, he has made a start toward changing the world.

In this situation, however, he will again soon find himself at an annoying disadvantage. I mentioned earlier the contingent character of facts, which could always have been otherwise, and which therefore possess by themselves no trace of self-evidence or plausibility for the human mind. Since the liar is free to fashion his "facts" to fit the profit and pleasure, or even the mere expectations, of his audience, the chances are that he will be more persuasive than the truthteller. Indeed, he will usually have plausibility on his side; his exposition will sound more logical, as it were, since the element of unexpectedness—one of the outstanding characteristics of all events—has mercifully disappeared. It is not only rational truth that, in the Hegelian phrase, stands common sense on its head; reality quite frequently offends the soundness of common-sense reasoning no less than it offends profit and pleasure.

We must now turn our attention to the relatively recent phenomenon of mass manipulation of fact and opinion as it has become evident in the rewriting of history, in image-making, and in actual government policy. The traditional political lie, so prominent in the history of diplomacy and statecraft, used to concern either true secrets—data that had never been made public—or intentions, which anyhow do not possess the same degree of reliability as accomplished facts; like everything that goes on merely inside ourselves, intentions are only potentialities, and what was intended to be a lie can always turn out to be true in the end. In contrast, the modern political lies deal efficiently with things that are not secrets at all but are known to practically everybody. This is obvious in the case of rewriting contemporary history under the eyes of those who witnessed it, but it is equally true in image-making of all sorts, in which, again, every known and established fact can be denied or neglected if it is likely to hurt the image; for an image, unlike an old-fashioned portrait, is supposed not to flatter reality but to offer a full-fledged substitute for it. And this substitute, because of modern techniques and the mass media, is, of course, much more in the public eye than the original ever was. We are finally confronted with highly respected statesmen who, like de Gaulle and Adenauer, have been able to build their basic policies on such evident non-facts as that France belongs among the victors of the last war and hence is one of the great powers, and "that the barbarism of National Socialism had affected only a relatively small percentage of the country." [21] All these lies, whether their authors know it or not, harbor an element of violence; organized lying always tends to destroy whatever it has decided to negate, although only totalitarian governments have consciously adopted lying as the first step to murder. When Trotsky learned that he had never played a role in the Russian Revolution, he must have known that his death warrant had been signed. Clearly, it is easier to eliminate a public figure from the record of history if at the same time he can be eliminated from the world of the living. In other words, the difference between the traditional lie and the modern lie will more often than not amount to the difference between hiding and destroying.

Moreover, the traditional lie concerned only particulars and was never meant to deceive literally everybody; it was directed at the enemy and was meant to deceive only him. These two limitations restricted the injury inflicted upon truth to such an extent that to us, in retrospect, it may appear almost harmless. Since facts always occur in a context, a particular lie—that is, a falsehood that makes no attempt to change the whole context—tears, as it were, a hole in the fabric of factuality. As every historian knows, one can spot a lie by noticing incongruities, holes, or the junctures of patched-up places. As long as the texture as a whole is kept intact, the lie will eventually show up as if of its own accord. The second limitation concerns those who are engaged in the business of deception. They used to belong to the restricted circle of statesmen and diplomats, who among themselves still knew and could preserve the truth. They were not likely to fall victims to their own falsehoods; they could deceive others without deceiving themselves. Both of these mitigating circumstances of the old art of lying are noticeably absent from the manipulation of facts that confronts us today.

What, then, is the significance of these limitations, and why are we justified in calling them mitigating circumstances? Why has self-deception become an indispensable tool in the trade of image-making, and why should it be worse, for the world as well as for the liar himself, if he is deceived by his own lies than if he merely deceives others? What better moral excuse could a liar offer than that his aversion to lying was so great that he had to convince himself before he could lie to others, that, like Antonio in *The Tempest,* he had to make "a sinner of his memory, To credit his own lie"? And, finally, and perhaps most disturbingly, if the modern political lies are so big that they require a complete rearrangement of the whole factual texture—the making of another reality, as it were, into which they will fit without seam, crack, or fissure, exactly as the facts fitted into their own original context—what prevents these new stories, images, and non-facts from becoming an adequate substitute for reality and factuality?

A medieval anecdote illustrates how difficult it can be to lie to others without lying to oneself. It is a story about what happened one night in a town on whose watchtower a sentry was on duty day and night to warn the people of the approach of the enemy. The sentry was a man given to practical jokes, and that night he sounded the alarm just in order to give the townsfolk a little scare. His success was overwhelming: everybody rushed to the walls and the last to rush was the sentry himself. The tale suggests to what extent our apprehension of reality is dependent upon our sharing the world with our fellow-men, and what strength of character is required to stick to anything, truth or lie, that is unshared. In other words, the more successful a liar is, the more likely it is that he will fall prey to his own fabrications. Furthermore, the self-deceived joker who proves to be in the same boat as his victims will appear vastly superior in trustworthiness to the cold-blooded liar who permits himself to enjoy his prank from without. Only self-deception is likely to create a semblance of truthfulness, and in a debate about facts the only persuasive factor that sometimes has a chance to prevail against pleasure, fear, and profit is personal appearance.

Current moral prejudice tends to be rather harsh in respect to cold-blooded lying, whereas the often highly developed art of self-deception is usually regarded with great tolerance and permissiveness. Among the few examples in literature that can be quoted against this current evaluation is the famous scene in the monastery at the beginning of *The Brothers Karamazov*. The father, an inveterate liar, asks the Staretz, "And what must I do to gain salvation?" and the Staretz replies, "Above all, never lie to yourself!" Dostoevski adds no explanation or elaboration. Arguments in support of the statement "It is better to lie to others than to deceive yourself" would have to point out that the cold-blooded liar remains aware of the distinction betwen truth and falsehood, so the truth he is hiding from others has not yet been maneuvered out of the world altogether; it has found its last refuge in him. The injury done to reality is neither complete nor final, and, by the same token, the injury done to the liar himself is not complete or final either. He lied, but he is not yet a liar. Both he and the world he deceived are not beyond "salvation"—to put it in the language of the Staretz.

Such completeness and potential finality, which were unknown to former times, are the dangers that arise out of the modern manipulation of facts. Even in the free world, where the government has not monopolized the power to decide and tell what factually is or is not, gigantic interest organizations have generalized a kind of *raison d'état* frame of mind such as was formerly restricted to the handling of foreign affairs and, in its worst excesses, to situations of clear and present danger. And national propaganda on the government level has learned more than a few tricks from business practices and Madison Avenue methods. Images made for domestic consumption, as distinguished from lies directed at a foreign adversary, can become a reality for everybody and first of all for the image-makers themselves, who while still in the act of preparing their "products" are overwhelmed by the mere thought of their victims' potential numbers. No doubt, the originators of the lying image who "inspire" the hidden persuaders still know that they want to deceive an enemy on the social or the national level, but the result is that a whole group of people, and even whole nations, may take their bearings from a web of deceptions to which their leaders wished to subject their opponents.

What then happens follows almost automatically. The main effort of both the deceived group and the deceivers themselves is likely to be directed toward keeping the propaganda image intact, and this image is threatened less by the enemy and by real hostile interests than by those inside the group itself who have managed to escape its spell and insist on talking about facts or events that do not fit the image. Contemporary history is full of instances in which tellers of factual truth were felt to be more dangerous, and even more hostile, than the real opponents. These arguments against self-deception must not be confused with the protests of "idealists," whatever their merit, against lying as bad in principle and against the age-old art of deceiving the enemy. Politically, the point is

that the modern art of self-deception is likely to transform an outside matter into an inside issue, so that an international or inter-
group conflict boomerangs onto the scene of domestic politics. The
self-deceptions practiced on both sides in the period of the Cold
War are too many to enumerate, but obviously they are a case in
point. Conservative critics of mass democracy have frequently out-
lined the dangers that this form of government brings to international affairs—without, however, mentioning the dangers peculiar
to monarchies or oligarchies. The strength of their arguments lies
in the undeniable fact that under fully democratic conditions deception without self-deception is well-nigh impossible.

Under our present system of world-wide communication, cover-
ing a large number of independent nations, no existing power is
anywhere near great enough to make its "image" foolproof. Therefore, images have a relatively short life expectancy; they are likely
to explode not only when the chips are down and reality makes its
reappearance in public but even before this, for fragments of facts
constantly disturb and throw out of gear the propaganda war between conflicting images. However, this is not the only way, or
even the most significant way, in which reality takes its revenge
on those who dare defy it. The life expectancy of images could
hardly be significantly increased even under a world government
or some other modern version of the Pax Romana. This is best
illustrated by the relatively closed systems of totalitarian governments and one-party dictatorships, which are, of course, by far the
most effective agencies in shielding ideologies and images from the
impact of reality and truth. (And such correction of the record is
never smooth sailing. We read in a memorandum of 1935 found in
the Smolensk Archive about the countless difficulties besetting this
kind of enterprise. What, for instance, "should be done with
speeches by Zinoviev, Kamenev, Rykov, Bukharin, *et al.,* at Party
Congresses, plenums of the Central Committee, in the Comintern,
the Congress of Soviets, etc.? What of anthologies on Marx-
ism . . . written or edited jointly by Lenin, Zinoviev, . . . and
others? What of Lenin's writings edited by Kamenev? . . . What
should be done in cases where Trotsky . . . had written an article

in an issue of the *Communist International?* Should the whole number be confiscated?" [22] Puzzling questions indeed, to which the Archive contains no replies.) Their trouble is that they must constantly change the falsehoods they offer as a substitute for the real story; changing circumstances require the substitution of one history book for another, the replacement of pages in the encyclopedias and reference books, the disappearance of certain names in favor of others unknown or little known before. And though this continuing instability gives no indication of what the truth might be, it is itself an indication, and powerful one, of the lying character of all public utterances concerning the factual world. It has frequently been noticed that the surest long-term result of brainwashing is a peculiar kind of cynicism—an absolute refusal to believe in the truth of anything, no matter how well this truth may be established. In other words, the result of a consistent and total substitution of lies for factual truth is not that the lies will now be accepted as truth, and the truth be defamed as lies, but that the sense by which we take our bearings in the real world—and the category of truth vs. falsehood is among the mental means to this end—is being destroyed.

And for this trouble there is no remedy. It is but the other side of the disturbing contingency of all factual reality. Since everything that has actually happened in the realm of human affairs could just as well have been otherwise, the possibilities for lying are boundless, and this boundlessness makes for self-defeat. Only the occasional liar will find it possible to stick to a particular falsehood with unwavering consistency; those who adjust images and stories to ever-changing circumstances will find themselves floating on the wide-open horizon of potentiality, drifting from one possibility to the next, unable to hold on to any one of their own fabrications. Far from achieving an adequate substitute for reality and factuality, they have transformed facts and events back into the potentiality out of which they originally appeared. And the surest sign of the factuality of facts and events is precisely this stubborn thereness, whose inherent contingency ultimately defies all attempts at conclusive explanation. The images, on the contrary, can always be explained and made plausible—this gives them their momentary advantage over factual truth—but they can never compete in stability with that which simply is because it happens to be thus and not otherwise. This is the reason that consistent lying, metaphorically speaking, pulls the ground from under our feet and provides no other ground on which to stand. (In the words of Montaigne, "If falsehood, like truth, had but one face, we should know better where we are, for we should then take for certain the opposite of what the liar tells us. But the reverse of truth has a thousand shapes and a boundless field.") The experience of a trembling wobbling motion of everything we rely on for our sense of direction and reality is among the most common and most vivid experiences of men under totalitarian rule.

Hence, the undeniable affinity of lying with action, with changing the world—in short, with politics—is limited by the very nature of the things that are open to man's faculty for action. The convinced image-maker is in error when he believes that he can anticipate changes by lying about factual matters that everybody wishes to eliminate anyhow. The erection of Potëmkin's villages, so dear to the politicians and propagandists of underdeveloped countries, never leads to the establishment of the real thing but only to a proliferation and perfection of make-believe. Not the past—and all factual truth, of course, concerns the past—or the present, insofar as it is the outcome of the past, but the future is open to action. If the past and present are treated as parts of the future—that is, changed back into their former state of potentiality—the political realm is deprived not only of its main stabilizing force but of the starting point from which to change, to begin something new. What then begins is the constant shifting and shuffling in utter sterility which are characteristic of many new nations that had the bad luck to be born in an age of propaganda.

That facts are not secure in the hands of power is obvious, but the point here is that power, by its very nature, can never produce a substitute for the secure stability of factual reality, which, because it is past, has grown into a dimension beyond our reach. Facts assert themselves by being stubborn, and their fragility is oddly combined with great resiliency—the same irreversibility that is the hallmark of all human action. In their stubbornness, facts are superior to power; they are less transitory than power formations, which arise when men get together for a purpose but disappear as soon as the purpose is either achieved or lost. This transitory character makes power a highly unreliable instrument for achieving permanence of any kind, and, therefore, not only truth and facts are insecure in its hands but untruth and non-facts as well. The political attitude toward facts must, indeed, tread the very narrow path between the danger of taking them as the results of some necessary development which men could not prevent and about which they can therefore do nothing and the danger of denying them, of trying to manipulate them out of the world.

V

In conclusion, I return to the questions I raised at the beginning of these reflections. Truth, though powerless and always defeated in a head-on clash with the powers that be, possesses a strength of its own: whatever those in power may contrive, they are unable to discover or invent a viable substitute for it. Persuasion and violence can destroy truth, but they cannot replace it. And this applies to rational or religious truth just as it applies, more obviously, to factual truth. To look upon politics from the perspective of truth, as I have done here, means to take one's stand outside the political realm. This standpoint is the standpoint of the truthteller, who forfeits his position—and, with it, the validity of what he has to say—if he tries to interfere directly in human affairs and to speak the language of persuasion or of violence. It is to this position and its significance for the political realm that we must now turn our attention.

The standpoint outside the political realm—outside the community to which we belong and the company of our peers—is clearly characterized as one of the various modes of being alone. Outstanding among the existential modes of truthtelling are the solitude of the philosopher, the isolation of the scientist and the artist, the impartiality of the historian and the judge, and the independence of the fact-finder, the witness, and the reporter. (This impartiality differs from that of the qualified, representative opinion, mentioned earlier, in that it is not acquired inside the political realm but is inherent in the position of the outsider required for such occupations.) These modes of being alone differ in many respects, but they have in common that as long as any one of them lasts, no political commitment, no adherence to a cause, is possible. They are, of course, common to all men; they are modes of human existence as such. Only when one of them is adopted as a way of life— and even then life is never lived in complete solitude or isolation or independence—is it likely to conflict with the demands of the political.

It is quite natural that we become aware of the non-political and, potentially, even anti-political nature of truth—*Fiat veritas, et pereat mundus*—only in the event of conflict, and I have stressed up to now this side of the matter. But this cannot possibly tell the whole story. It leaves out of account certain public institutions, established and supported by the powers that be, in which, contrary to all political rules, truth and truthfulness have always constituted the highest criterion of speech and endeavor. Among these we find notably the judiciary, which either as a branch of government or as direct administration of justice is carefully protected against social and political power, as well as all institutions of higher learning, to which the state entrusts the education of its future citizens. To the extent that the Academe remembers its ancient origins, it must know that it was founded by the polis's most determined and most influential opponent. To be sure, Plato's dream did not come true: the Academe never became a counter-society, and nowhere do we hear of any attempt by the universities at seizing power. But what Plato never dreamed of did come true: The political realm recognized that it needed an institution outside the power struggle in addition to the impartiality required in the administration of justice; for whether these places of higher learning are in private or in public hands is of no great importance; not only their integrity but their very existence depends upon the good will of the government anyway. Very unwelcome truths have emerged from the universities, and very unwelcome judgments have been handed down from the bench time and again; and these institutions, like other refuges of truth, have remained exposed to all the dangers arising from social and political power. Yet the chances for truth to prevail in public are, of course, greatly improved by the mere existence of such places and by the organization of independent, supposedly disinterested scholars associated with them. And it can hardly be denied that, at least in constitutionally ruled countries, the political realm has recognized, even in the event of conflict, that it has a stake in the existence of men and institutions over which it has no power.

This authentically political significance of the Academe is today easily overlooked because of the prominence of its professional schools and the evolution of its natural-science divisions, where, unexpectedly, pure research has yielded so many decisive results that have proved vital to the country at large. No one can possibly gainsay the social and technical usefulness of the universities, but this importance is not political. The historical sciences and the humanities, which are supposed to find out, stand guard over, and interpret factual truth and human documents, are politically of greater relevance. The telling of factual truth comprehends much more than the daily information supplied by journalists, though without them we should never find our bearings in an ever-changing world and, in the most literal sense, would never know where we are. This is, of course, of the most immediate political importance; but if the press should ever really become the "fourth branch of government," it would have to be protected against government power and social pressure even more carefully than the judiciary is. For this very important political function of supplying information is exercised from outside the political realm, strictly speaking; no action and no decision are, or should be, involved.

Reality is different from, and more than, the totality of facts and events, which, anyhow, is unascertainable. Who says what is— λέγει τὰ ἐόντα—always tells a story, and in this story the particular

facts lose their contingency and acquire some humanly comprehensible meaning. It is perfectly true that "all sorrows can be
borne if you put them into a story or tell a story about them," in
the words of Isak Dinesen, who not only was one of the great
storytellers of our time but also—and she was almost unique in
this respect—knew what she was doing. She could have added
that joy and bliss, too, become bearable and meaningful for men
only when they can talk about them and tell them as a story. To
the extent that the teller of factual truth is also a storyteller, he
brings about that "reconciliation with reality" which Hegel, the
philosopher of history *par excellence,* understood as the ultimate
goal of all philosophical thought, and which, indeed, has been the
secret motor of all historiography that transcends mere learned-
ness. The transformation of the given raw material of sheer happenings which the historian, like the fiction writer (a good novel is by
no means a simple concoction or a figment of pure fantasy), must
effect is closely akin to the poet's transfiguration of moods or movements of the heart—the transfiguration of grief into lamentations
or of jubilation into praise. We may see, with Aristotle, in the
poet's political function the operation of a catharsis, a cleansing or
purging of all emotions that could prevent men from acting. The
political function of the storyteller—historian or novelist—is to
teach acceptance of things as they are. Out of this acceptance,
which can also be called truthfulness, arises the faculty of judgment—that, again in Isak Dinesen's words, "at the end we shall be
privileged to view, and review, it—and that is what is named the
day of judgment."

There is no doubt that all these politically relevant functions are
performed from outside the political realm. They require non-com-
mitment and impartiality, freedom from self-interest in thought and
judgment. The disinterested pursuit of truth has a long history; its
origin, characteristically, precedes all our theoretical and scientific
traditions, including our tradition of philosophical and political
thought. I think it can be traced to the moment when Homer chose
to sing the deeds of the Trojans no less than those of the Achaeans,
and to praise the glory of Hector, the foe and the defeated man,

no less than the glory of Achilles, the hero of his kinfolk. This had happened nowhere before; no other civilization, however splendid, had been able to look with equal eyes upon friend and foe, upon success and defeat—which since Homer have not been recognized as ultimate standards of men's judgment, even though they are ultimates for the destinies of men's lives. Homeric impartiality echoes throughout Greek history, and it inspired the first great teller of factual truth, who became the father of history: Herodotus tells us in the very first sentences of his stories that he set out to prevent "the great and wondrous deeds of the Greeks *and* the barbarians from losing their due meed of glory." This is the root of all so-called objectivity—this curious passion, unknown outside Western civilization, for intellectual integrity at any price. Without it no science would ever have come into being.

Since I have dealt here with politics from the perspective of truth, and hence from a viewpoint outside the political realm, I have failed to mention even in passing the greatness and the dignity of what goes on inside it. I have spoken as though the political realm were no more than a battlefield of partial, conflicting interests, where nothing counted but pleasure and profit, partisanship, and the lust for dominion. In short, I have dealt with politics as though I, too, believed that all public affairs were ruled by interest and power, that there would be no political realm at all if we were not bound to take care of life's necessities. The reason for this deformation is that factual truth clashes with the political only on this lowest level of human affairs, just as Plato's philosophical truth clashed with the political on the considerably higher level of opinion and agreement. From this perspective, we remain unaware of the actual content of political life—of the joy and the gratification that arise out of being in company with our peers, out of acting together and appearing in public, out of inserting ourselves into the world by word and deed, thus acquiring and sustaining our personal identity and beginning something entirely new. However, what I meant to show here is that this whole sphere, its greatness notwithstanding, is limited—that it does not encompass the whole of man's and the world's existence. It is limited by those things which men cannot change at will. And it is only by respecting its own borders that this realm, where we are free to act and to change, can remain intact, preserving its integrity and keeping its promises. Conceptually, we may call truth what we cannot change; metaphorically, it is the ground on which we stand and the sky that stretches above us.

8

THE CONQUEST OF SPACE
AND THE STATURE
OF MAN

"**H**AS man's conquest of space increased or diminished his stature?"[1] The question raised is addressed to the layman, not the scientist, and it is inspired by the humanist's concern with man, as distinguished from the physicist's concern with the reality of the physical world. To understand physical reality seems to demand not only the renunciation of an anthropocentric or geocentric world view, but also a radical elimination of all anthropomorphic elements and principles, as they arise either from the world given to the five human senses or from the categories inherent in the human mind. The question assumes that man is the highest being we know of, an assumption which we have inherited from the Romans, whose *humanitas* was so alien to the Greeks' frame of mind that they had not even a word for it. (The reason for the absence of the word *humanitas* from Greek language and thought was that the Greeks, in contrast to the Romans, never thought that man is the highest being there is. Aristotle calls this belief *atopos,* "absurd.")[2]

This view of man is even more alien to the scientist, to whom man is no more than a special case of organic life and to whom man's habitat—the earth, together with earthbound laws—is no more than a special borderline case of absolute, universal laws, that is, laws that rule the immensity of the universe. Surely the scientist cannot permit himself to ask: What consequences will the result of my investigations have for the stature (or, for that matter, for the future). of man? It has been the glory of modern science that it has been able to emancipate itself completely from all such anthropocentric, that is, truly humanistic, concerns.

The question propounded here, insofar as it is addressed to the layman, must be answered in terms of common sense and in everyday language (if it can be answered at all). The answer is not likely to convince the scientist, because he has been forced, under the compulsion of facts and experiments, to renounce sense perception and hence common sense, by which we coordinate the perception of our five senses into the total awareness of reality. He has also been forced to renounce normal language, which even in its most sophisticated conceptual refinements remains inextricably bound to the world of the senses and to our common sense. For the scientist, man is no more than an observer of the universe in its manifold manifestations. The progress of modern science has demonstrated very forcefully to what an extent this observed universe, the infinitely small no less than the infinitely large, escapes not only the coarseness of human sense perception but even the enormously ingenious instruments that have been built for its refinement. The data with which modern physical research is concerned turn up like "mysterious messenger[s] from the real world." [3] They are not phenomena, appearances, strictly speaking, for we meet them nowhere, neither in our everyday world nor in the laboratory; we know of their presence only because they affect our measuring instruments in certain ways. And this effect, in the telling image of Eddington, may "have as much resemblance" to what they are "as a telephone number has to a subscriber." [4] The point of the matter is that Eddington, without the slightest hesitation, assumes that these physical data emerge from a "real world," more real by implication than the world we live in; the trouble is that something *physical* is present but never appears.

The goal of modern science, which eventually and quite literally has led us to the moon, is no longer "to augment and order" human experiences (as Niels Bohr,[5] still tied to a vocabulary that his own work has helped to make obsolete, described it); it is much rather to discover what lies *behind* natural phenomena as they reveal themselves to the senses and the mind of man. Had the scientist reflected upon the nature of the human sensory and mental apparatus, had he raised questions such as *What is the nature of man and what should be his stature? What is the goal of science and why does man pursue knowledge?* or even *What is life and what distinguishes human from animal life?*, he would never have arrived where modern science stands today. The answers to these questions would have acted as definitions and hence as limitations of his efforts. In the words of Niels Bohr, "Only by renouncing an explanation of life in the ordinary sense do we gain a possibility of taking into account its characteristics." [6]

That the question proposed here makes no sense to the scientist *qua* scientist is no argument against it. The question challenges the layman and the humanist to judge what the scientist is doing because it concerns all men, and this debate must of course be joined by the scientists themselves insofar as they are fellow citizens. But all answers given in this debate, whether they come from laymen or philosophers or scientists, are nonscientific (although not antiscientific); they can never be demonstrably true or false. Their truth resembles rather the validity of agreements than the compelling validity of scientific statements. Even when the answers are given by philosophers whose way of life is solitude, they are arrived at by an exchange of opinions among many men, most of whom may no longer be among the living. Such truth can never command general agreement, but it frequently outlasts the compellingly and demonstrably true statements of the sciences which, especially in recent times, have the uncomfortable inclination never to stay put, although at any given moment they are, and must be, valid for all. In other words, notions such as life, or man, or science, or knowledge are prescientific by definition, and the question is whether or not the actual development of science which has led to the conquest of terrestrial space and to the invasion of the space of the universe has changed these notions to such an extent that they no longer make sense. For the point of the matter is, of course, that modern science—no matter what its origins and original goals—has changed and reconstructed the world we live in so radically that it could be argued that the layman and the humanist, still trusting their common sense and communicating in everyday language, are out of touch with reality; that they understand only what appears but not what is behind appearances (as though trying to understand a tree without taking the roots into account); and that their questions and anxieties are simply caused by ignorance and therefore are irrelevant. How can anyone doubt that a science enabling man to conquer space and to go to the moon has increased his stature?

This sort of bypassing the question would be very tempting indeed if it were true that we have come to live in a world that only the scientists "understand." They would then be in a position of the "few" whose superior knowledge entitles them to rule the "many," namely, all non-scientists, laymen from the scientist's point of view—be they humanists, scholars, or philosophers—all those, in short, who raise pre-scientific questions because of ignorance.

This division between the scientist and the layman, however, is very far from the truth. The fact is not merely that the scientist spends more than half of his life in the same world of sense perception, of common sense, and of everyday language as his fellow-citizens, but that he has come in his own privileged field of activity to a point where the naïve questions and anxieties of the layman have made themselves felt very forcefully, albeit in a different manner. The scientist has not only left behind the layman with his limited understanding; he has left behind a part of himself and his own power of understanding, which is still human understanding, when he goes to work in the laboratory and begins to communicate in mathematical language. Max Planck was right, and the miracle of modern science is indeed that this science could be purged "of all anthropomorphic elements" because the purging was done by men.[7] The theoretical perplexities that have confronted the new non-anthropocentric and non-geocentric (or heliocentric) science because its data refuse to be ordered by any of the natural mental categories of the human brain are well enough known. In the words of Erwin Schroedinger, the new universe that we try to "conquer" is not only "practically inaccessible, but not even thinkable," for "however we think it, it is wrong; not perhaps quite as meaningless as a 'triangular circle,' but much more so than a 'winged lion.' " [8]

There are other difficulties of a less theoretical nature. Electronic brains share with all other machines the capacity to do man's work better and faster than man. The fact that they supplant and enlarge human brain power rather than labor power causes no perplexity to those who know how to distinguish between the "intellect" necessary to play good checkers or chess and the human mind.[9] This, indeed, proves no more than that labor power and brain power belong in the same category, and that what we call intelligence and can measure in terms of IQs has hardly any more to do with the quality of the human mind than being its indispensable *conditio sine qua non*. There are, however, scientists who state that computers can do "what a human brain cannot *comprehend*," [10] and this is an altogether different and alarming proposition; for comprehension is actually a function of the mind and never the automatic result of brain power. If it should be true—and not simply a case of a scientist's self-misunderstanding—that we are surrounded by machines whose doings we cannot comprehend although we have devised and constructed them, it would mean that the theoretical perplexities of the natural sciences on the highest level have invaded our everyday world. But even if we remain in the strictly theoretical framework, the paradoxes that have begun to worry the great scientists themselves are sufficiently serious to alarm the layman. Whereas the often mentioned "lag" of the social sciences with respect to the natural sciences or of man's political development with respect to his technical and scientific know-how is no more than a red herring drawn into this debate; it can only divert attention from the main problem, which is that man can *do,* and successfully do, what he cannot comprehend and cannot express in everyday human language.

It may be noteworthy that among the scientists it was primarily the older generation, men like Einstein and Planck, Niels Bohr and Schroedinger, who were most acutely worried about this state of affairs which their own work had chiefly brought about. They were still firmly rooted in a tradition that demanded that scientific theories fulfill certain definitely humanistic requirements such as simplicity, beauty and harmony. A theory was still supposed to be "satisfactory," namely, satisfactory to human reason in that it served to "save the phenomena," to explain all observed facts. Even today, we still hear that "modern physicists are inclined to believe in the validity of general relativity for aesthetic reasons, because it is mathematically so elegant and philosophically so satisfying." [11] Einstein's extreme reluctance to sacrifice the principle of causality as Planck's Quantum Theory demanded is well known; his main objection was, of course, that with it all lawfulness was about to depart from the universe, that it was as though God ruled the world by "playing dice." And since his own discoveries, according to Niels Bohr, had come about through a "remolding and generalizing [of] the whole edifice of classical physics . . . lending to our world picture a unity surpassing all previous expectations," it seems only natural that Einstein tried to come to terms with the new theories of his colleagues and his successors through "the search for a more complete conception," through a new and surpassing generalization.[12] Thus Max Planck could call the Theory of Relativity "the completion and culmination of the structure of classical physics," its very "crowning point." But Planck himself, although fully aware that the Quantum Theory, in contrast to the Theory of Relativity, signified a complete break with classical physical theory, held it to be "essential for the healthy development of physics that among the postulates of this science we reckon, not merely the existence of law in general, but also the strictly causal character of this law." [13]

Niels Bohr, however, went one step further. For him, causality, determinism, and necessity of laws belonged to the categories of "our necessarily prejudiced conceptual frame," and he was no longer frightened when he met "in atomic phenomena regularities of quite a new kind, defying deterministic pictorial description." [14] The trouble is that what defies description in terms of the "prejudices" of the human mind defies description in every conceivable way of human language; it can no longer be described at all, and it is being expressed, but not described, in mathematical processes. Bohr still hoped that, since "no experience is definable without a logical frame," these new experiences would in due time fall into place through "an appropriate widening of the conceptual framework" which would also remove all present paradoxes and "apparent disharmonies." [15] But this hope, I am afraid, will be disappointed. The categories and ideas of human reason have their ultimate source in human sense experience, and all terms describing our mental abilities as well as a good deal of our conceptual language derive from the world of the senses and are used metaphorically. Moreover, the human brain which supposedly does our thinking is as terrestrial, earthbound, as any other part of the human body. It was precisely by abstracting from these terrestrial conditions, by appealing to a power of imagination and abstraction that would, as it were, lift the human mind out of the gravitational field of the earth and look down upon it from some point in the universe, that modern science reached its most glorious and, at the same time, most baffling achievements.

In 1929, shortly before the arrival of the Atomic Revolution, marked by the splitting of the atom and the hope for the conquest of universal space, Planck demanded that the results obtained by mathematical processes "must be translated back into the language of the world of our senses if they are to be of any use to us." In the three decades that have passed since these words were written, such translation has become even less possible while the loss of contact between the physical world view and the sense world has become even more conspicuous. But—and in our context this is even more alarming—this has by no means meant that results of this new science are of no practical use, or that the new world view, as Planck had predicted in case the translation back into ordinary language should fail, "would be no better than a bubble ready to burst at the first puff of wind." [16] On the contrary, one is tempted to say that it is much more likely that the planet we inhabit will go up in smoke as a consequence of theories that are entirely unrelated to the world of the senses, and defy all description in human language, than that even a *hurricane* will cause the theories to burst like a bubble.

It is, I think, safe to say that nothing was more alien to the minds of the scientists, who brought about the most radical and the most rapid revolutionary process the world has ever seen, than any will to power. Nothing was more remote than any wish to "conquer space" and to go to the moon. Nor were they prompted by an unseemly curiosity in the sense of a *temptatio oculorum*. It was indeed their search for "true reality" that led them to lose confidence in appearances, in the phenomena as they reveal themselves of their own accord to human sense and reason. They were inspired by an extraordinary love of harmony and lawfulness which taught them that they would have to step outside any merely given sequence or series of occurrences if they wanted to discover the overall beauty and order of the whole, that is, the universe. This may explain why they seem to have been less distressed by the fact their discoveries served the invention of the most murderous gadgets than disturbed by the shattering of all their most cherished ideals of necessity and lawfulness. These ideals were lost when the scientists discovered that there is nothing indivisible in matter, no α-*tomos,* that we live in an expanding, non-limited universe, and that chance seems to rule supreme wherever this "true reality," the physical world, has receded entirely from the range of human senses and from the range of all instruments by which their coarseness was refined. From this, it seems to follow that causality, necessity, and lawfulness are categories inherent in the human brain and applicable only to the common-sense experiences of earth-bound creatures. Everything that such creatures "reasonably" demand seems to fail them as soon as they step outside the range of their terrestrial habitat.

The modern scientific enterprise began with thoughts never thought before (Copernicus imagined he was "standing in the sun . . . overlooking the planets")[17] and with things never seen before (Galileo's telescope pierced the distance between earth and sky and delivered the secrets of the stars to human cognition "with all the certainty of sense evidence").[18] It reached its classic expression with Newton's law of gravitation, in which the same equation covers the movements of the heavenly bodies and the motion of terrestrial things on earth. Einstein indeed only generalized this science of the modern age when he introduced an "observer who is poised freely in space" and not just at one definite point like the sun, and he proved that not only Copernicus but also Newton still required "that the universe should have a kind of center," although this center, of course, was no longer the earth.[19] It is, in fact, quite obvious that the scientists' strongest intellectual motivation was Einstein's "striving after generalization," and that if they appealed to power at all, it was the interconnected formidable power of abstraction and imagination. Even today, when billions of dollars are spent year in and year out for highly "useful" projects that are the immediate results of the development of pure, theoretical science, and when the actual power of countries and governments depends upon the performance of many thousands of researchers, the physicist is still likely to look down upon all these space scientists as mere "plumbers." [20]

The sad truth of the matter, however, is that the lost contact between the world of the senses and appearances and the physical world view has been re-established not by the pure scientist but by the "plumber." The technicians, who account today for the overwhelming majority of all "researchers," have brought the results of the scientists down to earth. And even though the scientist is still beset by paradoxes and the most bewildering perplexities, the very fact that a whole technology could develop out of his results demonstrates the "soundness" of his theories and hypotheses more convincingly than any merely scientific observation or experiment ever could. It is perfectly true that the scientist himself does not want to go to the moon; he knows that for his purposes unmanned spaceships carrying the best instruments human ingenuity can invent will do the job of exploring the moon's surface much better than dozens of astronauts. And yet, an actual change of the human world, the conquest of space or whatever we may wish to call it, is achieved only when manned space carriers are shot into the universe, so that man himself can go where up to now only human imagination and its power of abstraction, or human ingenuity and its power of fabrication, could reach. To be sure, all we plan to do now is to explore our own immediate surroundings in the universe, the infinitely small place that the human race could reach even if it were to travel with the velocity of light. In view of man's life span—the only absolute limitation left at the present moment—it is quite unlikely that he will ever go much farther. But even for this limited job, we have to leave the world of our senses and of our bodies not only in imagination but in reality.

It is as though Einstein's imagined "observer poised in free space"—surely the creation of the human mind and its power of abstraction—is being followed by a bodily observer who must behave as though he were a mere child of abstraction and imagination. It is at this point that all the theoretical perplexities of the new physical world view intrude as realities upon man's everyday world and throw out of gear his "natural," that is, earthbound, common sense. He would, for instance, be confronted in reality with Einstein's famous "twin paradox," which hypothetically assumes that "a twin brother who takes off on a space journey in which he travels at a sizable fraction of the speed of light would return to find his earthbound twin either older than he or little more than a dim recollection in the memory of his descendants." [21] For although many physicists had found this paradox difficult to swallow, the "clock paradox," on which it is based, seems to have been verified experimentally, so that the only alternative to it would be the assumption that earthbound life under all circumstances remains bound to a time concept that demonstrably does not belong among "true realities," but among mere appearances. We have reached the stage where the Cartesian radical doubt of reality as such, the first philosophical answer to the discoveries of science in the modern age, may become subject to physical experiments that would make short shrift of Descartes' famous consolation, *I doubt, therefore I am,* and of his conviction that, whatever the state of reality and of truth as they are given to the senses and to reason, you cannot "doubt of your doubt and remain uncertain whether you doubt or not." [22]

The magnitude of the space enterprise seems to me beyond dispute, and all objections raised against it on the purely utilitarian level—that it is too expensive, that the money were better spent on education and the improvement of the citizens, on the fight against poverty and disease, or whatever other worthy purposes may come to mind—sound to me slightly absurd, out of tune with the things that are at stake and whose consequences today appear still quite unpredictable. There is, moreover, another reason why I think these arguments are beside the point. They are singularly inapplicable because the enterprise itself could come about only through an amazing development of man's scientific capabilities. The very integrity of science demands that not only utilitarian considerations but the reflection upon the stature of man as well be left in abeyance. Has not each of the advances of science, since the time of Copernicus, almost automatically resulted in a decrease in his stature? And is the often repeated argument that it was man who achieved his own debasement in his search for truth, thus proving anew his superiority and even increasing his stature, more than a sophism? Perhaps it will turn out that way. At any event, man, insofar as he is a scientist, does not care about his own stature in the universe or about his position on the evolutionary ladder of animal life; this "carelessness" is his pride and his glory. The simple fact that physicists split the atom without any hesitations the very moment they knew how to do it, although they realized full well the enormous destructive potentialities of their operation, demonstrates that the scientist *qua* scientist does not even care about the survival of the human race on earth or, for that matter, about the survival of the planet itself. All associations for "Atoms for Peace," all warnings not to use the new power unwisely, and even the pangs of conscience many scientists felt when the first bombs fell on Hiroshima and Nagasaki cannot obscure this simple, elementary fact. For in all these efforts the scientists acted not as scientists but as citizens, and if their voices have more authority than the voices of laymen, they do so only because the scientists are in possession of more precise information. Valid and plausible arguments against the "conquest of space" could be raised only if they were to show that the whole enterprise might be self-defeating in its own terms.

There are a few indications that such might indeed be the case. If we leave out of account the human life span, which under no circumstances (even if biology should succeed in extending it significantly and man were able to travel with the speed of light) will permit man to explore more than his immediate surroundings in the immensity of the universe, the most significant indication that it might be self-defeating consists in Heisenberg's discovery of the uncertainty principle. Heisenberg showed conclusively that there is a definite and final limit to the accuracy of all measurements obtainable by man-devised instruments for those "mysterious messengers from the real world." The uncertainty principle "asserts that there are certain pairs of quantities, like the position and velocity of a particle, that are related in such a way that determining one of them with increased precision necessarily entails determining the other one with reduced precision." [23] Heisenberg concludes from this fact that "we decide, by our selection of the type of observation employed, which aspects of nature are to be determined and which are to be blurred." [24] He holds that "the most important new result of nuclear physics was the recognition of the possibility of applying quite different types of natural laws, without contradiction, to one and the same physical event. This is due to the fact that within a system of laws which are based on certain fundamental ideas only certain quite definite ways of asking questions make sense, and thus, that such a system is separated from others which allow different questions to be put." [25] From this he concluded that the modern search for "true reality" behind mere appearances, which has brought about the world we live in and resulted in the Atomic Revolution, has led into a situation in the sciences themselves in which man has lost the very objectivity of the natural world, so that man in his hunt for "objective reality" suddenly discovered that he always "confronts himself alone." [26]

The remarks of Heisenberg seem to me to transcend by far the field of strictly scientific endeavor and to gain in poignancy if they are applied to the technology that has grown out of modern science. Every progress in science in the last decades, from the moment it was absorbed into technology and thus introduced into the factual world where we live our everyday lives, has brought with it a veritable avalanche of fabulous instruments and ever more ingenious machinery. All of this makes it more unlikely every day that man will encounter anything in the world around him that is not man-made and hence is not, in the last analysis, he himself in a different disguise. The astronaut, shot into outer space and imprisoned in his instrument-ridden capsule where each actual physical encounter with his surroundings would spell immediate death, might well be taken as the symbolic incarnation of Heisenberg's man—the man who will be the less likely ever to meet anything but himself and man-made things the more ardently he wishes to eliminate all anthropocentric considerations from his encounter with the non-human world around him.

It is at this point, it seems to me, that the humanist's concern with man and the stature of man has caught up with the scientist. It is as though the sciences had done what the humanities never could have achieved, namely, to prove demonstrably the validity of this concern. The situation, as it presents itself today, oddly resembles an elaborate verification of a remark by Franz Kafka, written at the very beginning of this development: Man, he said, "found the Archimedean point, but he used it against himself; it seems that he was permitted to find it only under this condition." For the conquest of space, the search for a point outside the earth from which it would be possible to move, to unhinge, as it were, the planet itself, is no accidental result of the modern age's science. This was from its very beginnings not a "natural" but a universal science, it was not a physics but an astrophysics which looked upon the earth from a point in the universe. In terms of this development, the attempt to conquer space means that man hopes he will be able to journey to the Archimedean point which he anticipated by sheer force of abstraction and imagination. However, in doing so, he will necessarily lose his advantage. All he can find is the Archimedean point with respect to the earth, but once arrived there and having acquired this absolute power over his earthly habitat, he would need a new Archimedean point, and so *ad infinitum*. In other words, man can only get lost in the immensity of the universe, for the only true Archimedean point would be the absolute void behind the universe.

Yet even if man recognizes that there might be absolute limits to his search for knowledge and that it might be wise to suspect such limitations whenever it turns out that the scientist can do more than he is capable of comprehending, and even if he realizes that he cannot "conquer space," but at best make a few discoveries in our solar system, the journey into space and to the Archimedean point with respect to the earth is far from being a harmless or unequivocally triumphant enterprise. It could add to the stature of man inasmuch as man, in distinction from other living things, desires to be at home in a "territory" as large as possible. In that case, he would only take possession of what is his own, although it took him a long time to discover it. These new possessions, like all property, would have to be limited, and once the limit is reached and the limitations established, the new world view that may conceivably grow out of it is likely to be once more geocentric and anthropomorphic, although not in the old sense of the earth being the center of the universe and of man being the highest being there is. It would be geocentric in the sense that the earth, and not the universe, is the center and the home of mortal men, and it would be anthropomorphic in the sense that man would count his own factual mortality among the elementary conditions under which his scientific efforts are possible at all.

At this moment, the prospects for such an entirely beneficial development and solution of the present predicaments of modern science and technology do not look particularly good. We have come to our present capacity to "conquer space" through our new ability to handle nature from a point in the universe outside the earth. For this is what we actually do when we release energy processes that ordinarily go on only in the sun, or attempt to initiate in a test tube the processes of cosmic evolution, or build machines for the production and control of energies unknown in the household of earthly nature. Without as yet actually occupying the point where Archimedes had wished to stand, we have found a way to act on the earth as though we disposed of terrestrial nature from outside, from the point of Einstein's "observer freely poised in space." If we look down from this point upon what is going on on earth and upon the various activities of men, that is, if we apply the Archimedean point to ourselves, then these activities will indeed appear to ourselves as no more than "overt behavior," which we can study with the same methods we use to study the behavior of rats. Seen from a sufficient distance, the cars in which we travel and which we know we built ourselves will look as though they were, as Heisenberg once put it, "as inescapable a part of ourselves as the snail's shell is to its occupant." All our pride in what we can do will disappear into some kind of mutation of the human race; the whole of technology, seen from this point, in fact no longer appears "as the result of a conscious human effort to extend man's material powers, but rather as a large-scale biological process." [27] Under these circumstances, speech and everyday language would indeed be no longer a meaningful utterance that transcends behavior even if it only expresses it, and it would much better be replaced by the extreme and in itself meaningless formalism of mathematical signs.

The conquest of space and the science that made it possible have come perilously close to this point. If they ever should reach it in earnest, the stature of man would not simply be lowered by all standards we know of, but have been destroyed.

NOTES
INDEX OF NAMES

NOTES

Preface

1. For this quotation and the following, see René Char, *Feuillets d'Hypnos*, Paris, 1946. Written during the last year of the Resistance, 1943 to 1944, and published in the *Collection Espoir*, edited by Albert Camus, these aphorisms, together with later pieces, appeared in English under the title *Hypnos Waking; Poems and Prose*, New York, 1956.

2. The quotation is from the last chapter of *Democracy in America*, New York, 1945, vol. II, p. 331. It reads in full: "Although the revolution that is taking place in the social condition, the laws, the opinions, and the feelings of men is still very far from being terminated, yet its results already admit of no comparison with anything that the world has ever before witnessed. I go back from age to age up to the remotest antiquity, but I find no parallel to what is occurring before my eyes; as the past has ceased to throw its light upon the future, the mind of man wanders in obscurity." These lines of Tocqueville anticipate not only the aphorisms of René Char; curiously enough, if one reads them textually, they also anticipate Kafka's insight (see the following) that it is the future that sends man's mind back into the past "up to the remotest antiquity."

3. The story is the last of a series of "Notes from the year 1920," under the title "HE." Translated from the German by Willa and Edwin Muir, they appeared in this country in *The Great Wall of China*, New York, 1946. I followed the English translation except in a few places where a more literal translation was needed for my purposes. The German original—in vol. 5 of the *Gesammelte Schriften*, New York, 1946 —reads as follows:

Er hat zwei Gegner: Der erste bedrängt ihn von hinten, vom Ursprung her. Der zweite verwehrt ihm den Weg nach vorn. Er kämpft mit beiden. Eigentlich unterstützt ihn der erste im Kampf mit dem Zweiten, denn er will ihn nach vorn drängen und ebenso unterstützt ihn der zweite im Kampf mit dem Ersten; denn er treibt ihn doch zurück. So ist es aber nur theoretisch. Denn es sind ja nicht nur die zwei Gegner da, sondern auch noch er selbst, und wer kennt eigentlich seine Absichten? Immerhin ist es sein Traum, dass er einmal in einem unbewachten Augenblick—dazu gehört allerdings eine Nacht, so finster wie noch keine war—aus der Kampflinie ausspringt und wegen seiner Kampfeserfahrung zum Richter über seine miteinander kämpfenden Gegner erhoben wird.

1. Tradition and the Modern Age

1. *Laws* 775.

2. For Engels, see his *Anti-Dühring*, Zürich, 1934, p. 275. For Nietzsche, see *Morgenröte, Werke, München*, 1954, vol. I, aph. 179.

3. The statement occurs in Engels' essay on "The Part played by Labour in the Transition from Ape to Man," in Marx and Engels, *Selected Works*, London, 1950, vol. II, p. 74. For similar formulations by Marx himself, see especially "Die heilige Familie" and "Nationalökonomie und Philosophie" in *Jugendschriften*, Stuttgart, 1953.

4. Quoted here from *Capital*, Modern Library Edition, p. 824.

5. See *Götzendämmerung*, ed. K. Schlechta, München, vol. II, p. 963.

6. In *Das Kapital*, Zürich, 1933, vol. III, p. 870.

7. I refer here to Heidegger's discovery that the Greek word for truth means literally "disclosure"—ά-λήθεια.

8. Op. cit., Zürich, p. 689.

9. Ibid., pp. 697–698.

10. That "the Cave is comparable with Hades" is also suggested by F. M. Cornford in his annotated translation of *The Republic*, New York, 1956, p. 230.

11. See *Jugendschriften*, p. 274.

2. The Concept of History

1. Cicero, *De legibus* I, 5; *De oratore* II, 55. Herodotus, the first historian, did not yet have at his disposal a word for history. He used the

word ἱστορεῖν, but not in the sense of "historical narrative." Like εἰδέναι, to know, the word ἱστορία is derived from ἰδ-, to see, and ἵστωρ means originally "eyewitness," then the one who examines witnesses and obtains truth through inquiry. Hence, ἱστορεῖν has a double meaning: to testify and to inquire. (See Max Pohlenz, *Herodot, der erste Geschichtsschreiber des Abendlandes*, Leipzig and Berlin, 1937, p. 44.) For recent discussion of Herodotus and our concept of history, see especially C. N. Cochrane, *Christianity and Classical Culture*, New York, 1944, ch. 12, one of the most stimulating and interesting pieces in the literature on the subject. His chief thesis, that Herodotus must be regarded as belonging to the Ionian school of philosophy and a follower of Heraclitus, is not convincing. Contrary to ancient sources, Cochrane construes the science of history as being part of the Greek development of philosophy. See note 6, and also Karl Reinhardt, "Herodots Persegeschichten" in *Von Werken und Formen*, Godesberg, 1948.

2. "The Gods of most nations claim to have created the world. The Olympian gods make no such claim. The most they ever did was to conquer it" (Gilbert Murray, *Five Stages of Greek Religion*, Anchor edition, p. 45). Against this statement one sometimes argues that Plato in the *Timaeus* introduced a creator of the world. But Plato's god is no real creator; he is a demiurge, a world-builder who does not create out of nothing. Moreover, Plato tells his story in the form of a myth invented by himself, and this, like similar myths in his work, are not proposed as truth. That no god and no man ever created the cosmos is beautifully stated in Heraclitus, fragment 30 (Diels), for this cosmical order of all things "has always been and is and will be—an ever-living fire that blazes up in proportions and dies away in proportions."

3. *On the Soul*, 415b13. See also *Economics*, 1343b24: Nature fulfills the being-forever with respect to the species through recurrence (περίοδος) but cannot do this with respect to the individual. In our context, it is irrelevant that the treatise is not by Aristotle but by one of his pupils, for we find the same thought in the treatise *On Generation and Corruption* in the concept of Becoming, which moves in a cycle— γένεσις ἐξ ἀλλήλων κύκλῳ, 331a8. The same thought of an "immortal human species" occurs in Plato, *Laws*, 721. See note 9.

4. Nietzsche, *Wille zur Macht*, Nr. 617, Edition Kröner, 1930.

5. Rilke, *Aus dem Nachlass des Grafen C. W.*, first series, poem X. Although the poetry is untranslatable, the content of these verses might be expressed as follows: "Mountains rest beneath a splendor of stars, but even in them time flickers. Ah, unsheltered in my wild, darkling heart lies immortality." I owe this translation to Denver Lindley.

6. *Poetics*, 1448b25 and 1450a16–22. For a distinction between poetry and historiography, see ibid., ch. 9.

7. For tragedy as an imitation of action, see ibid., ch. 6, 1.

8. *Griechische Kulturgeschichte*, Edition Kröner, II, p. 289.

9. For Plato, see *Laws* 721, where he makes it quite clear that he thinks the human species only in a certain way to be immortal—namely insofar as its successive generations taken as a whole are "growing together" with the entirety of time; mankind as a succession of generations and time are coeval: γένος οὖν ἀνθρώπων ἐστί τι ξυμφυὲς τοῦ παντὸς χρόνου, ὃ διὰ τέλους αὐτῷ ξυνέπεται καὶ συνέψεται, τούτῳ τῷ τρόπῳ ἀθάνατον ὄν. In other words, it is mere deathlessness—ἀθανασία—in which the mortals partake by virtue of belonging to an immortal species; it is not the timeless being-forever—the ἀεὶ εἶναι—in whose neighborhood the philosopher is admitted even though he is but a mortal. For Aristotle, see *Nicomachean Ethics*, 1177b30–35 and further in what follows.

10. Ibid., 1143a36.

11. *Seventh Letter*.

12. W. Heisenberg, *Philosophic Problems of Nuclear Science*, New York, 1952, p. 24.

13. Quoted from Alexandre Koyré, "An Experiment in Measurement," *Proceedings of the American Philosophical Society*, vol. 97, no. 2, 1953.

14. The same point was made more than twenty years ago by Edgar Wind in his essay "Some Points of Contact between History and Natural Sciences" (in *Philosophy and History, Essays Presented to Ernst Cassirer*, Oxford, 1939). Wind already showed that the latest developments of science which make it so much less "exact" lead to the raising of questions by scientists "that historians like to look upon as their own." It seems strange that so fundamental and obvious an argument should have played no role in the subsequent methodological and other discussions of historical science.

15. Quoted in Friedrich Meinecke, *Vom geschichtlichen Sinn und vom Sinn der Geschichte*, Stuttgart, 1951.

16. Erwin Schroedinger, *Science and Humanism*, Cambridge, 1951, pp. 25–26.

17. *De nostri temporis studiorum ratione*, iv. Quoted from the bilingual edition by W. F. Otto, *Vom Wesen und Weg der geistigen Bildung*, Godesberg, 1947, p. 41.

18. No one can look at the remains of ancient or medieval towns without being struck by the finality with which their walls separated them from their natural surroundings, whether these were landscapes or wilderness. Modern city-building, on the contrary, aims at the landscaping and urbanization of whole areas, where the distinction between town and country becomes more and more obliterated. This trend could possibly lead to the disappearance of cities even as we know them today.

19. In *De doctrina Christiana*, 2, 28, 44.

20. *De Civitate Dei*, XII, 13.

21. See Theodor Mommsen, "St. Augustine and the Christian Idea of Progress," in *Journal of the History of Ideas*, June 1951. A close reading shows a striking discrepancy between the content of this excellent article and the thesis expressed in its title. The best defense of the Christian origin of the concept of history is found in C. N. Cochrane, op. cit., p. 474. He holds that ancient historiography came to an end because it had failed to establish "a principle of historical intelligibility" and that Augustine solved this problem by substituting "the *logos* of Christ for that of classicism as a principle of understanding."

22. Especially interesting is Oscar Cullman, *Christ and Time*, London, 1951. Also Erich Frank, "The Role of History in Christian Thought" in *Knowledge, Will and Belief, Collected Essays*, Zürich, 1955.

23. In *Die Entstehung des Historismus*, München and Berlin, 1936, p. 394.

24. John Baillie, *The Belief in Progress*, London, 1950.

25. *De Re Publica*, 1.7.

26. The word seems to have been rarely used even in Greek. It occurs in Herodotus (book IV, 93 and 94) in the active sense and applies to the rites performed by a tribe that does not believe in death. The point is that the word does not mean "to believe in immortality," but "to act in a certain way in order to assure the escape from dying." In the passive sense (ἀθανατίζεσθαι, "to be rendered immortal") the word also occurs in Polybius (book VI, 54, 2); it is used in the description of Roman funeral rites and applies to the funeral orations, which render immortal through "constantly making new the fame of good men." The Latin equivalent, *aeternare*, again applies to immortal fame. (Horace, *Carmines*, book IV, c. 14, 5.)

Clearly, Aristotle was the first and perhaps the last to use this word for the specifically philosophic "activity" of contemplation. The text reads as follows: οὐ χρὴ δὲ κατὰ τοὺς παραινοῦντας ἀνθρώπινα φρονεῖν, ἄνθρωπον ὄντα οὐδὲ θνητὰ τὸν θνητόν, ἀλλ᾽ ἐφ᾽ ὅσον ἐνδέχεται ἀθανατίζειν. . . . (*Nichomachean Ethics*, 1177b31). "One should not think as do those who recommend human things for those who are mortals, but *immortalize* as far as possible. . . ." The medieval Latin translation (Eth. X, Lectio XI) does not use the old Latin word *aeternare* but translates "immortalize" through *immortalem facere*—to make immortal, presumably one's self. (*Oportet autem non secundum suadentes humana hominem entem, neque mortalia mortalem; sed inquantum contingit immortalem facere*. . . .) Modern standard translations fall into the same error (see for instance the translation by W. D. Ross, who translates: "we must . . . make ourselves immortal"). In the Greek text, the word ἀθανατίζειν, like the word φρονεῖν, is an intransitive verb, it has no direct object. (I owe the Greek and Latin references to the kind help of Professors John Herman Randall, Jr., and Paul Oscar Kristeller of Columbia University. Needless to say, they are not responsible for translation and interpretation.)

27. It is rather interesting to note that Nietzsche, who once used the term "eternize"—probably because he remembered the passage in Aristotle—applied it to the spheres of art and religion. In *Vom Nutzen und Nachteil der Historie für das Leben*, he speaks of the *"aeternisierenden Mächten der Kunst und Religion."*

28. Thucydides II, 41.

29. How the poet, and especially Homer, bestowed immortality upon mortal men and futile deeds, we can still read in Pindar's *Odes*—now rendered into English by Richmond Lattimore, Chicago, 1955. See, for instance, "Isthmia" IV: 60 ff.; "Nemea" IV: 10, and VI: 50–55.

30. *De Civitate Dei*, XIX, 5.

31. Johannes Gustav Droysen, *Historik* (1882), München and Berlin, 1937, para. 82: *"Was den Tieren, den Pflanzen ihr Gattungsbegriff—denn die Gattung ist, ἵνα τοῦ ἀεὶ καὶ τοῦ θείου μετέχωσιν—das ist den Menschen die Geschichte."* Droysen does not mention author or source of the quotation. It sounds Aristotelian.

32. *Leviathan*, book I, ch. 3.

33. *Democracy in America*, 2nd part, last chapter, and 1st part, "Author's Introduction," respectively.

34. The first to see Kant as the theorist of the French Revolution was Friedrich Gentz in his "Nachtrag zu dem Räsonnement des Herrn Prof. Kant über das Verhältnis zwischen Theorie und Praxis" in *Berliner Monatsschrift*, December 1793.

35. *Idee zu einer allgemeinen Geschichte in weltbürgerlicher Absicht*, Introduction.

36. Op. cit., Third Thesis.

37. Hegel in *The Philosophy of History*, London, 1905, p. 21.

38. Nietzsche, *Wille zur Macht*, no. 291.

39. Martin Heidegger once pointed to this weird fact in a public discussion in Zürich (published under the title: "Aussprache mit Martin Heidegger am 6. November 1951," Photodruck Jurisverlag, Zürich, 1952): ". . . *der Satz: man kann alles beweisen* [ist] *nicht ein Freibrief, sondern ein Hinweis auf die Möglichkeit, dass dort, wo man beweist im Sinne der Deduktion aus Axiomen, dies jederzeit in gewissem Sinne möglich ist. Das ist das unheimlich Rätselhafte, dessen Geheimnis ich*

bisher auch nicht an einem Zipfel aufzuheben vermochte, dass dieses Verfahren in der modernen Naturwissenschaft stimmt."

40. Werner Heisenberg in recent publications renders this same thought in a number of variations. See for example *Das Naturbild der heutigen Physik,* Hamburg, 1956.

3. What Is Authority?

1. The formulation is Lord Acton's in his "Inaugural Lecture on the 'Study of History,'" reprinted in *Essays on Freedom and Power,* New York, 1955, p. 35.

2. Only a detailed description and analysis of the very original organizational structure of totalitarian movements and the institutions of totalitarian government could justify the use of the onion image. I must refer to the chapter on "Totalitarian Organization" in my book *The Origins of Totalitarianism,* 2nd edition, New York, 1958.

3. This was already noticed by the Greek historian Dio Cassius, who, when writing a history of Rome, found it impossible to translate the word *auctoritas:* ἑλληνίσαι αὐτὸ καθάπαξ ἀδύνατον ἔστι. (Quoted from Theodor Mommsen, *Römisches Staatsrecht,* 3rd edition, 1888, vol. III, p. 952, n. 4.) Moreover, one need only compare the Roman Senate, the republic's specifically authoritarian institution, with Plato's nocturnal council in the *Laws,* which, being composed of the ten oldest guardians for the constant supervision of the State, superficially resembles it, to become aware of the impossibility of finding a true alternative for coercion and persuasion within the framework of Greek political experience.

4. πόλις γὰρ οὐκ ἔσθ' ἥτις ἀνδρὸς ἐσθ' ἑνός. Sophocles, *Antigone,* 737.

5. *Laws,* 715.

6. Theodor Mommsen, *Römische Geschichte,* book I, chap. 5.

7. H. Wallon, *Histoire de l'Esclavage dans l'Antiquité,* Paris, 1847, vol. III, where one still finds the best description of the gradual loss of Roman liberty under the Empire caused by the constant increase of power of the imperial household. Since it was the imperial household and not the emperor who gained in power, the "despotism" which always had been characteristic of the private household and family life began to dominate the public realm.

8. A fragment from the lost dialogue *On Kingship* states that "it was not only not necessary for a king to become a philosopher, but actu-

ally a hindrance to his work; that, however, it was necessary [for a good king] to listen to the true philosopher and to be agreeable to their advice." See Kurt von Fritz, *The Constitution of Athens, and Related Texts,* 1950. In Aristotelian terms, both Plato's philosopher-king and the Greek tyrant rule for the sake of their own interest, and this was for Aristotle, though not for Plato, an outstanding characteristic of tyrants. Plato was not aware of the resemblance, because for him, as for Greek current opinion, the principal characteristic of the tyrant was that he deprived the citizen of access to a public realm, to a "market place" where he could show himself, see and be seen, hear and be heard, that he prohibited the ἀγορεύειν and πολιτεύεσθαι, confined the citizens to the privacy of their households, and demanded to be the only one in charge of public affairs. He would not have ceased to be a tyrant if he had used his power solely in the interests of his subjects— as indeed some of the tyrants undoubtedly did. According to the Greeks, to be banished to the privacy of household life was tantamount to being deprived of the specifically human potentialities of life. In other words, the very features which so convincingly demonstrate to us the tyrannical character of Plato's republic—the almost complete elimination of privacy and the omnipresence of political organs and institutions—presumably prevented Plato from recognizing its tyrannical character. To him, it would have been a contradiction in terms to brand as tyranny a constitution which not only did not relegate the citizen to his household but, on the contrary, did not leave him a shred of private life whatsoever. Moreover, by calling the rule of law "despotic," Plato stresses its non-tyrannical character. For the tyrant was always supposed to rule over men who had known the freedom of a polis and, being deprived of it, were likely to rebel, whereas the despot was assumed to rule over people who had never known freedom and were by nature incapable of it. It is as though Plato said: My laws, your new despots, will not deprive you of anything you rightfully enjoyed before; they are adequate to the very nature of human affairs and you have no more right to rebel against their rule than the slave has a right to rebel against his master.

9. "Eternal Peace," *The Philosophy of Kant,* ed. and trans. C. J. Friedrich, Modern Library Edition, 1949, p. 456.

10. Von Fritz, op. cit., p. 54, rightly insists on Plato's aversion to violence, "also revealed by the fact that, wherever he did make an attempt to bring about a change of political institutions in the direction of his political ideals, he addressed himself to men already in power."

11. Werner Jaeger's statement in *Paideia,* New York, 1943, vol. II, p. 416n; "The idea that there is a supreme art of measurement and

that the philosopher's knowledge of values (*phronesis*) is the ability to measure, runs through all Plato's work right down to the end" is true only for Plato's political philosophy. The very word φρόνησις characterizes in Plato and Aristotle the insight of the statesman rather than the "wisdom" of the philosopher.

12. *The Republic*, book VII, 516–517.

13. See especially *Timaeus*, 31, where the divine Demiurge makes the universe in accordance with a model, a παράδειγμα, and *The Republic*, 596 ff.

14. In *Protrepticus*, quoted from von Fritz, op. cit.

15. *Laws*, 710–711.

16. This presentation is indebted to Martin Heidegger's great interpretation of the cave parable in *Platons Lehre von der Wahrheit*, Bern, 1947. Heidegger demonstrates how Plato transformed the concept of truth (ἀλήθεια) until it became identical with correct statements (ὀρθότης). Correctness indeed, and not truth, would be required if the philosopher's knowledge is the ability to measure. Although he explicitly mentions the risks the philosopher runs when he is forced to return to the cave, Heidegger is not aware of the political context in which the parable appears. According to him, the transformation comes to pass because the subjective act of vision (the ἰδεῖν and the ἰδέα in the mind of the philosopher) takes precedence over objective truth (ἀλήθεια), which, according to Heidegger, signifies *Unverborgenheit*.

17. *Symposion*, 211–212.

18. *Phaedrus*, 248: φιλόσοφος ἢ φιλόκαλος, and 250.

19. In *The Republic*, 518, the good, too, is called φανότατον, the most shining one. Obviously it is precisely this quality which indicates the precedence which the beautiful originally had over the good in Plato's thought.

20. *The Republic*, 475–476. In the tradition of philosophy, the result of this Platonic repudiation of the beautiful has been that it was omitted from the so-called transcendentals or universals, that is, those qualities possessed by everything that is, and which were enumerated in medieval philosophy as *unum, alter, ens*, and *bonum*. Jacques Maritain, in his wonderful book, *Creative Intuition in Art and Poetry*, Bollingen Series XXXV, I, 1953, is aware of this omission and insists that beauty be included in the realm of transcendentals, for "Beauty is the radiance of all transcendentals united" (p. 162).

21. In the dialogue *Politicus:* "for the most exact measure of all things is the good" (quoted from von Fritz, op. cit.). The notion must have been that only through the concept of the good do things become comparable and hence measurable.

22. *Politics,* 1332b12 and 1332b36. The distinction between the younger and older ones goes back to Plato; see *Republic,* 412, and *Laws,* 690 and 714. The appeal to nature is Aristotelian.

23. *Politics,* 1328b35.

24. *Economics,* 1343a1–4.

25. Jaeger, op. cit., vol. I, p. 111.

26. *Economics,* 1343b24.

27. The derivation of *religio* from *religare* occurs in Cicero. Since we deal here only with the political self-interpretation of the Romans, the question whether this derivation is etymologically correct is irrelevant.

28. See Cicero, *De Re Publica,* III, 23. For the Roman belief in the eternity of their city, see Viktor Poeschl, *Römischer Staat und griechisches Staatsdenken bei Cicero,* Berlin, 1936.

29. *Annals,* book 43, ch. 13.

30. *De Re Publica,* 1, 7.

31. Cicero, *De Legibus,* 3, 12, 38.

32. *Esprit des Lois,* book XI, ch. 6.

33. Professor Carl J. Friedrich drew my attention to the important discussion of authority in Mommsen's *Römisches Staatsrecht;* see pp. 1034, 1038–1039.

34. This interpretation is further supported by the idiomatic Latin use of *alicui auctorem esse* for "giving advice to somebody."

35. See Mommsen, op cit., 2nd edition, vol. I, pp. 73 ff. The Latin word *numen,* which is nearly untranslatable, meaning "divine command" as well as the divine modes of acting, derives from *nuere,* to nod in affirmation. Thus the commands of the gods and all their interference in human affairs are restricted to approval or disapproval of human actions.

36. Mommsen, ibid., p. 87.

37. See also the various Latin idioms such as *auctores habere* for having predecessors or examples; *auctoritas maiorum,* signifying the authoritative example of the ancestors; *usus et auctoritas* as used in Roman law for property rights which come from usage. An excellent presentation of this Roman spirit as well as a very useful collection of the more important source materials are to be found in Viktor Poeschl, op. cit., especially pp. 101 ff.

38. R. H. Barrow, *The Romans,* 1949, p. 194.

39. A similar amalgamation of Roman imperial political sentiment with Christianity is discussed by Erik Peterson, *Der Monotheismus als politisches Problem,* Leipzig, 1935, in connection with Orosius, who related the Roman Emperor Augustus to Christ. "*Dabei ist deutlich,*

dass Augustus auf diese Weise christianisiert und Christus zum civis romanus *wird, romanisiert worden ist"* (p. 92).

40. *Duo quippe sunt . . . quibus principaliter mundus hic regitur, : auctoritas sacra pontificum et regalis potestas.* In Migne, PL, vol. 59, p. 42a.

41. Eric Voegelin, *A New Science of Politics*, Chicago, 1952, p. 78.

42. See *Phaedo* 80 for the affinity of the invisible soul with the traditional place of invisibility, namely, Hades, which Plato construes etymologically as "the invisible."

43. Ibid., 64–66.

44. With the exception of the *Laws*, it is characteristic of Plato's political dialogues that a break occurs somewhere and the strictly argumentative procedure has to be abandoned. In *The Republic*, Socrates eludes his questioners several times; the baffling question is whether justice is still possible if a deed is hidden from men and gods. The discussion of what justice is breaks down at 372a and is taken up again in 427d, where, however, not justice but wisdom and $εὐβουλία$ are defined. Socrates comes back to the main question in 403d, but discusses $σωφροσύνη$ instead of justice. He then starts again in 433b and comes almost immediately to a discussion of the forms of government, 445d ff., until the seventh book with the cave story puts the whole argument on an entirely different, nonpolitical level. Here it becomes clear why Glaukon could not receive a satisfactory answer: justice is an idea and must be perceived; there is no other possible demonstration.

The Er-myth, on the other hand, is introduced by a reversion of the whole argument. The task had been to find justice as such, even if hidden from the eyes of gods and men. Now (612) Socrates wishes to take back his initial admission to Glaukon that, at least for the sake of the argument, one would have to assume that "the just man may appear unjust and the unjust just" so that no one, neither god nor man, could definitely know who is truly just. And in its stead, he puts the assumption that "the nature both of the just and the unjust is truly known to the gods." Again, the whole argument is put on an entirely different level—this time on the level of the multitude and outside the range of argument altogether.

The case of *Gorgias* is quite similar. Once more, Socrates is incapable of persuading his opponent. The discussion turns about the Socratic conviction that it is better to suffer wrong than to do wrong. When Kallikles clearly cannot be persuaded by argument, Plato proceeds to tell his myth of a hereafter as a kind of *ultima ratio,* and, in distinction to *The Republic*, he tells it with great diffidence, clearly indicating that the teller of the story, Socrates, does not take it seriously.

45. Imitation of Plato seems to be beyond doubt in the frequent cases where the motif of apparent death recurs, as in Cicero and Plutarch. For an excellent discussion of Cicero's *Somnium Scipionis,* the myth which concludes his *De Re Publica,* see Richard Harder, "Ueber Ciceros Somnium Scipionis" (*Kleine Schriften,* München, 1960), who also shows convincingly that neither Plato nor Cicero followed Pythagorean doctrines.

46. This is especially stressed by Marcus Dods, *Forerunners of Dante,* Edinburgh, 1903.

47. See *Gorgias,* 524.

48. See *Gorgias,* 522/3 and *Phaedo,* 110. In *The Republic,* 614, Plato even alludes to a tale told by Ulysses to Alcinous.

49. *The Republic,* 379a.

50. As Werner Jaeger once called the Platonic god in *Theology of the Early Greek Philosophers,* Oxford, 1947, p. 194n.

51. *The Republic,* 615a.

52. See especially the *Seventh Letter* for Plato's conviction that truth is beyond speech and argument.

53. Thus John Adams in *Discourses on Davila,* in *Works,* Boston, 1851, vol. VI, p. 280.

54. From the draft Preamble to the Constitution of Massachusetts, *Works,* vol. IV, 221.

55. John Stuart Mill, *On Liberty,* ch. 2.

56. *The Prince,* ch. 15.

57. *The Prince,* ch. 8.

58. See especially the *Discourses,* book III, ch. 1.

59. It is curious to see how seldom Cicero's name occurs in Machiavelli's writings and how carefully he avoided him in his interpretations of Roman history.

60. *De Re Publica,* VI, 12.

61. *Laws,* 711a.

62. These assumptions, of course, could be justified only by a detailed analysis of the American Revolution.

63. *The Prince,* ch. 6.

4. What Is Freedom?

1. I follow Max Planck, "Causation and Free Will" (in *The New Science,* New York, 1959) because the two essays, written from the

standpoint of the scientist, possess a classic beauty in their nonsimplifying simplicity and clarity.

2. Ibid.

3. John Stuart Mill, *On Liberty.*

4. See "On Freedom" in *Dissertationes,* book IV, 1, § 1.

5. 1310a25 ff.

6. Op. cit., § 75.

7. Ibid., § 118

8. §§ 81 and 83.

9. See *Esprit des Lois,* XII, 2: *"La liberté philosophique consiste dans l'exercice de la volonté. . . . La liberté politique consiste dans la sûreté."*

10. *Intellectus apprehendit agibile antequam voluntas illud velit; sed non apprehendit determinate hoc esse agendum quod apprehendere dicitur dictare.* Oxon. IV, d. 46, qu. 1, no. 10.

11. John Stuart Mill, op. cit.

12. Leibniz only sums up and articulates the Christian tradition when he writes: *"Die Frage, ob unserem Willen Freiheit zukommt, bedeutet eigentlich nichts anderes, als ob ihm Willen zukommt. Die Ausdrücke 'frei' und 'willensgemäss' besagen dasselbe."* (*Schriften zur Metaphysik* I, "Bemerkungen zu den cartesischen Prinzipien." Zu Artikel 39.)

13. Augustine, *Confessions,* book VIII, ch. 8.

14. We find this conflict frequently in Euripides. Thus Medea, before murdering her children, says: "and I know which evils I am about to commit, but θυμός is stronger than my deliberations" (1078 ff.); and Phaedra (*Hippolytus,* 376 ff.) speaks in a similar vein. The point of the matter is always that reason, knowledge, insight, etc., are too weak to withstand the onslaught of desire, and it may not be accidental that the conflict breaks out in the soul of women, who are less under the influence of reasoning than men.

15. "Insofar as the mind commands, the mind wills, and insofar as the thing commanded is not done, it wills not," as Augustine put it, in the famous ch. 9 of book VIII of the *Confessions,* which deals with the will and its power. To Augustine, it was a matter of course that "to will" and "to command" are the same.

16. Augustine, ibid.

17. Pythian Ode IV, 287–289:

φαντὶ δ'ἔμμεν
τοῦτ' ἀνιαρότατον, καλὰ γινώσκοντ' ἀνάγκᾳ
ἐκτὸς ἔχειν πόδα.

18. *Esprit des Lois,* XII, 2 and XI, 3.

19. Op. cit., ibid.

20. Ibid.

21. See the first four chapters of the second book of *The Social Contract*. Among modern political theorists, Carl Schmitt is the most able defender of the notion of sovereignty. He recognizes clearly that the root of sovereignty is the will: Sovereign is who wills and commands. See especially his *Verfassungslehre*, München, 1928, pp. 7 ff., 146.

22. Book XII, ch. 20.

6. The Crisis in Culture

1. Harold Rosenberg in a brilliantly witty essay, "Pop Culture: Kitsch Criticism," in *The Tradition of the New*, New York, 1959.

2. See Edward Shils, "Mass Society and Its Culture" in *Daedalus*, Spring 1960; the whole issue is devoted to "Mass Culture and Mass Media."

3. I owe the story to G. M. Young, *Victorian England. Portrait of an Age*, New York, 1954.

4. For etymological origin and usage of the word in Latin, see, in addition to the *Thesaurus linguae latinae*, A. Walde, *Lateinisches Etymologisches Wörterbuch*, 1938, and A. Ernout & A. Meillet, *Dictionnaire Etymologique de la Langue Latine. Histoire des Mots*, Paris, 1932. For the history of word and concept since antiquity, see Joseph Niedermann, *Kultur—Werden und Wandlungen des Begriffes und seiner Ersatzbegriffe von Cicero bis Herder*, in *Biblioteca dell' Archivum Romanum*, Firenze, 1941, vol. 28.

5. Cicero, in his *Tusculan Disputations*, I, 13, says explicitly that the mind is like a field which cannot be productive without proper cultivation—and then declares: *Cultura autem animi philosophia est*.

6. By Werner Jaeger in *Antike*, Berlin, 1928, vol. IV.

7. See Mommsen, *Römische Geschichte*, book I, ch. 14.

8. See the famous chorus in *Antigone*, 332 ff.

9. Thucydides, II, 40.

10. Cicero, op. cit., V, 9.

11. Plato, *Gorgias*, 482.

12. *Critique of Judgment*, § 40.

13. Ibid., introduction, VII.

14. Aristotle, who (*Nicomachean Ethics*, book 6) deliberately set the insight of the statesman against the wisdom of the philosopher,

was probably following, as he did so often in his political writings, the public opinion of the Athenian polis.

15. *Critique of Judgment,* §§ 6, 7, 8.

16. Ibid. § 19.

17. For the history of word and concept, see Niedermann, op. cit., Rudolf Pfeiffer, *Humanitas Erasmiana,* Studien der Bibliothek Warburg, no. 22, 1931, and "Nachträgliches zu Humanitas" in Richard Harder's *Kleine Schriften,* München, 1960. The word was used to translate the Greek φιλανθρωπία, a word originally used of gods and rulers and therefore with altogether different connotations. *Humanitas,* as Cicero understood it, was closely connected with the old Roman virtue of *clementia* and as such stood in a certain opposition to Roman *gravitas.* It certainly was the sign of the educated man but, and this is important in our context, it was the study of art and literature rather than of philosophy which was supposed to result in "humanity."

18. Cicero, op. cit., I, 39–40. I follow the translation by J. E. King in Loeb's Classical Library.

19. Cicero speaks in a similar vein in *De Legibus,* 3, 1: He praises Atticus *cuius et vita et oratio consecuta mihi videtur difficillimam illam societatem gravitatis cum humanitate*—"whose life and speech seem to me to have achieved this most difficult combination of gravity with humanity"—whereby, as Harder (op. cit.), points out, Atticus's gravity consists in his adhering with dignity to Epicurus's philosophy, whereas his humanity is shown by his reverence for Plato, which proves his inner freedom.

7. Truth and Politics

1. *Eternal Peace,* Appendix I.

2. I quote from Spinoza's *Political Treatise* because it is noteworthy that even Spinoza, for whom the *libertas philosophandi* was the true end of government, should have taken so radical a position.

3. In the *Leviathan* (ch. 46) Hobbes explains that "disobedience may lawfully be punished in them, that against the laws teach even true philosophy." For is not "leisure the mother of philosophy; and Commonwealth the mother of peace and leisure"? And does it not follow that the Commonwealth will act in the interest of philosophy when it suppresses a truth which undermines peace? Hence the truth-

teller, in order to cooperate in an enterprise which is so necessary for his own peace of body and soul, decides to write what he knows "to be false philosophy." Of this Hobbes suspected Aristotle of all people, who according to him "writ it as a thing consonant to, and corroborative of [the Greeks'] religion; fearing the fate of Socrates." It never occurred to Hobbes that all search for truth would be self-defeating if its conditions could be guaranteed only by deliberate falsehoods. Then, indeed, everybody may turn out to be a liar like Hobbes' Aristotle. Unlike this figment of Hobbes' logical fantasy, the real Aristotle was of course sensible enough to leave Athens when he came to fear the fate of Socrates; he was not wicked enough to write what he knew to be false, nor was he stupid enough to solve his problem of survival by destroying everything he stood for.

4. Ibid., ch. 11.

5. I hope no one will tell me any more that Plato was the inventor of the "noble lie." This belief rested on a misreading of a crucial passage (414C) in *The Republic,* where Plato speaks of one of his myths— a "Phoenician tale"—as a ψεῦδος . Since the same Greek word signifies "fiction," "error," and "lie" according to context—when Plato wants to distinguish between error and lie, the Greek language forces him to speak of "involuntary" and "voluntary" ψεῦδος —the text can be rendered with Cornford as "bold flight of invention" or be read with Eric Voegelin (*Order and History: Plato and Aristotle,* Louisiana State University, 1957, vol. 3, p. 106) as satirical in intention; under no circumstances can it be understood as a recommendation of lying as we understand it. Plato, of course, was permissive about occasional lies to deceive the enemy or insane people—*The Republic,* 382; they are "useful . . . in the way of medicine . . . to be handled by no one but a physician," and the physician of the polis is the ruler (388). But, contrary to the cave allegory, no principle is involved in these passages.

6. *Leviathan,* Conclusion.

7. *The Federalist,* no. 49.

8. *Theologico-Political Treatise,* ch. 20.

9. See "What Is Enlightenment?" and "Was heisst sich im Denken orientieren?"

10. *The Federalist,* no. 49.

11. *Timaeus,* 51D–52.

12. See *The Republic* 367. Compare also *Crito* 49 D: "For I know that only a few men hold, or ever will hold, this opinion. Between those who do and those who don't there can be no common deliberation; they will necessarily look upon each other with contempt as to their different purposes."

13. See *Gorgias* 482, where Socrates tells Callicles, his opponent, that he will "not be in agreement with himself but that throughout his life, he will contradict himself." He then adds: "I would much rather that the whole world be not in agreement with me and talk against me than that I, *who am one,* should be in discord with myself and talk in self-contradiction."

14. For a definition of thought as the silent dialogue between me and myself, see especially *Theaetetus* 189–190, and *Sophist* 263–264. It is quite in keeping with this tradition that Aristotle calls the friend, with whom you speak in the form of dialogue an αὐτὸς ἄλλος, another self.

15. *Nicomachean Ethics,* book 6, especially 1140b9 and 1141b4.

16. See Jefferson's "Draft Preamble to the Virginia Bill Establishing Religious Freedom."

17. This is the reason for Nietzsche's remark in "Schopenhauer als Erzieher": "Ich mache mir aus einem Philosophen gerade so viel, als er imstande ist, ein Beispiel zu geben."

18. In a letter to W. Smith, November 13, 1787.

19. *Critique of Judgment,* Paragraph 32.

20. Ibid., Paragraph 59.

21. For France, see the excellent article "De Gaulle: Pose and Policy," in *Foreign Affairs,* July 1965. The Adenauer quotation is from his *Memoirs 1945–1953,* Chicago, 1966, p. 89, where, however, he puts this notion into the minds of the occupation authorities. But he has repeated the gist of it many times during his chancellorship.

22. Parts of the archive were published in Merle Fainsod, *Smolensk Under Soviet Rule,* Cambridge, Mass., 1958. See p. 374.

8. *The Conquest of Space and the Stature of Man*

1. This question was asked for a "Symposium on Space" by the editors of *Great Ideas Today* (1963) with special emphasis on what "the exploration of space is doing to man's view of himself and to man's condition. The question does not concern man as a scientist, nor man as a producer or consumer, but rather man as *human.*"

2. *Nicomachean Ethics,* book VI, ch. 7, 1141a20 ff.

3. Max Planck, *The Universe in the Light of Modern Physics,* 1929. Quoted from *Great Ideas Today,* 1962, p. 494.

4. As quoted by J. W. N. Sullivan, *Limitations of Science,* Mentor Books, 1949, p. 141.

5. See Sullivan's *Atomic Physics and Human Knowledge,* New York, 1958, p. 88.

6. Ibid., p. 76.

7. Planck, op. cit. p. 503.

8. See Planck's *Science and Humanism,* London, 1951, pp. 25–26.

9. John Gilmore, in a sharply critical letter when this article first appeared in 1963, puts the matter very nicely: "During the last several years we have in fact succeeded in writing computer programs that enable these machines to exhibit behavior that anyone not familiar with the makeup of the programs would unhesitatingly describe as intelligent, even highly intelligent. Alex Bernstein, for example, has devised a program that enables a machine to play spectacular good checkers. In particular, it can play better checkers than Bernstein. This is an impressive achievement; but it is Bernstein's and not the machine's." I had been misled by a remark of George Gamow—see note 10—and have changed my text.

10. George Gamow, "Physical Sciences and Technology," in *Great Ideas Today,* 1962, p. 207. Italics added.

11. Sergio de Benedetti, as quoted by Walter Sullivan, "Physical Sciences and Technology," in *Great Ideas Today,* 1961, p. 198.

12. Bohr, op. cit., pp.70 and 61 respectively.

13. Planck, op. cit., pp. 493, 517, and 514 respectively.

14. Bohr, op. cit., pp. 31 and 71 respectively.

15. Ibid., p. 82.

16. Planck, op. cit., pp. 509 and 505 respectively.

17. See J. Bronowski, *Science and Human Values,* New York, 1956, p. 22.

18. See *The Starry Messenger,* translation quoted from *Discoveries and Opinions of Galileo,* New York, 1957, p. 28.

19. See Einstein's *Relativity, The Special and General Theory* (1905 & 1916), quoted in *Great Ideas Today,* 1961, pp. 452 and 465 respectively.

20. Walter Sullivan, op. cit., p. 189.

21. Ibid., p. 202.

22. I quote from Descartes' dialogue "The Search after Truth by the Light of Nature," where his central position in this matter of doubting is more in evidence than in the *Principles.* See E. S. Haldane and G. R. T. Ross edition of his *Philosophical Works,* London, 1931, vol. I, pp. 324 and 315.

23. I owe this definition to John Gilmore's letter, mentioned in note 9. Mr. Gilmore, however, does not believe that this imposes

limitations on the knowledge of the practicing physicist. I think that Heisenberg's own "popular" statements bear me out on this point. But this is by no means the end of this controversy. Mr. Gilmore as well as Mr. Denver Lindley believes that the great scientists may very well be wrong when it comes to evaluating philosophically their own work. Mr. Gilmore and Mr. Lindley accuse me of using the scientists' statements uncritically, as though they could speak about the implications of their work with the same authority as they talk about their subjects properly speaking. ("Your confidence in the great figures in the scientific community is touching," says Mr. Gilmore.) This argument, I think, is valid; no scientist, no matter how eminent, can ever claim the same soundness for "philosophical implications" he or somebody else discovers in his work or in his utterances about it as he could claim for the discoveries themselves. Philosophic truth, whatever it may be, is certainly not scientific truth. Still, it is difficult to believe that Planck and Einstein, Niels Bohr, Schrödinger and Heisenberg, all of whom were puzzled and greatly worried about the consequences and general implications of their work as practicing physicists, should all have been subject to the delusions of self-misunderstanding.

24. In *Philosophic Problems of Nuclear Science,* New York, 1952, p. 73.

25. Ibid., p. 24.

26. In *The Physicist's Conception of Nature,* New York, 1958, p. 24.

27. Ibid., pp. 18–19.

INDEX OF NAMES

FOR THE BEST IN PAPERBACKS, LOOK FOR THE

In every corner of the world, on every subject under the sun, Penguin represents quality and variety—the very best in publishing today.

For complete information about books available from Penguin—including Pelicans, Puffins, Peregrines, and Penguin Classics—and how to order them, write to us at the appropriate address below. Please note that for copyright reasons the selection of books varies from country to country.

In the United Kingdom: For a complete list of books available from Penguin in the U.K., please write to *Dept E.P., Penguin Books Ltd, Harmondsworth, Middlesex, UB7 0DA.*

In the United States: For a complete list of books available from Penguin in the U.S., please write to *Dept BA, Penguin*, Box 120, Bergenfield, New Jersey 07621-0120.

In Canada: For a complete list of books available from Penguin in Canada, please write to *Penguin Books Ltd, 2801 John Street, Markham, Ontario L3R 1B4.*

In Australia: For a complete list of books available from Penguin in Australia, please write to the *Marketing Department, Penguin Books Ltd, P.O. Box 257, Ringwood, Victoria 3134.*

In New Zealand: For a complete list of books available from Penguin in New Zealand, please write to the *Marketing Department, Penguin Books (NZ) Ltd, Private Bag, Takapuna, Auckland 9.*

In India: For a complete list of books available from Penguin, please write to *Penguin Overseas Ltd, 706 Eros Apartments, 56 Nehru Place, New Delhi, 110019.*

In Holland: For a complete list of books available from Penguin in Holland, please write to *Penguin Books Nederland B.V., Postbus 195, NL-1380AD Weesp, Netherlands.*

In Germany: For a complete list of books available from Penguin, please write to *Penguin Books Ltd, Friedrichstrasse 10-12, D-6000 Frankfurt Main 1, Federal Republic of Germany.*

In Spain: For a complete list of books available from Penguin in Spain, please write to *Longman, Penguin España, Calle San Nicolas 15, E-28013 Madrid, Spain.*

In Japan: For a complete list of books available from Penguin in Japan, please write to *Longman Penguin Japan Co Ltd, Yamaguchi Building, 2-12-9 Kanda Jimbocho, Chiyoda-Ku, Tokyo 101, Japan.*

FOR THE BEST IN PSYCHOLOGY, LOOK FOR THE

FOR THE BEST IN PSYCHOLOGY, LOOK FOR THE

☐ **REDISCOVERING LOVE**
Willard Gaylin, M.D.

Using insights gleaned from great romantic writers, philosophers, and psychologists, Dr. Willard Gaylin explores the very essence of love and shows how we can recapture it in our everyday lives.

288 pages   ISBN: 0-14-010431-3   **$4.50**

☐ **KNOW YOUR OWN I.Q.**
H. J. Eysenck

The famous book describes clearly what an I.Q. (Intelligence Quotient) is, how it can be applied, and what its shortcomings may be, then enables readers to estimate and confirm their own rating through eight sets of problems.

192 pages   ISBN: 0-14-020516-0   **$4.95**

☐ **DEPRESSION AND THE BODY**
The Biological Basis of Faith and Reality
Alexander Lowen, M.D.

An eminent psychiatrist presents his revolutionary plan for conquering depression by activating dormant life forces and training mind and body to respond as a finely tuned instrument.   318 pages   ISBN: 0-14-021780-0   **$6.95**

☐ **LIVING THROUGH MOURNING**
Finding Comfort and Hope When a Loved One Has Died
Harriet Sarnoff Schiff

With understanding and wisdom, Harriet Sarnoff Schiff explores the complex feelings friends and relatives must cope with when someone dies and details the gradual process of grieving, offering aid to anyone facing the loss of a loved one.   300 pages   ISBN: 0-14-010309-0   **$6.95**

☐ **THE FARTHER REACHES OF HUMAN NATURE**
A. H. Maslow

Written by one of the foremost spokesmen of the humanistic, or "Third Force," psychologies, this wide-ranging book is a synthesis of Maslow's ideas on biology, synergy, creativity, and cognition.

408 pages   ISBN: 0-14-004265-2   **$6.95**

☐ **RELIGIONS, VALUES, AND PEAK-EXPERIENCES**
Abraham H. Maslow

One of the foremost spokesmen for the Third Force movement in psychology proposes that spiritual expression is both central to the "peak-experiences" reached by fully functioning persons and a rightful subject for scientific investigation.   124 pages   ISBN: 0-14-004262-8   **$4.95**